M000247565

POST-DIGITAL RHETORIC AND THE NEW AESTHETIC

NEW DIRECTIONS IN RHETORIC AND MATERIALITY
Barbara A. Biesecker, Wendy S. Hesford, and Christa Teston, Series Editors

POST-DIGITAL RHETORIC AND THE NEW AESTHETIC

JUSTIN HODGSON

THE OHIO STATE UNIVERSITY PRESS
COLUMBUS

Copyright © 2019 by The Ohio State University.
All rights reserved.

Library of Congress Cataloging-in-Publication Data
Names: Hodgson, Justin, author.
Title: Post-digital rhetoric and the new aesthetic / Justin Hodgson.
Other titles: New directions in rhetoric and materiality.
Description: Columbus : The Ohio State University Press, [2019] | Series: New directions in
    rhetoric and materiality | Includes bibliographical references and index.
Identifiers: LCCN 2018048555 | ISBN 9780814213940 (cloth ; alk. paper) | ISBN 0814213944
    (cloth ; alk. paper)
Subjects: LCSH: Rhetoric—Data processing. | Aesthetics. | Digital media.
Classification: LCC P301.5.D37 H63 2019 | DDC 801/.93—dc23
LC record available at https://lccn.loc.gov/2018048555

Cover design by Angela Moody
Text design by Juliet Williams
Type set in Adobe Minion Pro

This work was (partially) funded by the Office of the Vice Provost of Research and the Arts
and Humanities Council at Indiana University Bloomington through the Public Arts Grant.

♾ The paper used in this publication meets the minimum requirements of the American
National Standard for Information Sciences—Permanence of Paper for Printed Library
Materials. ANSI Z39.48-1992.

To NNF,
For the sleepless years, and the years to come.

CONTENTS

ILLUSTRATIONS

See image gallery following page 66 for color plates.

ACKNOWLEDGMENTS

WHAT BEGINS as a passing thought on a random Wednesday afternoon can grow, without warning, into a multiyear excursion. But that flicker of an idea is never a singularity; it is always the result of other ideas and experiences, which come from other conversations and encounters, which come from yet other flickers and flashes, memories and moments. Thus, it is difficult to discern, with any notable accuracy, precisely when a book project like this can be said to have begun. The formal development can be relegated to my time as a faculty member at Indiana University, where this work was aided by a semester of research leave, support of in-progress drafts from colleagues John Schilb, Christine Farris, Ivan Krielkamp, and Scott Herring, and many (far too many) invaluable conversations with Scot Barnett and Katie Silvester. I am grateful to these individuals and others for their support.

But I must acknowledge the University of Texas at Austin as well, for it was during my time as faculty there that I stumbled upon the critical focus of this project. Therefore, this work is also indebted to my former Department of Rhetoric and Writing colleagues who helped me understand what it means to be a scholar in the field of rhetoric. I would be remiss, however, not to especially give thanks to Diane Davis for her mentorship and friendship, Linda Ferreira-Buckley for her guidance and support, and Trish Roberts-Miller, who influenced me far more than I could have ever anticipated.

I also need to express gratitude to the Department of English at the University of Tennessee at Knoxville, particularly the Division of Rhetoric, Writing, and Linguistics, and Sean Morey, who offered me the chance to talk about ideas in art, technology, and media studies with a rhetorically oriented audience. Similarly, I am appreciative of the Rhetorics, Communication, and Information Design (RCID) doctoral program at Clemson University, particularly Jan Holmevik and Cynthia Haynes, for inviting me to discuss certain dimensions of rhetorical aesthetics with their graduate students. Both visits (to UT Knoxville and to Clemson) presented challenges and prompted conversations that improved my thinking on this project.

Further, one of the more significant contributions to this project came from the graduate students at IU who participated in my Post-Digital Aesthetics graduate course. Philip Choong, Jillian Gilmer, Becky Ottman, Laura Rosche, and Whitney Sperrazza helped push my inquiries into human–technology relationships—extending tenets and tensions central to this work. Additionally, I need to specifically thank Laura Rosche, whose Independent Study with me offered an unexpected opportunity to revisit key texts central to this work.

While the above acknowledgments trace the formative construction of the text, there are still yet others—too many others—who should be mentioned here. I want to thank Cynthia Cochran for influencing my life during my days at Illinois College—reminding me that I was capable of more. Most importantly, she opened my eyes to the world of rhetoric and writing studies. Her mentorship and continued friendship has been without measure. Second, I need to express appreciation for the late Carolyn Handa, who was pivotal in inviting me into the realm of visual rhetoric. Her compassion for students and willingness to support even the most outlandish of ideas (of which I had more than my share) allowed me to find a scholarly space to inhabit. And just as importantly, Carolyn encouraged me to pursue further studies with Victor J. Vitanza, a relationship that would change the trajectory of my life.

I have been privileged to learn from and study with some brilliant and talented individuals. But no one has been more influential in my intellectual development than Victor Vitanza. During my time as a student in the RCID program, Victor altered just about everything I knew to be. He rewired my thinking, pushed me outside my comfort zones, demanded more from me than I demanded of myself (which I did not think possible), and allowed me to find my own way even when he could see the path mapped in front of me. Victor also made it possible for me to spend a summer taking courses at the European Graduate School, which was a transformative experience—the effects of which permeate my personal and professional identities. Victor's mentorship and friendship was simply *more*—always some more—and for that I cannot thank him enough.

But Victor was not the only one at Clemson who influenced my scholarly formation. I mentioned Jan and Cynthia, whose research and teaching continue to influence me. I also need to acknowledge my cohort, the first-ever class in the RCID program—John Dinolfo, Xiaoli Li, Mac McArthur, and especially Amanda Booher, who pushed my engagements, challenged my assumptions, and added an unexpected richness to my inquiries (both during and well beyond our days together at Clemson). I also need to express my gratitude to select individuals in the immediate cohorts behind us "inaugurals": Jason Helms, Joshua Hilst, Joshua Abboud, Sergio Figeureido, Josie Walwema, and Anthony Collamati. This text is especially indebted to Anthony, who read early versions of the formative chapters of this book and provided support as the book entered production.

Beyond the above relationships, there are also multiple personal influences that need to be acknowledged, for without these individuals this project would not have been possible.

I am grateful for my in-laws, who supported my career, even when it has taken my wife, kids, and me four, eight, even fifteen hours away. I particularly want to thank my mother- and father-in-law, Nancy and Joe, who have regularly helped "hold down the fort" while I traveled for work or was buried in writing deadlines. Their presence has been immeasurably significant.

Second, turning to my own family, I am grateful to my mother, Brenda, for her unwavering belief in me as an individual, even when that support may have been unwarranted. I also need to express gratitude to my brother Travis, who in a memorable trip to PCA/ACA in Boston many moons ago served as an audience of one for a panel of burgeoning RCID students. I am also grateful to my sister, Andrea, who has been relentlessly supportive and who attended a presentation I delivered (though that talk was at the Digital Humanities conference in Parramatta, Australia, and involved an audience of well more than one). Additionally, I need to thank my father, Larry, who has asked every month for what seems like forever if this book was done yet. Beyond his motivational inquiries, he has also been the single most important figure in my life. He helped me understand the importance of being committed to the work, no matter what job you do. He helped me realize the importance of family and of being available to those who matter to you. And, most importantly, he helped me realize that it is okay to pursue your dreams with reckless abandon, even if those pursuits draw you away from home and transform everything about who you are and who you will be.

Finally, I want to say thank you to my two boys, Gavin and Ryan, who have enriched my life beyond belief and who routinely help me find levity and laughter amidst the most trying of writing times. And to my wife, Nicole, who has joined me on this long road and who has listened to all manner of ramblings about the New Aesthetic, digital rhetoric, pixels, and the like to the point that she deserves an honorary degree for her efforts. She is and forever remains my magnetic north.

Medial Orientations

A Cautionary Tale

AT THE END of the last millennium, in *Good Looking: Essays on the Virtue of Images,* visual studies scholar Barbara Maria Stafford called into question the long-standing supremacy of the "identification of writing with intellectual potency" (5). She argued that the dominant literate and linguistic perspectives in culture had led to a bias in which printed words were intrinsically (though by no means naturally) coupled with reason and "introspective depth," while visual aesthetics and image-based representations (i.e., the practice of imaging) were viewed as a kind of "dumbing down" (4). For Stafford this was problematic because it ignored the complex ways in which visual media functioned (from epistemic to aesthetic impulses) and actively reduced the visual register (among others) to a linguistic or literate order. She argued that "verbalizing binaries," like signifier/signified, "turned noumenal and phenomenal experience into the product of language" (5), which not only reinscribed a Cartesian separation of the mind and body but also routinely "collaps[ed] diverse phenomenological performances . . . into interpretable texts without sensory diversity" (6). What gets elided in these orientations, according to Stafford, is "the developmental link between perception and thought" (6), which is precisely what good imaging work attempts to foreground.

In challenging this bias, Stafford was not attempting to delegitimize writing (or the study of linguistics); rather, she was trying to grasp the "genuine nature" of a different set of representational and communicational values: creating a space for reimagining the power of imaging and, in so doing, freeing "graphicacy" and the realm of the visual aesthetic from its "subordinate [position] to literacy" (5). Moreover, Stafford was interested in reclaiming a certain value (and validity) to imaging itself—a rich and "fascinating modality for configuring and conveying ideas" (4)—as well as attempting to foster a better position from which to approach twenty-first-century thinking and engagement. If the *age of computerism,* as Stafford referred to the turn of the millennium, was to be dominated by image-based mediascapes, then a new order was required.

But while Stafford was so eloquently arguing for the [epistemic value of imaging—embracing the aesthetic dimension as a way of knowing and accounting for the various impacts of critical and creative media on human consciousness (70)—twenty-first-century academia continued to proliferate literacies (and literacy-ensconced orientations) with great fervor. Even a cursory glance around higher education today, now twenty-plus years removed from Stafford's efforts, reveals a world littered with literacies: digital literacies, computational literacies, multimodal literacies, gaming literacies, techno-literacies, screen literacies, and so on. (There seems a literacy for everything!) But for all their administrative appeal and cache, what resides at the core of these varied "literacies," as rhetoric and composition scholar Kathleen Blake Yancey intimated in "Made Not Only in Words: Composition in a New Key,"[1] is the attempt (among scholars) to bring "inside" the academy what is otherwise a series of techniques and techné developing and circulating among a digital public "outside" academic walls (see also Benkler[2]). There is, then, something else wanting (and something else at work) in today's rich mediascapes—which have only exponentially increased the visual saturations of media to which Stafford was responding.

Now, in making even a general appeal to something outside the literacy framework, I do not mean to discredit literacy, nor to dispense altogether with literacy-orientations—for the literacy frameworks should remain among the

---

1. This essay, which Yancey delivered as the 2004 CCCC Chair's address, takes stock of the vast types of writing (and writing practices) proliferated by writing technologies—inviting writing studies to reconsider its role and pedagogies in relation to "writing publics": those writing groups and practices that take shape and get distributed via participatory communities that form outside scholarly institutions.

2. In *The Wealth of Networks: How Social Production Transforms Markets and Freedom,* Yochai Benkler argues that the means of production are now held in common (no longer restricted to commercial owners), which means that what gets produced is no longer limited to the professional class and/or to the constraints of institutional platforms but rather reflects the coming together of "otherwise unconnected individuals" via network technologies to pursue common goals, engage in the sharing and distribution of knowledge, and facilitate new "condensation point[s] for human connection" and creation (375).

use

set of perspectives that individuals *might* draw from for thinking about, working with, and explaining various medial elements (particularly those actually grounded in literacy practices). But to adopt a literacy-orientation as the primary (and sometimes only) response to new mediating technologies and the human–technology relationships they introduce is, at best, short-sighted, and, at worst, egregious in how it limits thinking and practice. Let me offer the following analogy: In a 2008 Anheuser Busch Superbowl commercial, titled "Wheel Sucks," a group of cavemen attempt to push a large stone cooler full of Bud Light to a party. One caveman stops pushing the cooler, and, with exasperation, says, "We never make it to party." The cavemen all look despondent. Then another caveman (accompanied by heroic intro music) appears on the path in front of them. He boasts, "I invent Wheel!" and shoves the massive wheel over onto its side. As the stone wheel slams onto the dirt path, he says, with confidence and a sense of revelation, "Help get Bud Light to party." The cavemen all get very excited. But in the next scene, the three men who were pushing the cooler through the dirt are now standing, carrying the large, heavy stone wheel at shoulder height, using it as platform to transport the even heavier cooler full of beer. One caveman, struggling under the weight of the stone-wheel-cooler apparatus, says to the others, "Wheel suck!"

Aside from its humor, the commercial points to a particular way the cavemen relate to the technology of the wheel. To put it another way, despite the fuller range of affordances of the wheel, the cavemen failed to listen to the ways in which the wheel was calling to them to interact. Or rather, what they heard from the wheel and the manner in which they "listened" were conditioned by the ways in which they knew how to make sense of things in the world—how they made sense of the new technology (wheel) was framed in terms of older technologies (e.g., platform). This does make some sense given that "new technologies," as multimedia composition scholar Anne Wysocki has argued, always emerge "out of existing technologies and out of existing material economies, patterns, and habits" (8). Therefore, in its initial moment, the cavemen had little recourse but to think of the wheel in terms of a previous technology with which they were familiar: the platform. Of course, the wheel-as-platform does, in fact, "suck." But is being a platform part of its affordances? Yes. Can it work as a platform? Technically. Does it make sense that the cavemen made sense of the wheel as a platform? Absolutely. But does this make it any less absurd? No.

In a very correlative way, the current "caveman's wheel" is the advent of new mediating technologies. And much like the cavemen, when rhetoricians approach new mediating technologies from the perspective of literacy, they too end up trying to carry the wheel—inevitably leading to the realization *use*

that "Wheel suck!" What is needed instead, as rhetoric scholars Jenny Bay and Thomas Rickert argued in "Dwelling with New Media," is an engagement that affords new mediating technologies their own ontological weight and/or rhetorical agency[3]—approaches that allow one to attune to technologies on their own terms. Not only does this help avoid reinscribing a literacy imperative in a literal sense, but it better positions new mediating technologies as partners in a symbiotic engagement, not as neutral servants to a human will.

This work, then, does not (re)turn to any literacy impulse, nor does it merely embrace Stafford's new imagist figurations, but rather it attempts to afford a contemporary phenomenon its own ontological weight—attuning to the intuitions, implications, and insinuations of the techno-phenomenon known as the New Aesthetic as a way to expose new practices and proclivities for twenty-first-century rhetoricians. In turning to the New Aesthetic as focal entity, this work takes stock of contemporary mediascapes by immersing the inquiry in what media studies scholar and critical theorist David M. Berry refers to as the "inconspicuous surface-level expressions" and media artifacts of the everyday—which, he argues in "The Postdigital Constellation," allows one to better grasp the ontological, ideological, and epistemological dimensions of a given epoch (50).

NEW AESTHETIC: A FRAMING

The New Aesthetic will, of course, be more fully introduced in chapter 1, but something of a quick overview may help orient readers to the larger arc of this work. In 2011, after months of noticing a different kind of aesthetic sensibility and creative practice manifesting in art, culture, commerce, media, and the like, London-based artist James Bridle began capturing examples of what he saw as a "new aesthetic"—moments and manifestations that situated computationality and related elements of the network apparatus as increasingly aestheticized values. Bridle gathered these examples into a Tumblr[4] account, which he labeled the New Aesthetic. But as artist and designer Curt Cloninger argued in "A Manifesto for a Theory of the New Aesthetic," what Bridle ended up creating was an archive documenting the residue of the digital in people's

---

3. Bay and Rickert take up with philosopher Martin Heidegger's concept of *dwelling* as a way of thinking about fuller orientations to human–technology dynamics. Specifically, they argue that humans adopt the very perspectives of their mediating technologies, which, in turn, reshape the ways that humans see (and understand) themselves in the world.

4. Tumblr is a free social-media microblogging platform that allows users to post content, share media, and follow other Tumblr users.

everyday lives (n. pag.).[5] Although this "documentation" (and subsequent mediations) may not have resulted in an aesthetic movement *in proper,* what it demonstrated was the rich complexities in contemporary human–technology assemblages—adding depth to how one might understand the techno-human capacities that individuals possess for experiencing and making sense of the (mediated) world. To this end, my intent in this book is to explore, explicate, and expand the critical and creative impulses of the New Aesthetic (as archive and rhetorical ecology), doing so not simply as an extended examination of the New Aesthetic but rather to delineate and leverage its operative contours and position them as loose guides for the *doing* of rhetoric in a post-digital age.

Given this turning to the New Aesthetic and the attempt to offer it its own ontological weight, there may be value in contextualizing the considerations in relation to non-literacy medial orientations. One such frame is the pseudo-continuum that exists from new media studies to post-digital aesthetics to the New Aesthetic. To better situate this tripartite, I offer the following parallel with Web 1.0, 2.0, and 3.0 considerations. The web (or Web 1.0) was fairly static (primarily a client-based internet), while Web 2.0 moved the world toward a dynamic social web. Web 3.0 is yet something else, involving, as media arts scholar Virginia Kuhn has argued in "Web Three Point Oh: The Virtual Is the Real," at least three common approaches: a shift from indexical to semantic web, an attunement to an increasingly visually saturated culture (i.e., "imageworlds"; see also Stafford), and an orientation toward ubiquitous computing and the ways in which it breaks down any digital/real distinction (1).[6] Digital media scholar Lukasz Mirocha contends, in "Communication Models, Aesthetics, and Ontology of the Computational Age," that the New Aesthetic is "a movement rooted in Web 2.0 culture," owing to how it operationalizes the "logic[s] of the hyperlinked interface and freely shareable information" (63). But Mirocha's considerations are primarily grounded in the New Aesthetic's Tumblr home (more about *where* it is than about rhetorical considerations of *how* it is or ontological considerations of *what* it is). Instead, as I think one will more readily see in this work, there is greater correlation between Web 3.0 and the tenets of the New Aesthetic, particularly with

---

5. Cloninger situates the New Aesthetic as a process or orientation rather than as a singular aesthetic intentionality. For him it is fundamentally a matter of traces and residues being apperceived more readily in relation to affect than to any fixed line (or even fixing impulse) of critical theory.

6. Kuhn explicitly looks at how Web 3.0 technologies call into question the very distinctions between the virtual and the real. While she does not address the New Aesthetic in any capacity, many of the core gestures she makes of Web 3.0 have touchstones with the New Aestheticism explored in this work.

considerations of "imageworlds" and their composing elements as well as the blurring of boundaries associated with ubiquitous computing. But the point at this juncture is not to squabble over Web 2.0 or Web 3.0 orientations; rather, it is to set up the following (loose) comparative: new media (and new media principles) took shape on the front edge of Web 1.0 technologies and solidified, more or less, in the Web 2.0 era; post-digital (and post-digital aesthetics) took shape somewhere between the coming of Web 2.0 technologies and the Web 3.0 turn; and the New Aesthetic was of a different moment yet, taking shape in a culture operating in (if not beyond) the Web 3.0 mobile, technocultural scene.

What this parallel highlights is not only a kind of change in the operative tenets of networked (and mediating) technologies associated with each moment but also an additional tentativeness with how to proceed, especially from a rhetorical perspective. If this work does not move cautiously and critically with regard to certain assumptions (or even incongruities) across this medial spectrum, it could end up reproducing, at both theoretical and pragmatic levels, the technocommercial practices that regularly lead to massive computational glitches and vulnerabilities—offering something of a cautionary tale.

For example, on July 8, 2015, a technical glitch grounded, for the entire day, all United Airlines flights in the US. That same day, the New York Stock Exchange and the *Wall Street Journal* websites went down as well—also glitch-related. In addition to demonstrating how digital disasters have the potential to operate with the magnitude of a natural disaster, these events also revealed the scary reality that many major corporate glitches and computational mishaps are, as informatics scholar Zeynep Tufekci explained in "Why the Great Glitch of July 8th Should Scare You," the result of what happens when years of low-bid, adjunct, software laborers "make things work" with emerging systems (n. pag.). Meaning, as Tufekci explains, that companies regularly pay (often entry-level) programmers to patch their existing systems into newer protocols. This makes sense, as entire system changes can be extremely expensive (in cost, in time, and especially in training) and technologies evolve so quickly that new systems are essentially outdated the moment they go live. But the result of multigenerational patchwork, which is methodologically similar to much in the scholarly world (e.g., digital literacy), is that more than occasionally one is dealing with a major corporate computational structure operating on a piece of programming code written twenty to thirty years ago. That would be like hitching a Boeing 747 to a team of horses in order to get it up in the air—and what the New Aesthetic seems to be doing is highlighting the horseshit on the runway.

Therefore, while it is important to consider things like new media perspectives and even the nuances among post-digital orientations, this work will be attentive to the rhetorical limits of any patchwork concepts and structures that other medial orientations might provide. These other frameworks may help contextualize and even operationalize the rhetorical dimensions of the New Aesthetic, but the goal will be to explore the New Aesthetic as a rhetorical ecology and to articulate its circulating intensities as operative guides for post-digital rhetoric.] — question

THE ARCHITECTURE

This book unfolds across six chapters. Chapters 1 and 2 introduce New Aestheticism, situate the methodological orientations of the work, and rhetorically maneuver through the New Aesthetic ecology to identify its contours. Chapters 3 through 6 each pick up with one of the four contours identified and positions their value for contemporary rhetorical considerations.

Working with a bit more granularity, chapter 1, "The New Aesthetic and (Post-)Digital Rhetoric," provides a fuller outline of the New Aesthetic, situating its value for rhetorical studies and locating it within the formative tenets of digital rhetoric. It traces specific technological or medial implications through conversations in rhetoric, argues for the necessity of (if not recovery of) the aesthetic perspective (and a level of screen essentialism), and points to the underexplored rhetorical areas into which New Aestheticism pushes post-digital practices.

Chapter 2, "Rhetorical Ecologies and the New Aesthetic," introduces the methodology of this inquiry, which involves situating the New Aesthetic as a rhetorical ecology. To this perspective, the chapter adds the term *contour* as a way of capturing (and/or articulating) the circulating intensities among a given rhetorical ecology. Then, via rhetorical analysis, it explores the New Aesthetic ecology—specifically through the challenges lobbied at New Aestheticism—to give shape to its contours, which become the focus of the remaining chapters.

Chapter 3 picks up with the contour of *eversion as/of design*, explicitly showing how the dueling orientations of "making digital things real" and "making real things digital" opens greater capacities for post-digital rhetoricians. But more than that, this contour blurs the digital/real divide, moving post-digital considerations away from the rhetoric of couplings and binaries toward matters of ecology—showing why systems that operate through a complexity of relations (not either/or logics) are valuable. Specifically, it picks up

with the manners by which digital and nondigital materialities (and their cir-
culatory capacities) come to bear on post-digital rhetorical practices.

Chapter 4 picks up with the *pixel orientation* of the New Aesthetic to demonstrate the ways in which mediating practices, through the human–technology assemblage, have the capacity to transform the very root of human
sensibilities. But beyond accounting for how pixel aesthetics have become
intertwined with human sensibilities, this chapter also brings Jay David Bolter
and Richard Grusin's considerations of *remediation* to bear on (a) the very
experience of the pixel, and (b) how something like the New Aesthetic helps
situate the rhetorical value (and significance) of the pixel itself.

Chapter 5 takes up with the contour of *human–technology making,* which
resides at the very heart of New Aestheticism's contribution to rhetorical
studies. It attempts to demonstrate a more collaborative relationship between
humans and technologies, and it reconfigures the rhetorical practices of post-
digital making in terms of a *willingness to play* rather than the long-standing
orientation toward a *will to mastery.* This shift to play, in turn, invites new
considerations as well as altogether new kinds of representative figures (e.g.,
post-digital practitioners) for the *making* of rhetoric.

Finally, chapter 6 treats the *hyperawareness of mediation* that runs throughout most of the New Aesthetic. It returns the conversation to Bolter and
Grusin and the experiences of mediation to illuminate the rhetorical value of
hypermediation (in the artifacts themselves and in audience expectations), to
call attention to the potential of crafting hyperrhetorical mediations, and to
introduce the very necessity of moving away from practices rooted in *ekphrasis* toward those more firmly grounded in experience design.

Collectively, through these chapters, this work introduces the New Aesthetic, locates its value for rhetoric, situates it as its own rhetorical ecology,
and uses its rhetorical dimensions to help call to attention its operative contours. Then, working with each contour one by one, it introduces their complexities, unpacks their value for understanding the rhetorical capacities of
human–technology assemblages, and positions them as a guide for the practices of post-digital rhetoric. The first contour deals with the blurring of the
digital/real divide and the very need for an ecological orientation. The second
shows how technological values become human sensibilities and, in so doing,
reshape rhetorical practices. The third highlights an altogether different orientation to making—pointing to the collaborative (rather than controlling)
partnerships among human–technology productions as well as to the generative value of the novice and the need to focus on human–technology relations.
The fourth foregrounds the mediation itself and how contemporary media-

tions play within the hypermediacy of their own medial practices, fostering awareness, working rhetorically, and inviting specific kinds of relationships and expectations from specific kinds of audiences. Together, the contours offer something akin to "a rhetoric" for post-digital *knowing*, *doing*, and *making*, and unpacking those considerations is the focus of this work.

CHAPTER 1

The New Aesthetic and (Post-)Digital Rhetoric

IN *ORALITY AND LITERACY: The Technologizing of the Word,* media and culture theorist Walter J. Ong offered the following statement: "Technology, properly interiorized, does not degrade human life but on the contrary enhances it" (83). This statement echoes the core of this work, which seeks not to raise further alarm about the mechanization of human bodies, nor to reinscribe any particular tool/user paradigm, but rather to sincerely inquire after the human–technology relationships at the center of so many cultural and commercial activities today. As such, the intent of this inquiry is twofold: first, to understand the impact of emergent ordering principles, representational practices, privileged perspectives, and technological values (aesthetic or algorithmic, material or mathematical) on human ways of being in (and representing) the world; and second, to capture something of an "enhanced" posthumanism taking shape in today's digitally saturated moment. But to illuminate these considerations with any granularity requires more than just general gestures toward technology—as mediating condition or material apparatus. Therefore, this work will explicitly take up with the techno-aesthetic phenomenon known as the New Aesthetic, with the goal of situating its *contours* as heuretics for twenty-first-century critical and creative practices. I use the term *heuretics* here in the way it has been introduced by cybermedia scholar and critical theorist Gregory L. Ulmer: as the inventive counterpart to the process of interpretation (hermeneutics). Meaning that heuretics are intended to move rhetors (and their rhetorical inclinations) out of categorical imperatives tied to judgment and to instead situate them on a generative plane, one linked to intuition and affect as much as to any governing logics. Thus, while the focus of this work is on the intersections and interpenetrations of humans and technologies and the object is the New Aesthetic, the output (the contributions and scholarly interests) leans necessarily toward rhetoric, particularly the inventive practices central to rhetoric in a post-digital age.

The New Aesthetic was first introduced in May 2011 via a blog post[1] on the Really Interesting Group website. There, designer and digital futurist James Bridle wrote about a new aesthetic sensibility and creative practice manifesting in art, culture, commerce, media, and the like. The main thrust of this aesthetic involved everyday working creatives leveraging—as model, metaphor, and meme—the forms, functions, and infrastructures of computers and network culture. Bridle, in an attempt to demonstrate the nuances of this new aesthetic sensibility, embarked on a yearlong curatorial endeavor in which he gathered artifacts on a Tumblr account[2] (the New Aesthetic archive), with each artifact serving, in some capacity, as witness to one or more aspects of New Aestheticism. The problem, however, was that Bridle's artifacts varied so extensively in style, purpose, and delivery that there was little consistency among their critical features and aesthetic dimensions, making it difficult, if not impossible, to define. But as popular science fiction writer Bruce Sterling argued in "An Essay on the New Aesthetic," even without clear definition or categorical distinction, the archive itself (particularly when coupled with the many commentaries on the New Aesthetic) did gesture toward *something of significance* (n. pag.). That significance, as I will argue here, is a new kind of art practice and cultural critique—if not a twenty-first-century rhetorical orientation—calling attention to human relationships with technologies, human acts of mediation, the systems and protocols that produce particular computational representations, and the human viewpoints that frame those considerations.

Note, however, that my perspective (rhetorically infused as it is) stands notably in counterdistinction to mainstream treatments of New Aestheticism, which have primarily reduced the phenomenon to not much more than the novelty of pixelated representation—the use of 8-bit graphics (and their overtly pixelated qualities) in nondigital cultural spaces, as well as in things like screen glitches, downsampled satellite imagery, and the blurry squared

---

1. http://www.riglondon.com/2011/05/06/the-new-aesthetic/
2. http://new-aesthetic.tumblr.com

edges of render ghosts.[3] But for Bridle, the would-be André Breton of this movement, the pixelated imagery was and is merely a kind of visual short-hand—serving as a relay toward larger concerns: like the blurring bound-aries between the digital and the real, and the underlying systems that (a) produce those boundaries and (b) produce culture-specific understandings of such (Bridle, "#sxaesthetic," n. pag.). Or, said another way: while the New Aesthetic is attentive to the very media in which pixelated and glitched rep-resentations are being undertaken (and of which they are reflective), it is just as concerned with the human–technology assemblages that allow critics and working creatives alike to make sense of those attunements on multiple lev-els and scales. New Aestheticism may employ, in some cases, aesthetic sen-sibilities linked to 8-bit graphics, but what it is *about* (if one can make such a statement) are the overt and subtle impacts of computational mediation on representation, expression, and existence (three considerations important to rhetorical studies).

Bridle's curatorial Tumblr exercise was, then, more than just suggestive of a kind of network aesthetic (disruptive or otherwise). It was (and is), in many respects, a point of contact between what new media scholar Lev Manovich called Duchamp-land and Turing-land—a distinction offered in his 1996 arti-cle, "The Death of Computer Art," as a way of thinking through the contradic-tory orientations for art and computational technology present at the end of the last millennium. Duchamp-land, which Manovich named after the twen-tieth-century avant-garde artist Marcel Duchamp, pursued artistic practices and art objects that were oriented toward content, reveled in self-referentiality, and harbored a playful (if not destructive) impulse toward their own technic-ity and materiality (n. pag.). Turing-land, named after Alan Turing, a founding figure in theoretical computer science and artificial intelligence, was oriented toward technology rather than content, preferred simplicity of design (and often seamlessness as a governing quality), and deployed technology toward serious ends (n. pag.). For Manovich, these two "lands" were never to converge, because "Duchamp-land want[ed] art, not research into new aesthetic possi-bilities of new media" (n. pag.). Over a decade later, art scholar Claire Bishop reiterated some of these same tensions in her essay "Digital Divide," indicating that despite contemporary artists in the first decade of the new millennium using new technologies in their work, they had not "really confront[ed] the question of what it means to think, see, and filter affect through the digital"

---

3. *Render ghost* is the name given to the deployment of images of people in digital visual-izations—composite creations that use likenesses of individual people in decontextualized ways. This is particularly common in 2D and 3D architectural representations, where the designed spaces include human bodies as part of their visual representations (people in space, in action).

(436).[4] But the New Aesthetic, as art and design scholar Daniel ‖
suggested, points toward "confront[ing] these crucially important
precisely because it is situated in the convergences of these two "la
The New Aesthetic does this by (a) highlighting specific instances in which the
technological systems of Turing-land have come to produce the very aesthetic
mediascapes of contemporary Duchamp-land, and (b) demonstrating how the
aesthetic values of contemporary Duchamp-land have influenced the design,
practice, and experience of everyday (computational) objects in Turing-land.
To spin a line from journalist and art critic Josephine Bosma, the New Aesthetic may be art's very response to the merging of these two lands—offering
a screen-based way to perceive the art (and artistic tendencies and irruptions)
of the coding core of computational culture (n. pag.).[6]

What is important, then, is not any specific categorical order—nor, as
techno-culture scholar David M. Berry and his many collaborators[7] express
in *New Aesthetic, New Anxieties,* how the New Aesthetic might be funneled
into the "established divides of creative industries, art practice and theory"
(4)—but rather the larger complexity of relations among New Aestheticism
that proffer different avenues for critique, creativity, commentary, and conceptualization. Of course, if these "avenues" could be marshaled toward providing
structures, explanatory models, or representational techniques for designing
mediated experiences, then New Aestheticism would have much to offer a
range of critical and creative inquiry practices (for those in digital rhetoric
and digital humanities alike). But New Aestheticism seems to actively resist   *use*
the very codification needed for it to be "marshaled" anywhere. This is in
keeping, of course, with most aesthetic turns, which traditionally resist being
reduced to a set of tropes; but for Bridle the "resistance" is less tropological
hesitation and more that New Aestheticism is an ongoing process of critical

---

4. In this piece, Bishop argues that while artists may use computational technologies in
their processes, and while there is an entire subfield of new media art, turn-of-the-century
prognostications of the impact of "the digital" on mainstream art never fully manifested.

5. Pinkas's "A Hyperbolic and Catchy New Aesthetic" situates the New Aesthetic as
bringing together mediating technologies with human aesthetics and offering resolution to the
fourth great discontinuity in human history: the separation of humans and machines.

6. In "Post-Digital Is Post-Screen—Towards a New Visual Art," Bosma argues that as digital mediation is pervasive and persists, to speak of any "post" requires an altogether different
orientation, which she offers by extending visual thinking and critical art theory beyond the
screen (and/or the screenic-spectacle).

7. *New Aesthetic, New Anxieties* is a multiday, collaboratively written book sprint completed by Berry, Michel van Dartel, Michael Dieter, Michelle Kasprzack, Nat Muller, Rachel
O'Reilly, and José Luis de Vicente. This was the first extended treatment of the New Aesthetic,
which gave shape to its early lines of consideration and situated it as a mood (and/or collective
feeling) designed to mobilize network mediations.

and creative engagement (always in flux), born of a networked culture, taking place in/on/of networked worlds, and mirroring certain conditionalities of the network, which itself seems resistant to codification ("The New Aesthetic and Its Politics"). Take Sterling's attempt to give shape to New Aestheticism as one demonstration of this resistance. Sterling offered readers over thirty definitional statements, ranging from "The New Aesthetic is a native prod- uct of a modern network culture" to "it is rhizomic" to "the New Aesthetic is really a design fiction" (n. pag.). But aside from helping mainstream the New Aesthetic by lending his celebrity to the issue, Sterling came up short in providing any conceptual whole as to what the New Aesthetic is, what it may become, or how it may be deployed. And he most certainly did not provide a set of tropes (hermeneutic or heuristic) that might allow for the New Aes- thetic's "marshaling."

Part of the central tension to something like Sterling's engagement is that his impulse was one of definition, an orientation not well equipped to respond to something as in flux as the New Aesthetic. But another part of this ten- sion, in many ways connected to the larger concerns of New Aestheticism in general, is whether the New Aesthetic is (or wants to be) an aesthetic move- ment. As Sterling pointed out, and others, like games scholar Ian Bogost, have echoed: a year's worth of "eye-catching curiosities" curated by Bridle on a tumblr, though suggestive and significant, do not necessarily "constitute a compelling worldview" (Sterling n. pag.). The New Aesthetic collection may direct attention to things escalating in cultural and rhetorical significance— such as the increasingly computational worlds in which humans act, and the proliferation of hybrid "ways of seeing" manifesting with human–technology assemblages—but as a movement it simply does not have a handle on the particular types of perception, beauty, judgment, and value that it privileges. Or, to put it in Sterling's terms, the definitional frictions (if not anxieties) of the New Aesthetic result from its lacking a strong metaphysics. Instead of doing the work to establish itself on its own terms, the New Aesthetic has been getting by, as Sterling suggests, by hacking a modern (and postmodern) aesthetic—or, as artist Kyle McDonald critiques in "Personifying Machines, Machining Persons," by mining and employing aesthetics from the function- ally designed devices of everyday lives.

To be fair, Bridle never intended to launch an aesthetic movement. His project was merely a yearlong creative exercise, having little to do with mani- festos and revolution—(rhetorical) staples of aesthetic movements. Instead, his was an emergent "thing," tapping into the dynamics of networked cul- ture to gather together "images and things that seem[ed] to approach a new aesthetic" of the network itself (Bridle, "The New Aesthetic" n. pag.). Bridle

curatorial = discovery

adopted a "hey, look at this cool thing" methodology and pulled together artifacts that reveled in pixelated representation in nondigital/nonscreen spaces
(Plate A), that included "born digital" architecture and its impossible material structures (from the parametric school of architecture to more common
3D-printing practices; Plate B), that featured render ghosts (pixelated and
not) that populate the "virtual spaces of computer rendering software" (Bridle, "The Render"), that highlighted computational glitches and the displaced/
disrupted images and sounds they produce, and that capitalized on representational practices designed to circumvent "machine vision," like Adam Harvey's *CV Dazzle*,[8] one of the first entries on the New Aesthetic tumblr. [For all
images, see the image gallery.]

Although each artifact gathered offered its own visual cues, with many
possessing a notable degree of pixelation, what they all carried were markers
of their underlying systems, which are, as Bridle argues, "inseparable from
[the artifacts] and without which they would not exist" ("The New Aesthetic
and Its Politics" n. pag.). Given this relation, there is a rhetorical tension at
the core of New Aestheticism between (a) the visual elements that mark what
many see as nothing more than pixel aesthetics and (b) the computational,
social, and political systems that underlie those representations. Thus, while
Bridle's diverse collection of artifacts may resist being marshaled toward any
particular sociopolitical agenda, and while the New Aesthetic may not be or
may not represent a movement *in proper*—lacking a manifesto or revolutionary agenda—what it does offer is a set of gestures (and a collection of artifacts)
that quite overtly mark a place for thinking about how individuals situate
themselves in relation to particular technologies—a matter of critical significance for contemporary rhetorical arts.

To this end, part of what makes the New Aesthetic of value (and even
workable to a rhetorical context) is that despite the Tumblr archive being
continued by Bridle beyond his initial yearlong vision, the broader conversations around the New Aesthetic have tapered off: its moment has more or less
passed. But this distance is actually helpful because it allows one to approach
the emergence of the New Aesthetic as a marked rhetorical ecology—an entity
composed as much by its artifacts as by its surrounding arguments, with the
flows that manifest across its visual and verbal registers putting into relief its
varied shapes and shades. The New Aesthetic may not have coalesced into a
complete, compelling worldview, but it did generate an ecology whose granu-

---

8. Bridle was specifically working in relation to "Look #1" from Harvey's *CV Dazzle*, but
for a complete look at the project, visit https://cvdazzle.com.

larities illuminate significant qualities for rhetorical practices in a post-digital culture.

RHETORICAL MOTIVATIONS

That rhetorical studies should have interest in the practices and purposes (if not emerging paradigm) of the New Aesthetic should come as no surprise because rhetoric, as an art, as techné, has always been concerned with *making*—with how one produces discourse and/or artifacts for particular audiences, in and of specific moments in time, space, and culture, and through various materialities and mediations. In this regard, the New Aesthetic offers much for consideration, as it reflects a set of practices and aesthetic values of a contemporary moment. But there is more at stake here in the rhetorical flavor of this work, for what unfolds in the coming pages is a critical reciprocity: bringing rhetoric (and rhetorical perspectives) to bear on the New Aesthetic as a way of developing insights into New Aestheticism, and then extending those insights back into the practices of rhetoric as a way of guiding twenty-first-century knowing, doing, and making.

To more fully situate the rhetorical inflection of this work, let me offer something of a quadrangle of motivations. First, the major claims in this argument take shape by adopting a rhetorical approach to the New Aesthetic (a matter rooted not in the definitional impulse of Sterling but in the conceptual orientations offered by Jenny Edbauer's work on rhetorical ecologies, which are more fully explored in chapter 2). Second, rhetoric (as a mode of inquiry) has been quite absent from New Aesthetic conversations—with the overwhelming majority of its critical engagements coming out of new media studies, art criticism, and techno-culture perspectives. Third, as a kind of inversion of the previous point, the New Aesthetic has yet to be directly taken up in the field of rhetoric. This is especially interesting given how it so readily aligns with considerations of glitch, pixel art, dirty new media, computational subversion, digital representation, augmented installations, and the like, all of which have been touched on by rhetoric and composition scholars in recent years. As an orienting sample, in 2012 Alex Reid's "Composing Objects: Prospects for a Digital Rhetoric" focused on glitch ontology as a way of thinking/rethinking writing and rhetoric practices. In 2013, in "Reclaiming Experience: The Aesthetic and Multimodal Composition," Aimée Knight argued for a recovery of functional aesthetics as a critical orientation to techno-production—specifically grounded in multimodal composition practices. In 2015 Casey Boyle's "The Rhetorical Question Concerning Glitch" extended Reid's ontological orientation and situated glitch as rhetorical invention. Later that year, Steven Hammer argued, in "Writing (Dirty) New Media / Glitch Composition," that glitch and related dirty new media practices had a critical value for cultivating technical, rhetorical, and medial awareness among writers/rhetors. And in 2017 Sean Morey and John Tinnell published *Augmented Reality: Innovative Perspectives across Art, Industry, and Academia,* an edited collection on augmented reality that included a variety of rhetorical perspectives on how (and to what degree) digital technologies and physical/material spaces were converging. Collectively, this brief sample helps set up the fact that over the past half-decade or so, rhetoric and composition scholars have demonstrated (a) that rhetoric can critically inform how one thinks about techno-phenomena related to the New Aesthetic, and (b) that those insights can, in turn, be brought back into rhetoric, illuminating different conditionalities and practices relevant to today's emerging mediascapes.

The fourth and perhaps most significant motivation for the rhetorical consideration here is pragmatic—for mediating technologies, whether emergent or established, influence the very means, modes, and metaphors by which one does rhetoric in the everyday (in the *how* of making rhetorical artifacts). And this has impact beyond just the making of mediated representations, as new mediating technologies (and their related aesthetics) also introduce new models and conceptual structures for thinking about and accounting for things in the world—for example, from viewing the brain as computer (a perspective increasingly problematized) to seeing pixels in nonpixel representations and artifacts (a dynamic this work examines in chapter 4). More to the point, computational, screen-based, networked media have fundamentally altered, augmented, and expanded the materialities and modalities, figures and forms available to rhetoric, and the New Aesthetic offers a finer granularity by which to take stock of these changes. In looking at the artifacts and objects of the New Aesthetic, and situating those in relation to a larger rhetorical orientation, one can more readily grasp the privileged patterns, perspectives, and practices for knowing, doing, and making in and of post-digital culture; and, in turn, one can more easily put into relief current and emergent human and nonhuman conditions of being.

The latter (conditions of being) signals something of an essential concern for why any of this should matter to rhetorical studies. For as Boyle sets it up in "Writing and Rhetoric and/as Posthuman Practice," the current human condition is one increasingly "practiced in" and "more sensitive to being in relation" with various technological systems (540). This indicates something far more invasive than just an increased frequency, familiarity, and functionality for rhetors to do things with technology. Instead, it gestures toward and reflects a set of cultural circumstances in which the vast majority of day-to-day experiences are mediated experiences: where Western culture is so saturated by computational, screen-mediating technologies that *to be* is, in many ways, *to be mediated*—to relate to the world in mediated ways. Consequently, while mediating technologies undoubtedly augment technical capacities for expression (the classical "available means" line in rhetoric), what is more important is recognizing how new human–technology assemblages alter both the rhetorical practices by which people inhabit and interact with the world (and with things in the world) and the relationships that come to bear on how people make sense of those dynamics.[9] The issue is not just that technologies extend human capacities for action but rather that they also introduce entirely different ways for people to think about, describe, qualify, and explain those actions, those capacities, and their place within that rhetorical potentiality.

If mediating technologies are central to how one measures and (re)makes (and makes over) the world, then those individuals with greater access to and greater affluence with mediating technologies (and their rippling implications) possess greater rhetorical capacities for action. To put it another way: those rhetors most adept with technologically rooted acts of perception, interpretation, and representation are uniquely advantaged and can, in turn, potentially leverage more rhetorical/cultural power in the hypertechnologized mediascapes of the contemporary moment. What takes center stage, then, is not the degree to which techno-human assemblages may render a person more or less human but rather the degrees of fluency (if not intimacy) that one possesses with technologically enhanced ways of being in the world (an increasingly mediated condition).

Therefore, it is my contention that the most important issue facing rhetoric today is understanding the relationships between humans and mediating technologies. For these relationships, and how they are rhetorically situated, not only influence (and reflect) the practices and purposes championed in current rhetorical pedagogy but also shape the very performances and pragmatic engagements that working creatives (rhetoricians included) pursue in, with, or through screen-mediated discourse and the production of digital/cultural artifacts. In taking up with emergent mediating technologies (and related phenomena like the New Aesthetic), rhetoric must include more than

9. In "Dwelling with New Media," Bay and Rickert argue that "new media restructure our world" (118), which is not simply a matter of how new media help construct particular objects and artifacts in the world (and/or representations of such) but includes an ontological dimension that concerns "the totality of things and relations . . . within which we are situated" (118), including the conceptual ways in which one imagines and articulates her own technological relations.

just a concern for how digital tools expand the "available means" or how new mediating technologies introduce different forms of writing. Instead, what is needed is an increased attentiveness to the human–technology assemblage and, as Boyle intimates, to how minor and major techno-human alterations introduce fundamental transformations in the available capacities of rhetoric and rhetorical being ("Rhetorical"; "Writing").

To date, the scholarly area most concerned with technology's impact on this shift in rhetorical capacity has been digital rhetoric, which I pick up in the next section—particularly trying to retain the aesthetic dimension operative in the formative moments of digital rhetoric, which has been somewhat abandoned in more recent efforts (from histories to new trajectories).

DIGITAL RHETORIC

Digital rhetoric has taken shape through a number scholarly fields—computers and composition, humanities computing, media studies, new media studies, contemporary rhetoric, and the like—but its first known articulation comes from rhetoric scholar Richard Lanham, who coined the term in a lecture in 1992.[10] In this earliest of formations, Lanham made the case that computers were as much rhetorical devices as logical ones (*Electronic* 31). But what Lanham understood, perhaps better than most, was that computers were more than just (the sum of) their operative practices. They were media devices—the very "machine created for Art-about-Art" (47)—and the media they produced and the representational practices they made possible were ripe with rhetorical consideration. Instead of focusing on the "familiar Platonic, mathematical center of human reason," which manifested regularly in the proffering of the computer as a logic machine (31), Lanham paid attention to the "complete renegotiation of the alphabet/icon ratio" that was taking place through computational displays (34). What Lanham was doing, then, was not defining a digital rhetoric but rather drawing attention to "the extraordinary convergence of twentieth-century thinking with digital means . . . [of] expression" (51). Thus, his digital rhetoric (as one major root) was ultimately grounded in screen-based representation and the expressive capacities emergent between human and screen mediations; and the mediating practices manifest on/ through computational displays were, in Lanham's view, culturally situated

---

10. Lanham's lecture, "Digital Rhetoric: Theory, Practice, and Property," was originally published in 1992 in the journal *Literacy Online*. He republished that lecture in 1993 in *The Electronic Word*, under the chapter title "Digital Rhetoric and the Digital Arts."

ectly altering the practices of *ekphrasis*—an important element
ersation.

ig out of the rhetorical tradition as part of the progymnasmata (a
exercises designed to prepare students for the production and per-
nce of oral declamations), the *ekphrastic act* involved bringing (via
description) something visual, material, or experiential clearly before the eyes
or minds of an audience. This was the job of the rhetor, particularly in public
declamations: to present to an audience, via description, the scene or image or
act or object of importance / under question. In thinking about the practice
of *ekphrasis* more abstractly, however, one might understand its central act as
a kind of transmediation: the act of translating the essence and/or form of a
visual/material object, person, or experience from one medium or materiality into another—such as when one creates a painting of a sculpture or writes
a poem about a painting or puts into words an otherwise phenomenological
experience. By definition, then, *ekphrasis* is not limited to oral or alphabetic
representation but can manifest with any medium serving as its actor or its
object. In some respects, one might see the bulk of the arts as *ekphrastic,* as
they employ various techné to translate experience, imagination, feeling, and
the like.

Given Lanham's attunement to *ekphrasis,* it is not surprising that he was
quick to notice how computational media were altering established forms
of representation and introducing new representational practices as well as
making an array of old representational practices available in new ways. As
a simple example, Lanham looked at the increased ease and speed by which
one played with typography, color, font size, and layout on the personal computers of his era. He saw computer-inflected textuality as an extension of the
practices of previous avant-garde artists—particularly that of Italian Futurist
Filippo Tommaso Marinetti, with computers (hardware + software) essentially
making Marinetti's advanced techniques readily available to an entire class of
novices. But, of course, the changes to textuality via computationality did not
stop with typographical play or manipulation of format. Rather, the combination of increased affordances of manipulation (Marinetti in a machine) and
new functions for engagement (the promises of hyperlinks and algorithmic
augmentation) brought textuality alive in unprecedented ways—dramatically
altering the range (and impact) of *ekphrastic* practices (whether put to rhetorical ends or not).

But Lanham noted something else of significance: changes in mediating
technologies also necessitated the inhabiting of new perspectives. That is, new
practices of representation, computational or otherwise, required that one
adopt new perspectives for *making with* and *making sense of* those mediations.

Further, Lanham noticed that certain computational media ushered in a kind of self-conscious awareness of their own mediation (*Electronic* 82), which, in turn, called attention to the ways in which media created meaning. This increased awareness not only reflected tendencies in visual modernism[11] but also emerged by default from the juxtaposition of new media forms with older mediating technologies—exposing (via unavoidable comparison) the operative logics, functions, values, and limitations of the mediations involved. For Lanham, these developments shifted the focus away from specific mediating technologies toward the more transferable (and transversal) acts and practices of mediation (from certain devices of mediation to the rhetorical modes and manner of mediation). Meaning, what Lanham was taking stock of in the formative moments of digital rhetoric was less a matter of technological determinism and more a matter of cultural and rhetorical convergence—a focus on the practices of representation (as constrained by computational media) and how those practices set upon particular audiences, users, cultures. At the very beginning of digital rhetoric, then, one can find an important value in adopting a rhetorical orientation to something like the New Aesthetic: for what New Aestheticism exposes is not just radical change in the means of production (a condition that Western culture has been undergoing on a regular basis for two if not three decades now) but rather notable shifts in the practices of mediation and the corresponding aesthetic sensibilities of an audience. Which is to suggest that while the technologies and rhetorical practices involved are of interest in this work, one of the major implications of looking at the New Aesthetic is an increased attunement to contemporary audiences (small and large)—including both human and nonhuman members, particularly those who operate with a different set of expectations, sensibilities, and default conditionalities toward media (and mediations) than the new media audiences of yesterday and the print-media audiences of yesteryear.

It is important to note, therefore, that though Lanham opened much for rhetoric via the conceptual orientation of digital rhetoric—grounding, as he did, the computational mediascapes of the digital rhetoric 1990s in relation to avant-garde art practices, orienting digital rhetoric scholars toward medial experiences (and more abstract concerns of *ekphrasis*), and foregrounding screen mediation in particular ways—what he did not do was provide an operative definition for digital rhetoric. In fact, it would be more than another

---

11. In *Graphesis: Visual Forms of Knowledge Production,* Johanna Drucker argues that "the self-referential attention to the picture plane" is something that can be associated "with a phase of visual modernism" (30), and she uses this visual attentiveness to explore the epistemic dimensions of visual/graphic development.

decade before any formal scholarly attempt to take stock of digital rhetoric emerged.

In his 2005 article "Digital Rhetoric: Toward an Integrated Theory," rhetoric and media scholar James Zappen attempted to collate the various threads (and modes of inquiry) that had, to that point, been formative of the field of digital rhetoric. While he (indirectly) established a set of considerations for digital rhetoric—for example, how rhetorical strategies factor into production/analysis of digital text, the affordances and constraints of new media, the formations of digital identities, and the potential for digital technologies to contribute to social community formation—what he did not do was provide an actual integrated theory of digital rhetoric (nor a specific orientation to human–technology dynamics). Instead, Zappen took stock of a survey of contributions, and then raised considerations for the opportunities that a potential integrated theory *might* offer rhetoric.

Four years later, however, the nebulous formations of digital rhetoric would change as media histories and literacies scholar Elizabeth Losh, in her *Virtualpolitik: An Electronic History of Government Media-Making in a Time of War, Scandal, Disaster, Miscommunication, and Mistakes,* penned/pinned down a formalized articulation—offering something of a galvanizing point for the field of digital rhetoric. Up until Losh's book, digital rhetoric had been understood primarily as either rhetoric *about* digital practices, environments, ontologies, and the like or rhetoric *constructed in* or *conveyed by* digital platforms, screen-media interfaces, programming and code, and so on. To be fair, that loose structure served well enough to orient scholars in and around digital rhetoric—and is, in a general capacity, still quite functional, even for something like New Aestheticism: for not only is the New Aesthetic tied to digital, network practices (with Bridle and others intermittently referring to the New Aesthetic as a network aesthetic) but also its archive and its many commentaries reside on the network itself and are distributed via digital platforms. But as Losh argued, the *about/in/by* dynamic was not sufficient because it ignored, in her view, the rich epistemological and operative complexities that information culture brought to bear on communicative and cultural practices. Thus, Losh offered her own fourfold: positioning digital rhetoric as being concerned with (1) rhetorical conventions of digital genres of everyday discourse, (2) public rhetoric distributed via networks, (3) rhetorical analysis/criticism of new media (objects and scholarly communities), and (4) the rhetoric of information theory, rather than epistemic or institutional rhetorics (a rhetorical orientation to the theories and applications of informatics). This echoes Zappen in certain ways but also adds a strong consideration for information culture (and the ways in which information sciences come to bear on communication and knowledge-making in a computational era).

If one were to take up Losh's fourfold as an operative guide for digital rhetoric, the New Aesthetic would still have value, as (a) its artifacts are distributed online and curated in a digital archive, (b) it demarcates a set of objects (individually and as a collective) for rhetorical analysis, and (c) many of its artifacts bear what Losh might situate as the aesthetic markers of information culture—with things like glitch and pixelated imagery owing at least part of their aesthetic qualities to information theory's marriage with screen-based mediation. But Losh's fourfold for digital rhetoric introduces at least two tensions important to this work (one specific, one general): (a) an absence of consideration of the aesthetic, and (b) an implicit distance between rhetoric and digital rhetoric.

Absent Aesthetic

While Losh's categories offer considerations of genres, publics, analyses, and other staples of rhetorical studies, there is simply not much among them that accounts for the aesthetic (digital or otherwise) or for how the aesthetic plays out among her formulations (minus a few quick treatments in some of the website examples she analyzes). This absence is particularly interesting given how much of the early formations of digital rhetoric (and other substantive influences like Kathleen Welch's *Electric Rhetoric: Classical Rhetoric, Oralism, and a New Literacy* and Gregory L. Ulmer's corpus on *electracy*) were concerned with representation, with the screen, with a rhetorical aesthetic of computers, and so on. But this aesthetic absence is not specific to Losh. Many in the field of digital rhetoric have, in the last decade-plus, simply (though not simply) moved further and further inside the machine as a scholarly focus. In a recent example, James J. Brown Jr.'s *Ethical Programs: Hospitality and the Rhetorics of Software* offers an insightful and critical narrative about computationality, software, and network culture, with Brown deploying Jacques Derrida's concept of hospitality as a way of thinking about software-to-software processes. Or, as another contemporary example, David M. Rieder's *Suasive Iterations: Rhetoric, Writing, and Physical Computing* calls for a different kind of movement through the screen, toward critical considerations of hardware—sensors, circuits, actuators, microprocessors, and the like—which Rieder sees as the focal point of today's creative computing. Although both Brown and Rieder, like Losh, do offer significant contributions to digital rhetoric, Brown does not explicitly take up with the aesthetic, and when Rieder does it is often of secondary consideration to the techno-material and operative core of computationality. Interestingly enough, this absence is also reflected in Douglas Eyman's *Digital Rhetoric: Theory, Method, Practice,* which offers a fairly extensive history of the field of digital rhetoric (its evolution and trajectories). In that work, Eyman presents his definition of digital rhetoric (as a field/set of inquiry practices) that includes Losh's fourfold of considerations, but to which he adds the development of the rhetorics of technology, the use of rhetorical methods for interrogating digital works, the critical examinations of the rhetorical functions of networks, and the theorization of nonhuman agents (software interlocutors) that possess varying degrees of agency. But even in this extended Losh–Eyman four-by-four matrix, the aesthetic is secondary (if considered at all), which, again, is especially interesting given digital rhetoric's roots in screen representations and the sheer overtness of the visual (and its proliferating aesthetics) in today's screen-oriented culture.

Of course, pointing out the aesthetic as absent or as secondary consideration is not meant to denigrate any of these works, for they each offer an excellent scholarly engagement in their own right that expands current thinking about the intersections of computational technologies and rhetorical practices. Rather, it is merely to indicate that my efforts here may add (if not return) a necessary dimension to the conversation, a rhetorical-aesthetic dimension, which is paramount to actual human interactions with computationality. Meaning, as just one example within this aesthetic dimension, if one is operating in a world before the advent of the graphical user interface (GUI), then focusing extensively on computationality and even the numerical encoding (1s and 0s) at the base of digital computing makes a lot of sense. But in a GUI (if not post-GUI) culture, this can be somewhat problematic: for as technology and aesthetic critic Jonathan Openshaw suggests, while the screen (and screen-based visual aesthetics) may not be "the most important part of the computer," the screen is often "the most absorbing" (6).[12] Digital traces, programming, algorithms, microcodes, silicon, electric signals, and so forth may make up most of what comprises computationality, with code (and numerical encoding) being central to what makes the computational world go round, but the vast majority of people do not interact with everyday computationality at the level of code, nor at the level of digitization, but rather at the level of the screen: *making* or *making with* digital media primarily through

---

12. Openshaw explores the significance of screen mediation along with other material and technical considerations in *Postdigital Artisans: Craftsmanship with a New Aesthetic in Fashion, Art, Design and Architecture,* a beautifully designed work interspersing artworks with interviews with artists and curators as well as think pieces from techno-theorists and media and art scholars to capture something of the depths to which technologies are influencing the practices and performances of contemporary art and culture.

(and with) the visual and culturally laden metaphors of the screen (the logics, aesthetics, and rhetorics of the interface).[13] This is the point of what-you-see-is-what-you-get (WYSIWYG) and drag-and-drop editors, which allow everyday people to work from the screen up, so to speak (interacting routinely, if not ubiquitously, with screen-based, visual aesthetics). Even software engineers interact with the machine at the level of the screen—with their programming code represented on screens, manipulated on screens, and often executed on screens. Given today's visually saturated, social-media-infused, digital-camera-laden, techno-cultural moment, one might see the pixel of the screen, not the 1s and 0s of computationality, as the lowest common denominator among most human–computer interactions. This is not to disregard the value of pushing beyond the pixel-screen and into the machine and/or network apparatus—as algorithms and data processors help make digital and post-digital culture possible—but there is, I believe, much to be learned about human–technology dynamics from screen-based, aesthetic considerations; and here I am not alone. *access to technology affects*

As visual theorist and digital humanist Johanna Drucker argued in *Graph-* *rhet.* *esis: Visual Forms of Knowledge Production,* the visual and aesthetic elements of *punn* computational mediation are not just accoutrement; they introduce additional approaches to knowledge.[14] Similarly, Knight's scholarship on multimodal composition calls for reclaiming experience-based ways of knowing—arguing that the aesthetic dimension of multimedia operates rhetorically and that it necessarily opens different epistemological avenues ("Reclaiming"). Moreover, as I explored in the introduction to this work, in addition to introducing the problematic tensions of reducing visual forms of inquiry and understanding to linguistic and/or logocentric systems, Barbara Stafford's *Good Looking: Essays on the Virtue of Images* actually makes the case for visual ways of knowing, understanding, and engaging as being critical for a screen-saturated, visual

---

13. This is not meant to suggest that Rieder, Brown, and Losh do not offer rich considerations of everyday computationality and its impact on everyday rhetors or everyday cultural practices and values—for they each make notable contributions in these areas. Rather, it is to set up a greater consideration for attentiveness to the screen, which in many ways serves as the primary point of contact between humans and most computational technologies. Further, Western culture is ocular-centric, and the screen exists as the primary form of ocular-oriented mediation—although, as I also explore in chapter 4, the screen (and its pixels) operate in the haptic dimension as well.

14. Drucker makes an argument for the importance of visual epistemology and traces out the implication of visual approaches to knowledge for screen-mediated culture. She offers a solid history of graphic, visual design, considered from multiple perspectives and across multiple media, with a particular humanist orientation that calls into question certain values and practices. Her work addresses the rhetorical dimensions of visual media, though it is surprisingly devoid of scholarship on visual rhetoric.

culture. What these authors establish in their own unique manner is that there has been (and continues to be) a long-standing bias against visual and other aesthetic forms of knowledge, particularly when considered in relation to logocentric and numerocentric attitudes toward computational, screen-based mediation—not only privileging a disconnected dynamic between humans and computational media but also necessitating something of a recovery of an aesthetic orientation to knowing (and situating that knowing as part of a human–technology relationship)—a matter to which I more fully attend in the "Recovering the Aesthetic" section below.

A second reason for the recovery of an aesthetic dimension here is that the few limited orientations to visual ways of knowing that are in general circulation have, as Drucker argues, taken shape not from art history, nor the humanities more generally, but primarily from computational engineers and user-oriented production experts who routinely design interfaces or digital environments for efficient action (151), approaching the screenic-visual in terms of function first, aesthetics second, and epistemic value third (if ever at all). Interestingly, it is this very condition that establishes part of the value (if not rhetorical necessity) of the New Aesthetic, which features an assortment of products and performances that serve as a kind of return of the repressed: for example, an aesthetic (if not epistemic) dimension that pushes back into and destabilizes the controlling impulse of functional computationality. But the aesthetic dimension has more to offer than just an interrupting of the ways that computers have been made to organize content/culture or structure interfaces and user engagements; as Lanham's work demonstrates and as Berry argues, the aesthetic can be employed to further "explore the computational practices that underwrite and mediate" the relational dynamic between screen-based representation and function ("Postdigital" 51). And this reiterates Bridle's take on the value of the visual cues of New Aestheticism—seeing them not as definitive qualities representative of an aesthetic movement but as directing attention to matters of computationality, culture, techno-human conditionalities, and the like, which all come into play as changes in mediating technologies generate new capacities for being in the world.

Although I do not agree with Berry's championing of computationality as the focal lens for all things New Aesthetic ("Postdigital"), what his and Bridle's take on New Aestheticism point to is the critical relationality between aesthetics and architecture, ornamentation and function, or screen-based representation and programming, all of which are central to developing and understanding contemporary mediascapes. Given this critical relationality, it would seem that the more effectively one might engage, conceptualize, and articulate aesthetic considerations of practices and experiences tied to screen-based (or screen-inspired) representation, the more readily one might explore, position, and even contextualize the computational underpinnings of those screen mediations and their related rhetorical implications. But before I turn more fully to this aesthetic dimension, let me first address the second tension hinted at above: a rhetoric/digital rhetoric divide.

Rhetoric / Digital Rhetoric

The second tension introduced by Losh's work is not exclusive to her efforts but more of a general concern reflected in her deployment of the term *digital rhetoric*: that is, the potential construction of a rhetoric/digital rhetoric divide. The term *digital rhetoric* is clearly a marker for the conversations in which this work hopes to participate (and valuable for locating this work among a specific subfield, in a particular history, and/or for a target readership), but it is equally important to note the perspective gap that emerges when using the term *digital rhetoric* (a gap that simply may no longer serve rhetoric's best interests). For example, Rieder's work on *suasion* moves across this tension by offering views in which physical computing is seen not as a digital-other but very much as part of the material experiences of everyday culture; and Morey and Tinnell's collection on augmented reality moves beyond this division by dealing with things that emerge when digital representations and the physical world fold into one another. Part of what this work offers, then, is not only a muddying of the digital/real divide and its rippling implications (more fully addressed in chapter 3) but, by extension, a muddying of the rhetoric/digital rhetoric divide—situating this conversation in a different rhetorical ecology.

However, keeping the above tensions in mind, I do understand the necessity of offering a working definition of digital rhetoric in a text like this, which draws from rhetoric as much as from aesthetic and new media perspectives. To this end, as I deploy it here, digital rhetoric means the study of and practice concerned with (1) acts and artifacts of mediation, (2) systems (computational, cultural, communicative, etc.) that produce or allow for particular types of digital and nondigital creations, and (3) human–technology assemblages at the center of contemporary making practices—with the latter being the primary impetus of this inquiry. Now, there are, of course, opportunities for slippage in this definition, as (a) the aesthetic dimension will manifest in all three areas, and (b) nearly all forms of rhetorical production today are intertwined with the material and conceptual practices of "the digital,"[15] but

15. "The digital" here refers to the more popular usage that situates the concept as a metonym for all things computational and networked. It includes everything from new materialities and technological devices to social media platforms and broadcast signals. Additionally,

manipulation opposed to use

hopefully the above definition offers enough of an orientation to allow readers to move forward in meaningful ways—particularly as I allow the New Aesthetic to inform digital rhetoric and digital rhetoric to help contextualize (and locate) the contours of the New Aesthetic.

Part of what this overview sets up, however, is that digital rhetoric in its formative moments and digital rhetoric in its more contemporary articulations may not be sufficient in their individual orientations for framing, thinking about, or working through something like the New Aesthetic, which uses the aesthetic dimension to illuminate particular computational conditionalities, leverages computationality as aesthetic style (often deployed for rhetorical purposes), and mobilizes an attentiveness to mediation through a rhetorical-aesthetic experientiality. What is needed, then, as I suggested in the introductory chapter, are additional lenses through which one might trace and triangulate the multitude of human–technology relations. But turning to the New Aesthetic as one of those potential lenses necessitates something of a recovery of the aesthetic dimension, for it is often held at arm's length (if not given second-class status) in rhetorical studies and/or in critically rooted approaches to knowledge.

RECOVERING THE AESTHETIC

In the eighteenth century, in his *Reflections on Poetry,* German philosopher Alexander Gottlieb Baumgarten offered a split between *things known* and *things perceived*—with the known falling under the faculty of logic and things perceived under the science of perception (the aesthetic) (17). What he attempted there (and in subsequent works) was to draw attention to the role that the aesthetic plays in how individuals perceive and understand the world, as well as to provide rules for aesthetic judgment. But Baumgarten's movement toward a theory of aesthetic experience (see Knight, "Reclaiming") was relatively short-lived. For philosopher Immanuel Kant, writing a couple decades later, would firmly re-ensconce the aesthetic under the banner of reason and would, in the process, establish the modern disposition toward the aesthetic: grounding the aesthetic in *a priori* conditions—"truths" that can be determined via reason and which appeal to a common sense, rather than in *posteriori* (experience-based) knowledge of the world. As Knight has argued, the aesthetic in a post-Kantian frame was to be understood "in other terms,

---

"the digital" often serves as a substitute for related concepts like the virtual of virtual reality and notions of cyberspace (all matters I more critically address later in this work).

with other criteria" ("Reclaiming" 150), and aesthetic ways of ⌐
to be "subsumed by other ways of knowing and relating to the wo⌐

Given Kant's influence, the aesthetic has been shrouded in this
intellectual and disembodied aestheticism ever since—leading to an
philosophized aesthetic whereby the aesthetic is understood not as a spec
thing or value, nor even as a set of qualities, nor tied explicitly to the human
sensorium, but instead as an abstracted kind of "sense" (e.g., to be sensible, to
make sense of). Although pursuing this philosophized "sense" in any depth is
beyond the scope of this work, the primary evolution for this "sense" (and the
aesthetic understood in this way) has been for it to function as the grounds
on which particular community formations take shape: in other words, as
Jacques Rancière argues in *The Politics of Aesthetics,* as that condition or quality or thing that creates clear divisions between what is acceptable (sensible)
and what is not (nonsense) for specific groups of people; or, as Pierre Bourdieu framed it in *Distinction: A Social Critique of the Judgment of Taste,* as
that which is productive and/or reflective of particular social/class inequali-
ties. There remains, of course, much to do with the aesthetic in this vein,
particularly as related to matters of *axiology* and considerations of the *polis,*
but the larger result of this orientation is that the aesthetic has ceased to be
"an acceptable way of knowing the world" (Knight, "Reclaiming" 150; see also
Stafford). But this works directly in contrast to the earliest formations and
understandings of the aesthetic.

To follow Knight's efforts, the etymological roots of the aesthetic come not
from Greek concepts of *logos* or *techné* but rather from *aisthetike* (noun) and
aisthanomai (verb). The *aisthetike* marks that which pertains to sense perception, while *aisthanomai* refers to knowing through an embodied sensorium.
Together they situate the aesthetic as being rooted, fundamentally, in sense
perception (and/or a general condition of perceptibility)—to a bodily sense-
ability operating as a basis for understanding. Of course, the Greeks would go
on to create a sense hierarchy, elevating sight and hearing over smell, taste,
and touch because the former revealed the world external to the body and
were simply more objectively verifiable than the latter (see Aristotle's *Metaphysics*). But the outcome of this sense hierarchy was, as Knight argues, the
"favor[ing of] *a priori* knowledge, based on logic, over posteriori knowledge,
based on experience" ("Reclaiming" 149). And this simple crack began the
long march to Kant's intellectual and disembodied aestheticism. But as the
postcritical turn set up over a half-century ago, and as has been reflected in
posthumanism and new materialism considerations since, any disembodied, intellectual-focused approaches are, at minimum, incomplete given the
greater complexities in which human actions, agencies, and even aesthetics
take shape.

Here is where turning to someone like American pragmatist and educational theorist John Dewey can help; for unlike his transcontinental philosophy contemporaries, who in the 1930s had taken up with matters of mechanical reproduction and aesthetics as related to a body politic (particularly that of fascism), Dewey was concerned with the establishment of the rhetorics by which the aesthetic became isolated from the very human conditions of their making and from their contexts and consequences of daily life. In *Art as Experience,* Dewey writes, "Objects that were in the past valid and significant because of their place in the life of a community now function in isolation from the condition of their origin"; and it is this setting apart, this "disconnect[ing aesthetic experience] from other modes of experience," that is the very movement that makes possible the aesthetic branch of philosophy and the specialized secularities of art (9). But this separation is by no means inherent in the aesthetic itself; it is a constructed position (much like the computationality/aesthetic divide) that has come to completely infect cultural institutions and habits of practice, and it has created the very rhetorical conditions from which arises the illusion of a group of master thinkers and master artisans who can speak to (and speak into existence) the aesthetic.

What is needed, then, is a "recovering [of] the continuity of [a]esthetic experience with normal processes of living," because, as Dewey presents it, "even a crude experience, if authentically an experience, is more fit to give a clue to the intrinsic nature of [a]esthetic experience than is an object already set apart from any other mode of experience" (9). This is doubly the case for the New Aesthetic, which points to an emerging (if not emerged) aesthetic sensibility that is captured not only through objects (and practices) set apart in art galleries and museums but also (perhaps more so) in everyday manifestations: in advertisements and architecture, digital signals and digital design, cultural artifacts and creative expressions. Which is to say, in Dewey's perspective, that a glitched broadcast signal on one's home television reveals as much about aesthetic experience and current human conditions as do the art installations of Kello (Plate A) or Aram Bartholl (Plate C). This is not to suggest that Kello's or Bartholl's works are not more poignant, but to point out that the underlying conditions to which the everyday glitch draws attention possesses equal magnitude in its ability to illuminate Western culture's current, digitally saturated conditionality.

Naturally, Dewey recognized that returning the aesthetic (and aesthetic experience) to everyday materiality and ordinary practices would "seem to some unworthy" (10), and I expect the efforts of this work to encounter some of the same dismissiveness given the traditional distance between rhetoric and the aesthetic. But the very implication of "unworthiness" is only pos-

sible as a designation if one is already operating from a p
ded within the very separative rhetoric that Dewey finds pr
understanding the aesthetic, the experiencing of the aesthe[
an aesthetic outside of the very practices, contexts, and cc
from which that aesthetic arises seems an impoverishe
contends:

> No amount of ecstatic eulogy of finished works can of itself assist the under-
> standing or the generation of such works. Flowers can be enjoyed without
> knowing about the interactions of soil, air, moisture, and seeds of which they
> are the result. But they cannot be *understood* without taking these interac-
> tions into account. . . . It should be commonplace that [a]esthetic under-
> standing—as distinct from sheer personal enjoyment—must start with the
> soil, air, and light out of which things [a]esthetically admirable arise. (11)

Thus, to understand the aesthetic experience and/or to embrace aesthetic ways
of understanding the world, including those offered by the New Aesthetic,
one must begin, then, not with abstracted, *a priori* principles, but rather, as
Dewey says, "in the raw; in the events and scenes that hold the attentive eye
and ear" (3). In this regard, the aesthetic experience to which Dewey directs
attention is not the product of any will to mastery of aesthetic principles but
is instead "determined by the essential conditions of life"—the very conditions of being; in other words, the aesthetic is something that emerges out
of humans undergoing/initiating "interchanges with [their] environments" in
the "most intimate way" (12). Human values (aesthetic or otherwise) emerge,
then, in balance with the environmental and essential conditions in which and
by which they live, and any surge in these conditions (e.g., changes introduced
by new mediating technologies) both necessitates and allows for transition-
ing to new equilibriums of interchange—with one's own values, expectations,
sense-perceptions, and rhetorical tendencies and practices reforming and
restabilizing in relation to these new equilibriums.

This is one of the many reasons for turning to the New Aesthetic. For
while contemporary mediascapes are littered with flash, whiz, bang; with
smart agents and anticipatory algorithms; with echo chambers and ubiquitous
computing narratives, Bridle's Tumblr archive showcases everyday artifacts
and occurrences that captivate the senses (as representations and interruptions, simulations and interventions). In other words, the New Aesthetic
collection presents, as Dewey might articulate it, "objects of intense admi-
ration" that intensify through awareness and acquiescence of one's "sense of
immediate living" (5). In the New Aesthetic, that "sense" not only depends

human–nonhuman interaction but, as Curt Cloninger argues, reflects the unequal distributions of the digital (its pockets of intensities)—offering at least one alternative to the delusion of democratic distribution through ubiquitous computing (n. pag.).[16] Thus, in touching upon any number of aesthetic considerations (proper and improper alike), the New Aesthetic (and its related post-digital siblings[17]) may serve, in varying capacities, to expose, to reflect, to highlight, and possibly even to provide a language and/or set of responses for describing new equilibriums of interchange.

Once we begin to rethink (and reclaim) the aesthetic as an embodied understanding through sensory perception, the role of mediating technologies (and their related artifacts) becomes extensively more profound. For as media studies pioneer Marshall McLuhan argued in *Understanding Media: The Extensions of Man* (resonating with Dewey's new equilibriums of interchange), new mediating technologies and their related practices of expression and mediation transform human sensory perceptions—that is, they change the ways (and scales) by which individuals make sense of the world around them. Writing a couple decades after McLuhan, cultural theorist Paul Virilio would include a further gesture: proffering, in *Open Sky*, that new mediating technologies introduced changes to how people make sense of things in the world by altering the very intervals of time and space against which all manner of human understanding occurs.[18] New mediating technologies, then, do more than just introduce new aesthetics and new aesthetic experiences; they also alter the very measures and perspectives by which one understands experience itself.

On its own, this would be important for rhetorical studies, as it would indicate a need for rhetorical practices and theories to evolve as new equilibriums are introduced or as new sensory perceptions (and intervals) shape how people make sense of their world. But N. Katherine Hayles suggested that something more essential might be taking place. In her foundational works on

---

16. In "Manifesto for a Theory of the 'New Aesthetic,'" Cloninger offers gestural orientations for the New Aesthetic. While his efforts do not formalize into any traditional sense of a manifesto, he does foreground the New Aesthetic as an orientation rather than a singular aesthetic, with its value stemming from how it puts its finger on certain intensities that result from and constitute the digital residue of daily life.

17. The post-digital not only marks a set of practices and orientations but also, more recently, serves as a cultural marker—as in the post-digital is what comes after the new media era. To this end, as media art scholar Caroline Bassett has argued, many contemporary media/art constructions get lumped under the heading of the post-digital (the New Aesthetic, Accelerationism, Glitch Art, Dirty New Media, etc.).

18. For Virilio, time and space are giving way to the interval of light, and when the world operates at the speed of light (through electronic tele-technologies), standard measures of duration and distance become compressed, and events and experiences get dispersed instantaneously and everywhere at one and the same moment.

cybernetics and posthumanism, she argued that working with new mediating technologies like virtual reality (headsets and interfaces) does not just extend one's sensory world in new ways, but rather has the potential to actually alter the neural configurations of the brain (*How We Became*; "Hyper")—in other words, technological change has the capacity to lead to physiological change. Hence, changes in mediating practices and technologies are not simply externalized in a tool or object, or simply extensions of a human sensorium, but instead can become embodied, material, biological. It is not just that people use technologies, nor that humans exist as part of the circuitry in which mediating technologies operate, but that there is a capacity for people to internalize (in multiple senses) technologized ways of representing, measuring, and mapping the world. This suggests that it is no longer sufficient to think of the human as the dominant measure; rather, as critical design architect and filmmaker Liam Young claims in his short piece "Shadows of the Digital: An Atlas of Fiducial Architecture," what now defines how people make their worlds and make sense of their worlds is "the technologies through which . . . [they] see and experience the world" (15).[19]

Given this framework of the aesthetic, if we understand the aesthetic as an intellectual, disembodied, *a priori* value beholden to a Kantian truth, or if the aesthetic is situated as merely the techniques invented and controlled by a master class (yet another element of the separatist rhetoric Dewey resisted), then the New Aesthetic has notably limited value. But if the aesthetic is tied to embodied sensory perception—to embodied, experience-based ways of knowing—then what the New Aesthetic does, and what it has the potential to expose, becomes crucial for aesthetics and rhetorics alike. This is because the New Aesthetic not only illuminates (and reflects) computational-infused aesthetic sensibilities but also foregrounds changes in audience expectations of the experience of media.

Dispositions and Apperception

One way to approach something like the New Aesthetic, following Dewey, would be to take keen interest in our "motor dispositions": the orientations toward particular mental and physical preferences that form in people in

---

19. Critical to Young's position is the call for a new design sensibility that has the capacity to "resonate across both human and machinic experience" (15). To this end, he turns to the machinic vision concept "fiducial" (a recognizable marker in an environment that functions as reference or measurement) to describe a new genre of architecture that is machine-readable (anchor point for augmented reality systems), that possesses a representational value that circulates (as image) in network platforms, and that occupies/inhabits a physical space on earth.

the production and/or reception of everyday aesthetic artifacts (101). For, to extend an earlier metaphor, in taking stock of the "soil, air, and light" of aesthetic considerations (the larger material, social, cultural, and environmental complexities necessary for any attempt to *understand* particular aesthetics), motor dispositions reveal the particular types of attentiveness that one possesses in relation to different materialities and media (and their potential manipulations). This is demonstrated most expertly in Steph Ceraso's "(Re) Educating the Senses: Multimodal Listening, Bodily Learning, and the Composition of Sonic Experiences," which introduces a realignment of the motor dispositions associated with listening. Ceraso seeks to move out from under ear-sound binarism so as to reconfigure contemporary dispositions toward listening around a multisensory ecology and, in so doing, highlight the greater complexity of relations between individual bodies and sound.

Like this work, Ceraso picks up with Dewey's aesthetic (and the experience of the aesthetic), but does so to situate listening as an embodied way of knowing. She argues that ignoring the multitude of ways in which sound penetrates the body or is perceptible to other parts of the human sensorium notably delimits the rhetorical capacities of sound. To counter this position, she calls for *multimodal listening,* which not only "draw[s] attention to listening as an expansive multisensory practice" (104) but which is intended to (a) defamiliarize students' listening habits/practices (112) in order to (b) prepare them "to become sensitive, reflective participants in and designers of sonic experiences" (103). At its core, Ceraso's *multimodal listening* invites a reinventing of the field's motor dispositions toward sound—advocating for "a bodily retraining" that can help rhetors (students and working creatives alike) "learn to become more open to the connections between sensory modes, materials, and environments" (120).

What Ceraso offers, beyond a smart take on multimodality and listening, is a contemporary work in rhetorical studies that uses Dewey's aesthetic inflection to counter habituated motor dispositions. More succinctly, her work is grounded in human apperception (and/or the human sensorium more broadly), and she offers one approach (*multimodal listening*) by which to extend the rhetorical capacities available to varying sensory modalities (in this case, matters of sonic writing/making).

The argument at the center of this book operates in a similar capacity, turning to the New Aesthetic precisely because it exposes, as communication scholar Geoff Cox argues, "the limits of human apperception" (152). But whereas Ceraso's work uses Dewey's embodied aesthetic (among others) to push against the habituated practices championed in listening, inviting a more nuanced orientation to the experience of sound, this work turns to the New

Aesthetic to push against apperception itself, to grasp how changes in human–technology assemblages (related to both changes in technology and changes in the human condition) introduce new capacities and new expectations for human experience and perception more broadly.

Additionally, while Ceraso's aesthetic and embodied orientations to sound find resonance with the holistic listening practices of solo percussionist and composer Dame Evelyn Glennie—which Ceraso employs as a means to help others attune to synesthetic convergences in sound, to experience sound in embodied ways, and to be attentive to the formation of bodily habits—the New Aesthetic is, at least on the surface, less available for this kind of leveraging. For as art and aesthetic scholar Katja Kwastek indicated, the New Aesthetic is not really concerned with matters of critique or even creative explanation; it appears content to just present its objects and their aesthetics "largely without classifying them, judging or theorizing them" (80). However, this does not mean the New Aesthetic is without critical value. For while it may not operate in terms of criticism, or in the established methods of an expert practitioner (e.g., Glennie), or in clearly delineated categories or methodological operations, it does, as Kwastek argues, provide commentary and critical insight from its "fuzzy areas"—on the margins and in the vibrating intensities among its example artifacts and myriad conversations (80). Or, to put it another way, the contributions of the New Aesthetic emerge not from any categorical order but rather, as Kwastek indicates, from the rhetorical resonances that manifest in the margins of its demarcated objects and objections. To grasp the New Aesthetic with any significance, then, one must take stock of its rhetorical dimensions as much as its archive.

Therefore, what the New Aesthetic presents, at least in part, is an element of rhetorical awareness specific to human apperception itself (and the related motor dispositions that reveal such apperception). But that awareness and its qualities are difficult to track because New Aestheticism was *located in, part of,* and *emergent from* the very techno-human apperception it helped illuminate. Thus, to take stock of the New Aesthetic with any validity requires that one be attentive to its flux, its fuzzy areas, its margins and vibrating intensities, as these are where its constitutive dimensions reside. Which means that one must adopt (or adapt) methods of engagement and inquiry that allow for degrees of fluidity (in perspective, in perception, and in procedure). To this end, in chapter 2 I turn to a rhetorical ecologies methodology, deploying this framework as a way for understanding the complexities operating within the New Aesthetic and for identifying its critical contributions to any post-digital rhetorical practice.

CHAPTER 2

Rhetorical Ecologies and New Aestheticism

MAKING SENSE of the New Aesthetic presents a bit of a challenge. For one, it actively resists codification, as James Bridle has argued in "The New Aesthetic and Its Politics"; two, it emerges as part of a larger collection of tendencies and tensions, conversations and critiques—encompassing not only its tangible artifacts (digital and non) but its many fleeting and competing discourses (its rhetorical dimension). More succinctly, the New Aesthetic takes shape as part of an ongoing rhetorical ecology: one that includes its artifacts, representative practices, and intentional and unintentional techniques of expression, as well as the particular ways in which these entities have been taken up, positioned, challenged, and co-opted in the commentaries on and criticisms of New Aestheticism. Thus, any approach to the New Aesthetic that does not take into account its rhetorical dimensions ends up presenting something of a limited perspective.

For example, filmmaker and media scholar Michael Betancourt's "Automated Labor: The 'New Aesthetic' and Immaterial Physicality" employs a critical Marxian perspective to position the New Aesthetic (particularly its archive) as documenting the shift from a machine labor that *augments* human action (amplifying and extending human action) to a machine labor that *supplants* human action. But then he reduces the New Aesthetic archive to four overlapping categories of artifacts:

1. autonomously generated images that contain markers of the digital;
2. physical constructions employing signifiers of digital forms;
3. translations of digital forms into visual style; and
4. dynamic, interactive data visualizations ("Automated" n. pag.).

While these groupings have potential, I hesitate to extend them because they are so tied to (inconsistent) surface patterns of the archive that they ignore the larger conversations in which the New Aesthetic participates as well as the underlying structures central to the very ways in which meaning can be made of the "patterns" themselves (the rhetorical dimensions). Additionally, part of what I am arguing here is not that humans have undergone a loss of agency, as Betancourt suggests, but rather that shifts in human–technology assemblages have reconfigured human and nonhuman structures altogether.

What is needed is not a decree of the loss of some agential condition, nor the imposition of a categorical order on an otherwise instable archive, but a mapping of the larger rhetorical ecology of the New Aesthetic, which gives shape and depth to the reconfigurations themselves. In focusing on the intricate relationships among its many components and momentary performances, the goal is to investigate, through rhetorical means, what the New Aesthetic *is* and how it can be meaningfully leveraged for rhetorical purposes. To get at these more abstract patterns, however—these shadows and silhouettes of momentary figurations—one must ignore the impulse to critically define a set of objects among a fluid and sometimes frivolous archive and instead post-critically drift among the gestures and gyrations of the New Aesthetic rhetorical ecology.

RHETORICAL ECOLOGIES

The term *ecology* stems from the discipline of biology, particularly in relation to the study of organisms and their interactions with one another. But in the early 1970s anthropologist Gregory Bateson's *Steps to an Ecology of Mind* helped open ecology to a larger set of metaphorical and modular considerations, as he used ecology as a conceptual orientation for understanding certain acuities, capacities, and processes of the mind. Some twenty years later, in the late 1990s and early 2000s, Bateson's extensions found resonance in rhetorical studies—with the ecological perspective offering rhetoric scholars an explanatory power that aligned with the impulses of late postmodernism and early posthumanism that were proliferating in contemporary thinking. For example, in *The Wealth of Reality: An Ecology of Composition*, Margaret Syverson adopted an ecological perspective to locate rhetoric/writing as a practice distributed across a complexity of networks and relations, from material nodes to varying social fields; this situated rhetoric/writing as involving greater complexity than what had been presented by the dogmatic rhetorical triangle. As such, Syverson's work was foundational in creating inroads for ecology in rhetoric—with her going so far as to offer an analytical matrix for working with ecology as an expansive framework for writing studies (7–20). My particular approach to rhetorical ecologies, however, is grounded not in Syverson but in Jenny Edbauer's extension of Syverson: for what Edbauer offers is not a set of analytical (and/or operative) heuristics but rather a concentrated focus on the flows and connections among the elements of a given ecology. Edbauer's attempt to take stock of and give articulation to that which is invariably "in flux" is crucial because the New Aesthetic, as Bridle suggest, is itself *in flux* and *of* the flux ("New Aesthetic" n. pag.). It is critical, therefore, to further unpack Edbauer's work and more fully situate how it contributes to and/or shapes this explication.

In "Unframing Models of Public Distribution: From Rhetorical Situation to Rhetorical Ecologies," Edbauer calls for rhetorical studies to adopt an ecological rather than a situational orientation. She argues that while Lloyd Bitzer's classical construct of rhetorical situation[1] has served as a valuable hermeneutic, it and its counterrhetorics inherently frame rhetoric as a collection of discrete elements: audience, exigence, constraints, and so on (7)—similar to Syverson's tensions with the rhetorical triangle. Element-based approaches like Bitzer's do possess "important explanatory power," but they are, in Edbauer's view, insufficient for taking stock of the "wider sphere of active, historical, and lived processes" as well as the material and medial influences in which rhetoric (and rhetorical artifacts) take shape (8). There is, Edbauer contends, always a complexity operating in excess of any given elemental framework, which is especially the case with rhetorical artifacts and utterances because

---

1. In 1968 Bitzer's "The Rhetorical Situation" argued not only that rhetorical discourse was situational but that it was actively called into existence by situation. He defined situation as a "complex of persons, events, objects, and relations" that took shape in relation to an exigence (or potential exigence) that called for particular kinds of discourse (3). This discourse and the human decisions associated with it were, in turn, constrained by the situation. Bitzer went on to identify the constituent parts that compose any rhetorical situation: exigence (problem existing in the world), audience (those capable of enacting change), and constraints (persons, events, objects, relations, and the like that limit decisions and discourse as well as any resulting actions).

they take on different degrees of significance as they traverse across different social constructions and purposes—what she refers to as the "'constitutive circulation' of rhetoric in the social field" (7). We can see Edbauer's concerns similarly operating in Betancourt's categories: while the categories do offer an explanatory framework for specific tendencies among aspects of the New Aesthetic, they are not sufficient for accounting for the "wider sphere" in which (nor the underlying substrate from which) the artifacts take shape— from technical considerations to the social field. Moreover, the categories also seem surprisingly devoid of connections with Betancourt's own framework (his Marxian orientations), which suggests that they are themselves in excess of his own explanatory moves.

What Edbauer argues is that rhetors should consider elemental orientations like Bitzer's or Betancourt's frameworks (and the larger arc of situational rhetoric in general) as part of "an ongoing social flux" (9). In this reorientation, the rhetorical power comes not from the imposition (or fit) of a particular categorical order (nor its related cause–effect logics) but rather from describing the fibers and fissures that formulate the flux: the relations, flows, and points of contact among the entities and organisms of a rhetorical ecology, and the social, institutional, and historical backdrops against which artifacts and utterances move. Rhetoric (and/or the rhetorical significance of any artifact or utterance) becomes constituted, then, not through declamation by a critical hermeneutist but rather as emergent among/through networked "flows and connections" (9). Moreover, and this is perhaps the most significant element of Edbauer's orientation, these flows and connections accrete over time, creating specific "intensities and mutations" that (a) transform and condition the network itself (including human participants), (b) orient the social flux toward particular perspectives and purposes, and (c) generate new rhetorical ecologies, which, in turn, further expand via counterrhetorics, co-optation, circulation, and the like (10; 20).

To demonstrate her position, Edbauer tracks the evolution of the "Keep Austin Weird" slogan, now central to the identity of Austinites in/from Austin, Texas. She shows how the slogan, which was initially enacted as a form of small business resistance to big-box corporate infiltration, came to participate in a multitude of rhetorics in and around Austin—from city government proceedings to street art, from academic branding to counterculture irruptions. In tracing "Keep Austin Weird," what she sets up is an articulation of how utterances, artifacts, and events are able to move fluidly through social and institutional discourses, forming their own networks and ecologies while remaining rhetorically pliable. For Edbauer, being attentive to the pliability of rhetorical artifacts in and across networks allows scholars to ask different questions and take stock of different considerations, all while situating the rhetor as both transformative of and conditioned by the ecology.

By tracing "Keep Austin Weird" across a set of artifacts, discourse communities, counterpublics, and other rhetorical manifestations, Edbauer offered not just a narrative of the slogan but also a loose description of its accretions. There was no definitive articulation to be had (nor was that Edbauer's intent); rather, by exploring the motility of "Keep Austin Weird," Edbauer showed how an ecological rather than situational (or even categorical) perspective provided access to material and medial effects and processes as well as to the everyday, lived capacities associated with a given object of study. In adopting a rhetorical ecology orientation to the New Aesthetic, I inherently consider the designated artifacts of the New Aesthetic archive but also, as suggested above, the ways in which the artifacts are given meaning, circulate among various discourses, and manifest in relation to different materialities, social fields, historical moments, and institutional structures. What takes center stage in this approach is not the imposition of a particular (external) hermeneutical order onto a relatively nebulous archive (à la Betancourt) but rather an increased attunement to the circulating intensities that constitute (and reflect) the New Aesthetic rhetorical ecology. The challenge, however, is finding a way to put into relief the circulating intensities, as they are themselves in flux and somewhat resistant to the description that Edbauer situated as part of the power of this model.

My response, then, is not to describe any circulating intensity itself but to glimpse its edges and outlines, colors and contrasts, which accrete as the intensities move across different flows and connections, conversations and contentions. This allows, in my view, one to articulate the contours of the accretions, which in turn can offer something of a tentative shape to particular circulating intensities. As *contour* is a key term in this work, let me take a moment to better situate its meaning and use in this context, which draws from a multitude of its potential meanings.

WHAT IS A CONTOUR?

First, *contour* is commonly used to refer to the general shape or form of something (e.g., the contour of the hood of a car). Second, it is associated with malleability—as when used as a verb (e.g., to contour something [mold into specific shape] so as to fit it into something else). Third, contour is a practice used in cartography to denote multiple levels of elevation (i.e., mapmakers use contour lines to indicate height or depth). While the critical impulse would be to situate contour in relation to a single meaning (as concept), the postcritical move here is "punceptual," a neologism introduced by Gregory L. Ulmer in *Heuretics: The Logic of Invention,* which, like the pun, allows for thinking with all the meanings of a term (and all its registers) simultaneously. In this way, the contours of the New Aesthetic are meant to (1) denote general shapes and shades, (2) demarcate entities that can readily be made to fit into/with other registers (e.g., digital rhetoric), and (3) designate the depths and intensities of New Aestheticism. They are not part of a fixed categorical order, nor of a singularity, but rather are more akin to the shifting silhouettes of an evening dress (as its wearer dances in the moonlight).

If working from a traditional critical perspective, constructs like contours are hard to deal with because they do not satisfy the hermeneutic imperative (they are not necessarily stable). But I am attempting something different here, with the contours of the New Aesthetic meant to function rhetorically: serving as a set of operative guides for mediated beings *making* in a mediated world. While they may offer something akin to "a rhetoric" (perhaps a post-digital rhetoric), I stop short of such a label, as the contours themselves possess notable degrees of instability. Further, as I demonstrate in the remaining chapters, New Aesthetic artifacts can at one and the same moment be seen to fit with multiple contours, apply to different contours in contradictory ways, and even point toward the inevitable excess of the ecology (that which resides beyond what the contours here can provide). By focusing on the individual contours (and not approaching them as a stable collective), I aim to keep open the possibility of adding new contours or, as is more likely, completely remaking the contours as the postcritical winds continually shift the dress's silhouette.

To put the contours into relief, then, one must work in relation to the objects of the New Aesthetic as well as its many arguments and articulations. For not only does moving through the rhetorical dimension in which New Aesthetic artifacts participate help one develop a richer context for understanding the contours that emerge, but it is the very process that must be undergone to glimpse the contours in the first place. Thus, the next sections pick up with key challenges to the New Aesthetic, offering responses to those challenges while using the depths they provide to better illuminate particular contours and considerations.

As a kind of pre-first step to this rhetorical ecology orientation, however, it seems important to acknowledge the online dynamic of the majority of sources in this chapter (and in subsequent chapters when dealing explicitly with commentary on New Aestheticism), for most of the rhetorical elements of New Aestheticism live in blogs, online journals, video-recorded talks, book sprints, and electronic as well as print versions of magazines like *Atlantic* and *Wired*. While it has, of course, become more common for academics to work in relation to sources from the blogosphere, it seems nonetheless important to note this element here because (a) the degree of online source material involved may feel different from most academic writing practices, and (b) the online, networked quality of the sources is central to the engagement: that is, central to what media culture historicist and theorist Anne Friedberg would have called the "born digital"[2] quality of New Aestheticism.

RHETORICAL DIMENSIONS

For all of its faults, failures, and finicky manifestations, the myriad engagements on the New Aesthetic collectively serve in at least one capacity: testimony to its existence, to its potential value, and to the need to continue working it through. For whatever it is, has been, or may become, the New Aesthetic did manage to put its finger on the pulse of something—something, as Bruce Sterling suggested, that only emerges in a world increasingly defined and organized by human–technology relations. If there were not *something* to the New Aesthetic, it would not have spawned such a variety of presentations, keynotes, and responses (from bloggers and artists to popular writers and ivory-tower academics). But the range of reactions suggests that while there may be value in New Aestheticism, there are also many tensions that cannot be ignored.

The primary charge levied at the New Aesthetic begins with the most fundamental of rhetorical components, its label: whether the New Aesthetic is an aesthetic movement at all. More than a few critics and public intellectuals do not see the New Aesthetic as a movement—maybe as a *meme,* as techno-theorist Robert Jackson argued in "The Banality of the New Aesthetic," or perhaps a *vibe,* as media studies scholar Lukasz Mirocha suggested in "Communication Models, Aesthetics, and Ontology of the Computational Age Revealed," but not a movement. Even Bridle, as indicated in chapter 1, hesitated to call it a movement. And Sterling did the same, though on different grounds (e.g., metaphysics). But whether a movement or not, what the various challenges to its stature reveal are different potential understandings of aesthetic movements themselves as well as why New Aesthetic artifacts operate and inculcate the way they do. To this end, the myriad of challenges to its movement status include

---

2. When digital artifacts and objects are not produced as a transmediation of a text but rather are conceived and constructed from the start in digital platforms, they are, as Friedberg argues in "On Digital Scholarship," born digital: inception, conception, and reception all taking shape in and through digital materialities.

the world now being too fragmented and dispersed to sustain a movement (or any type of avant-garde for that matter), the New Aesthetic being a "backward-facing" aesthetic and lacking any sense of futurecasting, or it being all about style, having no content or politics of its own. Further concerns include the New Aesthetic's lack of history (or any sustained sense of history) or its pursuit of human aesthetics (and/or that it focuses too much on the human element) at the expense of objects or an object-oriented aesthetic. This, of course, is by no means an exhaustive list, but together these rhetorical maneuvers provide the backdrop and flux upon which the New Aesthetic's circulating intensities accrete; that is, they offer the discursive and material points of contact from which one might begin to draw out the contours of New Aestheticism.

To begin this rhetorical engagement, let me focus first on the challenges to whether the New Aesthetic is a movement, for that claim (and its related contentions) establishes a comparative dynamic by which one can further investigate the other rhetorical challenges to the New Aesthetic.

Movement

Avant-garde artists and other aesthetic movements have traditionally used creative works as *ruptures of* or *exceptions to* established practices and values. That is to say, as freelance writer and techno-critic Kyle Chayka argued in "The New Aesthetic: Going Native," aesthetic movements typically use dissidence to "shock a society" into an (often revolutionary) aesthetic shift or to draw critical attention to a prevailing cultural condition they are confronting (n. pag.). The Dadaists, for example, used a range of tactics to respond to the violence and trauma of World War I, the industrialized technology of the early twentieth century, and the prevailing standards of modernity. They championed irrationality and the nonsensical, took up an anti-art culture, and laid the groundwork for abstract art. The Surrealists, as an extension of Dada, pursued instinctive thinking as art practice. In a very Freudian sense, they intended to reconcile dreams and depth psychology with reality in order to break the chains imposed on imagination. Both Dadaism and Surrealism challenged the aesthetics and rhetorics of rationalism (particularly excessive rationalism) and offered a different future, one where imagination, instinctual thinking, and the nonsensical qualities of human beings had space to flourish in and through representational practices. The artists in these movements created works that showcased a different value set, "shocked" an overly rational cultural ideology, and pointed toward a different future-to-come.

If one takes Dada and Surrealism as possible models, the question becomes how might the New Aesthetic stack up? And here the matter is not a measure of impact, for that would be an unfair equation on a number of accounts. Rather, the issue is in determining what makes an aesthetic movement an aesthetic movement. In this regard, one element commonly aligned with aesthetic movements is the notion of shock or a revolutionary spirit that challenges well-established practices and paradigms, seeking to exchange the familiar with the unfamiliar. But in thinking of the New Aesthetic as a rhetorical ecology, operative in a particular historical and cultural context, the reality is that the beginning of the twenty-first century is nothing like the beginning of the twentieth; there have been major cultural, ideological, epistemological, ontological, and technological shifts in the past one hundred years. It is simply more difficult to shock a society in a post-, post- moment because the fragmentation and dispersion ushered in by postmodernism and poststructuralism coupled with the affordances and ubiquity of networked culture make it difficult to find anything solid enough to work against, anything established enough to legitimately be "shocked" by something. As digital humanist Caroline Bassett has argued in "Not Now? Feminism, Technology, Postdigital," the "enchantment with the technological as new" has passed, no longer functioning "as a privileged site," at least not in the same ways (137).[3] Instead, what the New Aesthetic is doing, as Chayka claimed, is "respond[ing] to a[n already] shocked society and turn[ing] the changes we're confronting into critical creation" (n. pag.). The New Aesthetic is not replacing or subverting an established order so as to "shock" society or culture; rather, it is showcasing artifacts and attunements, practices and preferences that draw critical attention to the technological "shock" that the developed, Western world has already undergone.

Interestingly, Marshall McLuhan, writing in the 1960s, provided a way to understand this New Aesthetic function. In *Understanding Media: The Extensions of Man*, he argued that people are often numbed to the actual impact of technologies. That is to say, the public gets distracted by particular relational understandings of technologies (e.g., the conventional user–used relationship) and fails, McLuhan says, to take stock of the effects that those technologies have on human patterns of perception and/or ways of being in the world (18). People so readily adopt, use, and internalize the logics and *new ways of being* afforded by technologies that they typically are unable to take stock of how technologies alter their sense ratios, aesthetic preferences, and worldly sensibilities. Of course, the crazy thing about McLuhan's claims is that radio and television were the dominant emerging media when he was writ-

---

3. Bassett's work here attempts to account for a variety of medially aware responses to contemporary technological developments (and the different ways in which those might be read).

ing. These were unidirectional broadcast technologies, blanketing a relatively stable consumer culture. But today's technology and media no longer exist as singular entities. They function as networked devices that communicate with one another as much as with humans—a mediated world where *to be* has become intertwined with *to make,* where cultural participation is enmeshed with producing digital/network artifacts. Therefore, there may be no position for a general public to take up with other than what McLuhan calls "the numb stance of the technological idiot" (18). For when people are saturated by (and infatuated with) their technological devices, they may not be equipped to fully attune to new mediating technologies or to the changes in the human condition ushered in by those technologies. And the reasons are at least twofold. First, as Walter Ong suggested in *Orality and Literacy: The Technologizing of the Word,* one needs the highest technology available to be able to assess the ways in which previous technologies set upon the human condition. For what newer technologies reveal are not only the blips and imperfections of previous representational practices but also the depth and degree to which those technologies influence human ways of being/thinking in the world (80). This suggests, on some level, that it may be impossible to take stock of the impacts of the highest technological forms themselves; but part of what the New Aesthetic is doing, specifically in relation to its larger rhetorical ecology, is prompting a particular kind of awareness of these human–technology considerations—revealing the assemblage through manifestations of its own granularity.

Second, the "numbed stance" to which McLuhan refers results from sociocultural practices that have conditioned people to put technologies to use, to do things with them, and, perhaps more importantly, to use them for what they were designed. This conditioning has created a general hesitancy to employ technologies differently and to play with them critically (processes that allow for intervening in technological assumptions and logics and attuning to the ways in which technologies set upon the human condition). Being indoctrinated in this way is, perhaps, a remnant of industrial/machinic culture, which saw a decrease in multifunctional tools and an increase in specialized artifacts for specialized purpose: one tool (one worker) for one job (one task). But while the more recent hacker/tinkerer/do-it-yourself (DIY) mentality coming into mainstream culture may be changing this orientation—the kind of hacker-bricoleur to which media and technology scholar Jan Holmevik refers[4]—by and large people still commonly relate to technologies with

---

4. The hacker, of course, is something of a cult figure—coming to mainstream culture through literature and cinema narratives that position her as a subversive, one who can intervene in various technological systems and/or expose what is hidden by black-boxed computa-

the numbed stance: ubiquitously using technologies while failing to take stock of how they alter individual and collective patterns of perception.

But artists, "serious artists," as McLuhan might say, are a different breed. Unlike the average Jane or Jimmy, they are "able to encounter technology with impunity" because they are experts at accounting for "changes in sense perception" (18)—which includes taking stock of the "shock" already undergone. Dutch media art critic Arjen Mulder echoed these sentiments, arguing that artists are "able to be conscious of the present" and possess the ability to make the rest of culture more aware of present, technologized sensibilities (in Brouwer, Mulder, and Spuybroek; qtd. in Berry et al. 15). And while I agree, to a certain degree, about the role that "artists" may play in helping the larger culture more readily attune to how technologies influence sense perception, I would move outward from the specific class of working creatives designated by McLuhan's and Mulder's "artist." For example, the New Aesthetic itself is tied to this consciousness of the present; its artifacts and occurrences come as much from maker culture, industry, and commerce as from art-proper. And part of the very value of the New Aesthetic is that it highlights how changes in human–technology assemblages reconfigure structures of attention that lead, in turn, to differently attuned types of awareness on the part of everyday working creatives and rhetors who *make* as part of an operative assemblage. For what is taking shape in the New Aesthetic is less a transition from no awareness to awareness, and more a change in the level of attunement that results from shifts in human–technology assemblages—with contemporary assemblage formations directing human and nonhuman attention alike toward a root condition of mediation as well as opening access to a level of awareness that would be otherwise obfuscated by the sense of immediacy or emersion in one's own techno-cultural moment (Ong's highest technology position). Thus, the capacity of the "artist" to take stock of the present and to encounter technology with impunity may be true of any individual who possesses a certain attunement to the technologies and materialities with which she works (and/or to how they set upon her and her upon them); and part of what makes the New Aesthetic valuable to rhetoric is that it helps foster this attunement in everyday rhetors by exposing core elements of mediation and/or by subverting human expectations of mediation, which are also part of the

---

tionality. The bricoleur, coming from French anthropologist Claude Levi-Strauss, is a tinkerer, an assembler, an individual who improvises with the material and nonmaterial possibilities at hand. The hacker-bricoleur, then, as Holmevik presents it, is one who "works with what is available to create new and exciting possibilities" that allow for new representations in the world and for interventions into socio-culturo-political orders (44). What limits this figure is not materialities but her abilities to imitate, simulate, replicate, and leverage aesthetics, objects, and artifacts in, of, and through computational systems.

ecology in which it participates. Thus, on at least one level, part of the very purpose and value of this work is in helping everyday rhetoricians attune to reconfigured structures of attention by working in relation to the contours of the New Aesthetic so as to move away from McLuhan's *numbness* and open heuretic avenues for rhetorical practices in post-digital culture.

It seems important to acknowledge, however, that the New Aesthetic—a "particular kind of sensibility" attuned to a ubiquitous computing and networked present (Berry et al. 11)—does actually come into existence via Bridle and other digital futurists (artists) playing in the digital and nondigital art galleries and streets of London. As post-digital artists who work among and through digital and nondigital medial interfaces, these folks are highly sensitive to changes in patterns of perception with regard to mediation. They do possess something of an orientation to seeing, hearing, and feeling dissidence in media in ways that a general population may not, at least not without prompting; and this is a vital component of what the New Aesthetic contributes—the prompt—as it exists, at least in part, to make the rest of culture more aware of present, technologized (in)sensibilities.

What this also suggests, from a rhetorical analysis perspective, is that Bridle's "hey, look at this cool thing" approach to gathering artifacts is not as *arhetorical* as it may seem. It is a trained practice of recognition by an individual attuned to particular human–technology tensions. Further, his project, which launched the New Aesthetic but is not totalizing of it, was a curatorial act; and as Berry et al. argue in *New Aesthetic, New Anxieties,* this "implies a public gesture and a subject position" that "frames the collection" and "produces connections" among the artifacts (32–33). So, games scholar Ian Bogost's joke that the New Aesthetic can be defined as "things Bridle posts to its tumblr" is not as flippant as it may appear ("New Aesthetic" n. pag.). Even that reductive view still situates the New Aesthetic as curatorial practice, gathering examples of emergent patterns of representation that help foster a kind of attunement—patterns that have not, up to this point, coalesced enough into an articulable platform or paradigm but nonetheless remain recognizable as (a) touching on something of importance and (b) helping others attune to the implications of human–technology shifts (particularly as reflected in the forms and materialities of mediations). This is partly why it is important to try to grasp the accretions among the New Aesthetic ecology, for what is being introduced by New Aestheticism is not a definitive set of categories for making sense of contemporary art and media but rather a rhetorical attunement to how shifts in human–technology assemblages, and the new patterns of perception they introduce, are themselves ushering in a kind of mindfulness that realigns (if not counters) McLuhan's *numbness.*

One example of the "new" patterns to emerge among the reconfigured structures is something of a destabilization of an old dichotomy: the digital/ real divide. Bridle, as indicated in chapter 1, was pretty consistent on the fact that much in and of the New Aesthetic was blurring the boundaries between the digital and the real. This is echoed, of course, in the many commentaries on the New Aesthetic but is also demonstrated in things like (a) pixel aesthetics manifesting on T-shirts, in hairstyles, and as exterior building designs; (b) cityscapes becoming blanketed by a digital layer of maps, reviews, check-ins, and so forth; and (c) digital interfaces themselves being constituted by the metaphors and images of everyday reality (from icons to social media feeds). In other words, the first accretions that one might identify among the New Aesthetic ecology involve the ways that New Aesthetic objects and ostentations direct attention to the rhetorical interplay across the digital/real divide—revealing, on the one hand, that the digital and the real were perhaps not as separate as originally thought and, on the other, that each operates in an aesthetic as well as material and representational dimension for today's working creatives. As I explore more fully in the next chapter, science fiction writer William Gibson referred to this blurring as *eversion*—the eversion of cyberspace into the real—but in the New Aesthetic it functions as a two-way orientation (the digital everting into the real; the real everting into the digital), offering the overarching gesture of the first contour: *eversion as/of design*.

But before moving on to that (and other) contours, it is important to continue with this rhetorical exploration of the tensions of the New Aesthetic, for the more deeply one can understand New Aestheticism, the more significantly one will be able to position (and leverage) the contours for rhetorical considerations.

Challenging the Challenge

The first response above situates the New Aesthetic as an awareness aesthetic rather than a revolutionary one—suggesting that the New Aesthetic is intended not to shock a society into a particular mode or order but rather to draw attention to (a) the technological shock that everyday culture has already undergone and (b) the reconfigured attention structures that this undergoing has introduced. The second potential response, in contrast, is to make the case that the New Aesthetic does in fact respond to a prevailing cultural condition. Of course, the triggers of this responsivity do not carry the political and/or rationalist overtones to which Dadaism and Surrealism responded, but they nonetheless function as a counter to the widespread, McLuhan-esque "technological idiotism" indicated above—large-scale populations increasingly unaware of the screen-mediated, computationally constructed, and network-oriented patterns of perception and representation rampant in their current moment. Not only unaware, but unaware that they are unaware—which, again, may simply be a position that one cannot occupy without some sort of prompt (e.g., the New Aesthetic) or trained sensibility (McLuhan's and Mulder's artist). A popular, commercial example of this "unaware" mentality is demonstrated in the marketing strategy of the iPad 2 release. In the same year as Bridle's launch of the New Aesthetic, Apple aired a television commercial for the iPad 2 that included the following voiceover: "When technology gets out of the way, everything becomes more delightful, even magical. That's when you leap forward. That's when you end up with something like this" ("We Believe" iPad 2 Commercial). Here, technology "getting out of the way" refers not to the technological device itself but specifically to keeping the technical, computational, machinic interruptions from intervening in regular user-tool dynamics (the numbed stance). The more the technology "gets out of the way"—the more black-boxing that occurs with corporate/commercial technologies—the more people can remain oblivious to the device, its functions, and its impact. It is difficult to grasp the patterns and practices of representation when one is disconnected from the operative logics that produce them (which is as true for writing as it is for computational media). But the simple reality is that the more difficult it is for one to intervene in a given technology (device, system, practice, or other), the harder it is to take any position other than the numbed stance of the technological idiot. Hence, there is a rhetorical value in fostering awareness: creating opportunities for individuals not only to intervene in the human–technology coupling but also to grasp shifts in their very own sensibilities. For when interventions are possible or when interruptions occur—technical, cultural, political, or otherwise—these instances draw attention to the technology, to its mediating acts, to the device as device (no longer merely a window or portal to the digital world), as well as to the role, function, and position that humans may take up in relation to these matters. They ask, in Richard Lanham's terms, that users look *at* the human–technology assemblage (its technological and human components alike) rather than merely operate *through* it. Or, to put this in philosopher Martin Heidegger's terms: in those moments of intervention or interruption, the iPad2 becomes "present-at-hand" (*vorhandenheit*) and Apple wants them to be or remain "ready-to-hand" (*zuhandenheit*). That is, Apple (as corporate metonym here) wants users to use the device, to move through it to access or make digital content in the ways that Apple has designed, and not necessarily to be aware of the device's computational workings or of it as computational device, prone to all sorts of miscues, malfunctions, and misfortunes.

In counterdistinction, part of the very rhetorical function of the New Aesthetic is making "present-at-hand" (via aesthetic triggers) a litany of mediating practices that general culture associates with network activity and drawing attention to the operations of the systems of digital culture. For example, one might look at something like computational artists Jon Satrom and Ben Syverson's sOS operating system, which is an extension of their earlier collaboration Satromizer. sOS is basically a corrupted version of Apple's operating system, which merges glitch practices with problem-based (if not problem-inducing) operations. As users tap the iPad screen, they have no real way of anticipating what the operating system will do. The un-anticipatable outcome of the operative system calls into question, as Casey Boyle suggests, the assumptions (as well as epistemological order) most people have with computer systems ("Rhetorical" 14). While this particular example is not part of the New Aesthetic curation, how it works to destabilize expectations of a device's operative system—by turning glitch itself into a procedural methodology for operation—foregrounds much of what people take for granted in human–computer relationships. Or, put another way: the very experience of sOS, like most New Aesthetic artifacts, creates an awareness of (or at least attentiveness to) the medial platform, process, or product of which it is a parody, including the human dimension within that assemblage.

Therefore, one way to understand New Aestheticism (and, by extension, its contours) is not as an *arhetorical* entity, devoid of the political fervor of Dadaism, but rather as a direct response to the medial numbness that has served as default cultural position. This numbness exists, however, not only in relation to computational systems of mediation but also in relation to the very underlying assumptions of those technologies and how they shape human perception. Further, the more that people fetishize technologies and the more "the real" gets inundated with "the digital," the more significant the need for something like the New Aesthetic (whether movement or not) and its rhetorical implications. For, as McLuhan argued, the change ushered in by technologies does not require cultural consent (19). The change occurs, regardless. It may unfold differently depending on the technologies and degree of general (dis)approval, but it unfolds nonetheless. All one can do is try to attune oneself to its effects, take stock of the patterns of perception being introduced, and work to understand how technologies alter (and can be made to alter) one's conditions of being in the world. Of course, in twenty to thirty years, this *awareness* may simply be part of everyday life—similar to the way Dadaism opened the world to abstract art and readymades as leverageable artifacts. But in the meantime, the New Aesthetic reflects the reconfigured attention structures introduced by new/different human–technology assemblages and serves as one postcritical engagement of today's increasingly technologized conditions.

Perhaps this is why the general consensus on the New Aesthetic is that it functions primarily by pointing to the technologized reality of contemporary lives: people are living a technologized reality—living in it, of it, and becoming beings through it. What Bridle has been doing, then, is merely (though, to be sure, not merely) pointing to things in the world *as they already are*—and what makes this central for rhetoric is that it offers an attunement to practices and relations, preferences and representations reflective of a contemporary condition. To enact change in/on/of/through networked discourses, which are as much visual and textual (as well as volatile and tactile) as they are computational, one needs to be attuned to a perspective in which the aesthetic dimension not only directs attention to mediation but also operates as *suasive*.

In mapping or merging an aesthetic dimension with a rhetorical orientation, one needs to consider the larger set of expectations and anticipations that are part of both registers. This includes, on the one hand, understanding the value of the aesthetic to rhetorical practice—the kind of Dewey-based pragmatism presented in chapter 1, where the aesthetic refers not simply to an artistic or cultural style (deemed as such by a master class) but rather fundamentally introduces, as Steph Ceraso's and Aimée Knight's work echo, another mode of knowing central to the experience of (and making of meaning through) everyday artifacts in a media-saturated culture. On the other hand, this also includes grasping the rhetorical tenets of the aesthetic tradition, which includes, in this case, discursively constructed tensions raised by the New Aesthetic. While I will address the former throughout this work, particularly in relation to each contour and its rhetorical implications, I want to continue to sketch out the latter, as knowing how the New Aesthetic complements and counters the very rhetoric of aesthetic movements helps flesh out its contributions to both cultural and rhetorical frameworks.

If aesthetic movements are defined, in part, by the futures they envision, then as artist and academic Carla Gannis argues in "A Code for the Numbers to Come," the New Aesthetic is simply not an aesthetic movement (n. pag.).[5] Or, as critic Hrag Vartanian put it in "A Not-So-New Aesthetic, or Another Attempt at Technological Triumphalism": because the New Aesthetic functions with a backward-facing orientation, it lacks any "ability to dream into

---

5. Gannis argues that as the digital comes to saturate culture, artists will no longer be limited to working in the gaps between life and art but will start to work in the gaps between 1s and 0s, exposing not simply an aesthetic but something of contemporary digital and nondigital substrates.

the future" (n. pag.). Now, while Gannis and Vartanian are just two among the many, they reflect a larger sentiment, which rejects the New Aesthetic as movement precisely because it does not adhere to this future-to-come conditionality. But that very conditionality is beholden to the aesthetic traditions of yore, and so there is, first, a question as to the actual necessity of this futurecasting quality for a contemporary aesthetic movement and the rhetorical ecologies in which the New Aesthetic participates. Second, if one does see futurecasting as a required element, then rather than maintain that New Aestheticism lacks any future sensibilities, perhaps it would be of greater rhetorical value to ask what kind of future it does suggest even with its backward-facing orientation. Below I offer a few responses intended to address these considerations, which, in turn, illuminate additional circulating intensities among the New Aesthetic ecology.

Futurecasting

If the New Aesthetic is a movement, the simple reality is that it may not require the same kind of futurecasting as previous aesthetic movements. As rhetoric scholar Arabella Lyon has argued in her work *Deliberative Acts,* "a future-oriented theory minimizes what is happening in the moment of engagement" (36); and the New Aesthetic, if anything, is rooted in the conditions of the here and now of its own manifestation. This echoes Dewey's implications from chapter 1 that any considerations of the aesthetic must begin with "the events and scenes" connected to essential conditions of one's everyday life (3; 12), which manifest in and through a moment of engagement and not as conjecture for a future-to-come. Of course, while Lyon's work is on deliberative rhetoric rather than aesthetics or technology, her positioning of the futurecasting issue provides an unexpected but important parallel. According to Lyon, theories steeped in futurecasting ignore how the acts and events "in the present"—what one might see as Dewey's immediate sense of living—"create a current worldview that is always already constructing the future in an infinite procession" (36). Thus, New Aestheticism's attunement to the lived digital and nondigital materialities of the present signals to the importance of how the conditions and practices of today necessarily participate in the construction of any future-to-come (11). What is "new" about the New Aesthetic, then, is perhaps that it introduces a different kind of aesthetic movement—being not of the revolutions or subversions of Cubism, Surrealism, Constructivism, and the like, but rather being an awareness aesthetic, one more aligned with "renegotiat[ing] the relationship between human-subject and non-human-object" (Cloninger n. pag.) than with overthrowing any representational dogma. As an awareness aesthetic,[6] what it presents is not a future-yet-to-come but a Deweyan attentiveness to the present-as-it-is, which is increasingly important in an overtly aestheticized and overly technologized world where understandings of the material world are filtered through (if not only accessible through) layers and layers of mediation.

Now, while the New Aesthetic may not stem from a revolution-oriented politic, Bridle does often work quite explicitly to associate the New Aesthetic with particular political (and even military) interests—specifically his work connected to drones, which is also rooted in this conditional awareness. In his 2012 work *Drone Shadow 002*,[7] which was commissioned for the Istanbul Design Biennale, Bridle used chalk and tape to create a 1:1 representational outline of the MQ-1 Predator drone. The goal in this installation was to make the military drone visible in an exacting way: to give it representation, a pseudo-tangibility; and to create a kind of critical awareness of its magnitude (i.e., attempting to put into perspective its size, scale, and mass, things that most nonmilitary personnel have no way of experiencing[8]). While Bridle's interest in drones has led some to position the drone as the nonofficial symbol of the New Aesthetic, what Bridle's work pursues is an attempt to account for things that are generally invisible to human sensibilities alone (whether technologically or politically constructed invisibilities). There is, to put it mildly, an immense amount that exists outside the human sensorium.

That is to say, things exist—particularly technological things—that are nonsensible to humans without the aid of a technology and/or without a particular human condition saturated by computational media and materialities. Some of these invisibilities include the digital layers that permeate culture, the wireless networks that facilitate everyday activities, and the computational mechanisms at work in myriad devices. But outside specific human–technology assemblages, many of these things or processes or signals go unseen, unnoticed, and unknowable. Part of what the New Aesthetic involves is bringing these things to attention (revealing something of the present-as-it-is) as well

6. By "awareness aesthetic" I mean that (a) it uses the aesthetic dimension to draw attention to (make one aware of) the underlying systems (human and non) that give particular mediations value, meaning, and even existence; and (b) it highlights the reconfigured structures that make human–technology assemblages attentive to different configurations and patterns of perception.

7. An image of this work can be seen at http://jamesbridle.com/works/drone-shadow-002.

8. The MQ-1 Predator Unmanned Aerial Vehicle, for example, is not like the toy helicopter at the mall with a camera on it; its wingspan is the size of a typical cargo trailer of a commercial semi-truck, and Bridle gives this visibility by chalking out a real-size outline of the drone on the ground.

as highlighting the ways in which humans and technology must collaborate and cooperate to give them visibility, tangibility, and understanding. Hence, what lies at the heart of New Aestheticism is not pixels or drones, nor even what future-may-come, but rather the various acts or artifacts manifesting in and of contemporary mediascapes that make the larger public aware of the prolific volume of things that (1) cannot be detected or created by human sensibilities alone and (2) cannot be understood in any meaningful capacity by nontechnologized cultures (or even less or differently technologized cultures). While the former points to different capacities for action and expression, the latter reflects the changes in assemblage conditions that allow one to be attentive in particular ways and to make sense of reconfigured structures and relations accordingly. Meaning that human–technology assemblages not only inform human perspectives on the world but also structure the very practices by which humans make meaning through mediation (shaping our ways of both seeing and understanding). For example, as Sterling put it, much (if not all) of the New Aesthetic imagery would not have made "any sense to anyone in 1982, or even in 1992," as they lacked the adequate metaphors, models, or means for making sense of what they were seeing—matters germinated from particular human–technology assemblages (n. pag.).

Although the New Aesthetic may be backward-facing in the ways that Vartanian suggested (which only reaffirms McLuhan's position that cultures typically drive into the future looking into the rearview mirror), it nonetheless reveals or reflects or responds to a current change in human relationships to technology, which, by extension, alter the human condition (and, correspondingly, how one does rhetoric). By focusing on the present-as-it-is, what the New Aesthetic reveals is (a) the digitally crafted realities of people's everyday lives (from architecture to identity formation); (b) the human–technology relationships that reside in, make possible, and make sense of the different attention structures and conceptual configurations (i.e., the digital/real divide and its blurring); and (c) the human–technology assemblages that grant one access (in terms of general awareness and in terms of rhetorical possibilities) to that which resides outside the human sensorium alone. As such, what this present-as-it-is condition points to is a number of accretions that will manifest in (and in relation to) the four contours that this work identifies. But while this conditional orientation helps to give them shape (and adds a layer of consideration to contour 1), it is not enough on its own to give contours 2, 3, and 4 figuration. Therefore, I want to work through a few additional challenges to the New Aesthetic, including its relationship to any particular sense of history and to its object-oriented possibilities, to better identify and introduce the remaining contours.

Short-Term Memory

Vartanian chides the New Aesthetic for having only short-term memory, arguing that it focuses on the recent past as a way of seeing the contemporary as nothing more than *retro-present*. He comes to this conclusion by using Elizabeth E. Guffey's *Retro: The Culture of Revival,* where the concept of retro is tied to consumable objects/products—an object orientation that renders recent history as objects possessing discernable style and function markers. In this view, the New Aesthetic may be seen as doing nothing more than using the nostalgia of the recent past (leveraging the style and function markers of engineered technological devices) to distance itself from the immediacy of yesterday. For Vartanian, this retro-present approach is a short-term-memory fix to a short-term-memory problem, all of which takes place at the expense of long-term-memory (historical) sensibilities. Although I return to a longer historical trajectory later in this work, as Vartanian does raise a matter of some consideration, I want to first respond to two critical issues looming in the short-term-memory challenge, as they have increasing value in contemporary rhetorical arts: the danger/value of the retro-present and the potential impact of the compression of memory/history.

Retro-present

For Vartanian, the idea of the retro-present appears to be a negative thing, at least in terms of is potential for understanding New Aestheticism as a movement. That is, the focus on the style and function markers of recent history comes, Vartanian suggests, at the expense of more richly historical narratives. But a retro-oriented practice, as articulated by Guffey, actually has much to offer current thinking about media engagement and representation in the digital age. For the art of remix, which has proliferated exponentially in/through computational media, is one contemporary practice that thrives on leveraging and reusing recent (and not-so-recent) style and function considerations. But more than that, repurposing, remaking, or reinventing (with) recent digital artifacts (and processes) is both central to digital/cultural participation and valuable to rhetorical forms of networked-based engagement.

To begin, while Lanham recognized more than twenty years ago that the tenets and tendencies of electronic media were offering something of a return, if not fulfillment, of classical rhetoric, he also foregrounded new sets of practices in computational media that were chock-full of rhetorical significance, like appropriation, replication, repetition, and juxtaposition (all vital to any "retro-present" and all cornerstones of remix) (*Electronic* 39–43). Virginia Kuhn extended this idea further, showing not only how acts of appropriation, for example, are central to the practices of the digital age but also how those acts (and actions) are themselves transformative ("Rhetoric"; "Web"). She argues that when one engages in these practices (ripping, editing, rendering a new artifact, leveraging the styles of a recent past for a contemporary representation, etc.), one transforms into a rhetor/artist capable of intervening in the truth claims of those artifacts as well as the truth claims of one's own ("Rhetoric" par. 5.3). Therefore, something as superficial as appropriating 8-bit pixel aesthetics may operate as a nostalgic nod to a pre-to-early networked culture but it also allows rhetors to intervene in the truth claims of that aesthetic, in the meaning-making practices associated with it, and in the ways those practices can be leveraged to offer new insights, comments, or critique. The New Aesthetic, then, is not simply mired in a kind of retro-present; rather, the style and function markers of "recent history" are simply ripe with rhetorical potential, and practitioners of the New Aesthetic leverage that potential to great effect and affect—often directed at understanding or illuminating mediation itself.

Kuhn goes on to argue that one of the most interesting aspects of these practices, particularly as they manifest in relation to something like the art of remix, is their "tendency to subvert the dominant discursive field and its reified genres" ("Rhetoric" par. 5.4). Which means that the techniques associated with remix (and shared by the sensibilities of a "retro-present") involve, as artist Paul Miller contends in *Rhythm Science,* identifying what something is or means (or how it means) and then flipping the script, pushing the meanings in different directions, and/or subverting the very structures from which the sample emerges. On the one hand, the New Aesthetic itself reflects these tendencies: in other words, subverting the "reified genre" of aesthetic movements. On the other hand, this suggests that the retro-present that Vartanian associates with New Aestheticism is actually a positive value, gesturing not toward what the New Aesthetic lacks but toward the rhetorical manner in which the borrowing of aesthetic markers can be transformative, participatory, immediate.

However, while the retro-present conditionality includes gestures to a range of cultural objects in and of the New Aesthetic—like Bruno Pasquini's Coin Block (Plate D), which materializes the coin block (and its function) from Nintendo's *Super Mario Bros.* videogame series—the primary retro-present among Bridle's collection is, as mainstream treatments suggest, the use of 8-bit graphics (particularly forms of pixelation) in contemporary mediations. With many New Aesthetic artifacts deploying a pixel aesthetic (intentionally or otherwise), the pixel becomes one retro-present marker by which objects get included in the archive. Interestingly, however, what makes the aesthetic aspects of pixelation retro in the first place is not the passage of time (often the case with retro conditionalities), as pixels remain at the root of contemporary screen representations. Rather, the retro condition manifests because hardware and software improvements have essentially effaced the pixel—rendering pixelation as either the result of a technical failure (human and nonhuman alike) or, increasingly, an intentional aesthetic choice. Therefore, the function of any pixel aesthetic in New Aestheticism is as much about calling attention to a medial conditionality (and what it reflects) as it is a nostalgic nod to a retro-present.

Thus, the attentiveness to the pixel as an example of retro-present is as much a matter of its being a material condition as an aesthetic choice. This includes, as I argued in chapter 1, the pixel serving as the lowest common denominator for most in a digitally saturated (and often screen-mediated) culture; for even the ever-watchful *computational eye* is oriented around pixels—seeing and sensing the world via a pixel-based grid (the world rendered as pixels as data). All of which suggests an accretion of pixels and, in turn, a pixel orientation functioning as the second contour among the circulating intensities of the New Aesthetic.

Now, I use the phrase *pixel orientation* here rather than *pixel aesthetic* because, as I further demonstrate in chapter 4, the ever-present dynamic of the pixel (as naturalized element of screen mediation) has led to a condition in which the pixel not only exists as an aesthetic element that one can deploy rhetorically but also has become intertwined with a reconfigured way of seeing introduced by contemporary human–technology assemblages: pixels and pixelation offer a pattern of representation that shapes and reflects how techno-human assemblages make sense of the world—and do so to the point that many often see (or assume) pixels where they are not.

Memory Compression

The second critical dimension to Vartanian's challenge (and the many who share this perspective) is a sense of holding on to the unquestioned (if not unchanging) value of long-term memory: the value of history, of archives, of the depth of records and traceable pasts. While this archive drive seems somewhat fundamental to Western human existence, the reality is that given the human–technology assemblages constructed by or as part of the current media-saturated world, long-term memory or traditional historical sensibilities may no longer apply—or at least not in the same way. As Paul Virilio argued in *Open Sky,* where he explores the cultural and individual impacts of global electronic mediation, the electronic perspectives in today's moment have dissolved the very "scale of the human environment" (40): the traditional intervals of time and space are now being infused by a third interval, the interval of light (the light of the pixel) via fiber optics and screen mediation; and life itself has become computationally compacted (see also Lanham, *Economics* 21). Simply put, today's hybrid worlds operate at the speed of light—where the speed of light acts as the standard and not the limit (Virilio 14)—and thus time and space get compressed to such a degree that connection and (near) instantaneity replace distance (space) and duration (time) as de facto, privileged values. While space/time retained a privileged position in the nineteenth and twentieth centuries, where tele-technologies (radio, telegram, television, telephone, etc.) allowed people to hear and see at a distance, the underlying values of duration and distance simply become *destabilized* in twenty-first-century assemblages operative at the speed of light. Thus, history, long-term memory, or more generally any sense of "past" oriented around the concept of duration (time), become suspect in the compressed moment of the digital now.

One way to think about this reconfiguration of time (and/or the sense/ experience of time) is in relation to the compression of *production duration* that occurs when *making* operates at the speed of light (and/or primarily through light-based, pixel representations). Meaning, it becomes increasingly important to be able to take stock of the crafting-time of an artifact as well as the duration associated with the depth and skill of the engagement, for these qualities influence how one understands or experiences a given creation. For example, the creations of post-digital artist Gehard Demetz, who uses small, rough-cut woodblocks and polished parts to craft wood sculptures of children, capitalizes on the play between surface types and shapes.[9] His amazing works could be produced using 3D-printing technologies and, in turn, completed in a fraction of the time—he says as much. But the extended production time of hand-carving his sculptures is critical to the work. It creates an intimacy and identification with the work on his part by allowing his "mind to develop with the piece over time" (qtd. in Openshaw 76). What the viewing public experiences with Demetz's work includes not just the finished wood artifacts but a kind of *thickness of time* (duration, labor, etc.) associated with the production of his sculptures.

---

9. See http://www.geharddemetz.com.

Of course, this thickness is not exclusive to wood sculpture, nor to the specific practices of cutting-edge artists today; it can be found in the mundane as well, particularly in everyday digital photography. In this regard, not only do images provide visual culture with visual histories—one sense of time—but also they carry their own thickness (or thinness, more accurately) of time as well as their own sense of history (and a changing sense, at that). For example, if one thinks about the distance and duration between taking a photo and viewing it as captured image, one can readily grasp how the photographic process in digital culture is incredibly compressed: there is a near simultaneity between capture and view-ability. But if one backs up just a few years ago or turns to non-digital materialities (e.g., chemical, film-based photography), this process or sense of production (and its related duration) expands considerably by adding in other considerations of time, equipment, and even the labor needed to develop the film before artist/audience can view the photos.

Let me offer something of an extended example. In the mid 1980s, the process of popular photography included first taking enough photos to complete the roll of film and then getting the film developed. If the everyday-photographer was using was a 24-exposure roll of film and only took five pictures at Jackson's Party (photographic event A), then she would likely wait until all twenty-four pictures had been taken (often spread across multiple events, like Josie's bridal shower [event B] or Jeremy getting a tattoo [event C], and so on) before going to get the film developed. Second, getting film developed involved traveling to a location/business that could develop the film (like the Fotomat kiosks spread throughout the country or the photo department at Wal-Mart stores) and then returning to pick up the pictures when they were done. Prior to 1-hour development options, which are still offered today, the duration between drop-off and pick-up was often a day or more. Thus, from the moment of the camera click (at event A) to the point where people were able to actually see what was captured in the photos (i.e., what was produced), there was already a distance, a real passage of time ("Oh, that's Jackson's party from last month. What a great time!").

But today the mechanical and chemical processes that produce material photographic artifacts have been subject to algorithmic replacement and rupture. Digital cameras capture and display in real time, whether on smartphones or LCD camera viewfinders. The "captured" is near instantaneous with the capturing. The distancing that existed as part of the production duration has been all but removed, and this renders the image as an element of both *then* and *now* because it is of a past moment yet located in the present: not something one *will* see, but something one *is* seeing. What once was the inherent nostalgia built into viewing photos, stemming from the distance created by the production duration between the capturing and viewing of the images, which naturally produced a kind of longing for the moment gone by, is now replaced by an uncanny simulation of nostalgia; it is an instantaneous simulacrum of a nostalgia *one will have had* at some future moment. An individual takes a picture, views it, and thinks, "That's *going to be* a great memory."

What is more, in today's speed-of-light, fiber-optic, networked world, a person's friends, family, and even acquaintances now too share in the experience of the images nearly instantaneously with their capture. For example, I take a picture of my kids, post it to Facebook, and within seconds (sometimes, I swear, even before the upload is complete) people have "liked" the photo. The once-standard dynamic of getting together with friends and retelling stories of the "things we have done" has given way (to a noticeable degree) to the shared posting of the "things we are doing." People participate in each other's lives not by "getting caught up" (bringing personal histories forward in the form of narratives and artifacts) but by "following" along in the self- and machine-selected and crafted digital representations of the lives each of them lead. And while there is surely far more at work here than this brief treatment can account for, hopefully this illuminates, through considerations of digital production and production duration, some of the small tangents with how changes in human–technology relationships also change how people understand, experience, or even privilege matters of history/time.

Although a richer sense of history could be helpful in locating New Aestheticism in a particular trajectory of art practice and/or technological development, the fact that it is coming-to-be in a world with perspectives and sensibilities compressed from always operating at the speed of light might give pause, once again, to positioning it in the expectations of previous aesthetic movements. Further, if one key element of New Aestheticism is connected to creating an awareness of McLuhan's *numbness*, then whether New Aestheticism works with the mediations of yesterday (short-term memory) or the established practices of yore (long-term memory) only matters insofar as the degree to which those positions help draw attention to the perspectives needed to make sense of particular acts and artifacts of mediation.

Championing the short-term-memory approach allows for grounding the New Aesthetic in a future-now, where the "retro-present" is a significant practice for playing with a culture compressed by and saturated with digital artifacts. Championing the long-term-memory approach, in contrast, necessitates a fuller sense of the movements and practices and technologies from a medial past to see whether they might inform the tenets and tendencies of New Aesthetic ideologies. The former is aligned with a trajectory of the New Aesthetic being of a different kind of aesthetic and taking shape in a different kind of cultural moment; the latter establishes threads and touch points for the myriad practices at play in New Aesthetic artifacts and objects. As such, both approaches are needed, and ignoring one is not necessarily a shortcoming of the other. To this end, I more notably return to long-term considerations as part of chapter 4, but before moving to the contour chapters more fully, I want to address one additional challenge to the New Aesthetic, which emerges as much from the seeming popularity of object-oriented ontology (OOO) as it does from any New Aesthetic connection to machinic agency. Moreover, this challenge, when considered in relation to the larger maneuvers of this chapter, will help put into relief the remaining contours, which is where this chapter concludes.

Object-Oriented Aestheticism

The more the New Aesthetic gets situated in terms of objects and/or object-relations, the more there is a wanting connection between it and recent trends in rhetoric scholarship tied to OOO (and/or to the larger theoretical frame of speculative philosophy). As part of the posthuman and nonhuman turns, some rhetoric scholars have turned to OOO because it offers a metaphysical perspective that suspends the privileging of the human at the expense of objects—beginning from a position in which (a) both humans and nonhumans are understood as coming to bear on objects in equal magnitude, and (b) objects are understood as existing independently of human perception, with an existence that can never be fully exhausted (or accounted for) by an object's relations to humans, nor to other objects. Rhetorical trajectories that pick up with OOO do so because it allows rhetors to envision new human–nonhuman and nonhuman–nonhuman relations (many of which were closed off by the philosophies of Immanuel Kant).

Given the New Aesthetic's ties to an object-oriented archive, it is not surprising that one would find (or want to find) resonance between New Aestheticism and OOO. As artist and author Greg Borenstein has argued in "What It's Like to Be a 21st Century Thing," both "strive toward a fundamentally new way of imagining the relations between things in the world" (n. pag.). But one must move cautiously with folding them together, for, as Bogost contends in "The New Aesthetic Needs to Get Weirder," the New Aesthetic is simply too concerned with human ways of relating to and experiencing objects in the world to genuinely fit with (or within) an OOO paradigm. It is, as Berry et al. have suggested, a "profoundly human problem," which prevents it from becoming any kind of "aesthetic agenda grounded in the specific material workings" (and desires?) of the technologies themselves (19).

For the two to be reconciled, Bogost writes, the New Aesthetic must "get weirder" and become a kind of object-oriented aesthetic (OOA): that is, rather than asking how humans might see/situate their worlds differently as they work with computational technologies "that themselves 'see' the world in various ways," what one should be asking, according to Bogost, is how (and to what extent) "computers [and other objects] . . . develop their *own* aesthetics" ("New" n. pag.). To use Bogost's example, one might speculate about the aesthetic preferences of a pastry toaster and about how it understands itself in the world. While the pastry toaster may seem like an unusual example, this kind of speculating stems from the primary view that all objects exist equally and that there is always a withdraw present in the ways in which individuals engage, understand, and think with any object: an object is never fully present to humans, particularly not in how it (the object) might understand that presence. Nor is it ever fully absent from humans. Meaning, the pastry toaster is always more than just a pastry toaster but never less than the gathering of human relations with it. It includes a multitude of possibilities—those relations one can readily imagine (as toaster, as paperweight, as projectile-weapon, etc.) and those one cannot (where some future-to-come is needed to create conditions that might help reveal new engagements or relationships). Further, individuals can never understand the object (pastry toaster, computer, other) in the ways in which it understands itself. This is simply a position the human cannot occupy. All one can do, as Borenstein suggests, is to speculate about the "secret inner lives" of objects—how they imagine themselves as objects, what aesthetic values they privilege, how they understand their own relations, and so on (n. pag.).

But like many of the other perspectives operating in this chapter, one should hesitate in using OOO to understand (and/or situate) the New Aesthetic. For, on the one hand, this approach fetishizes the New Aesthetic object and makes it all too convenient, as Cloninger suggests, to "ignore the ethical ways" that humans are "implicit" in the very production of the New Aesthetic object as well as in the production of the machinic agents that often produce New Aesthetic images (n. pag.). On the other hand, this lens colonizes the New Aesthetic in particular ways and shifts (if not dismisses) what appears central to its endeavor: the human–technology assemblage. The OOO frame applied here, as Bogost does, would pursue a nonhuman aesthetic, speculating with regard to objects (e.g., pastry toasters), and, intentionally or not, would end up removing, as Bassett argues, all too important distinctions among humans from the equation in exacting ways.[10] This is not to imply that OOO

---

10. Bassett argues that "the priorities" of OOO or even OOA "render irrelevant a series of questions concerning 'humans,' their relationships with each other and with technologies, and

is explicitly dismissive of the human condition but rather that the rhetorical dimension it has contributed to the New Aesthetic ecology has, to this point, largely marginalized the human element.

Whereas OOO is concerned with objects and their materiality (and, particularly, their withdraw), the New Aesthetic is concerned with representational moments that suggest practices, procedures, and preferences of which people are often unaware (or to which they are numbed). OOO introduces a different ontological stance/space, while New Aestheticism introduces an awareness of the mediations operating upon (and with) individuals at any given point. OOO is a philosophical issue, tied to speculation and phenomenological concerns; the New Aesthetic is a media studies and art issue, tied to the aesthetics of a human–technology assemblage and the degrees of awareness present in mediating acts (which also mediate human beings). The two are not of, nor after, the same things. However, the two might be brought together in interesting ways, as each is attuned to particular frequencies emitted by things "born of contemporary technological culture" (Borenstein n. pag.). For example, the visual cues of New Aestheticism might serve as markers for where to speculate about the secret inner lives of objects. Or the tenets of OOO might help facilitate an inquiry into the wants, desires, and preferences of the technological devices that make New Aesthetic artifacts possible: What does the digital camera find beautiful? What does the pixel desire? What does my iPhone want from me? Even McLuhan went so far as to suggest that humans were the sex organs of technology, which asks for a certain degree of speculative conceptualization on behalf of the object. The point is that there is still much to explore in understanding technology, in human relationships with technology, and in the emergent understandings of those relationships.

But in considering the gestures of OOA (and/or its OOO parent) in relation to the New Aesthetic, what specifically gets put into relief is that the New Aesthetic is (and remains) overtly concerned with the human–object or human–nonhuman collaborations—particularly those, as filmmaker and speculative fictionist Jonathan Minard argues, that provide "access [to] new experiences and augment our creative capacities" (n. pag.). In this regard, what is at stake is not a condition of being more or less human (or more or less a thing) but rather, as anthropologist Daniel Miller has put it in "Technology and Human Attainment," the emergence of a "form of humanity that coexists with [the] collusion of digital and analogue forms" (199). What the New

how each of these is articulated and mediated by the other" (142). This means that the "divisions between humans, founded in bodies, and elaborated over 2,000 years as a sex/gender system" (142) simply become inconsequential. Thus, if the New Aesthetic deals with human experience in any meaningful way, then retaining attentiveness to and a perspective that allows for the experiences (and understandings) of differently abled and differently immersed bodies is vital.

Aesthetic highlights is not "the destruction of everything that was authentic and integral to being human" (199) but rather an opening of a previously unattainable humanity—one where there is a ready acknowledgment that the world around humans changed and that the human condition itself has been reconfigured (including shifts in how we understand things in the world and their relations to us). And a key part of this transformation involves an increased attentiveness to the ways in which human and nonhuman entities come together as symbiotic components that create unprecedented capacities for engagement and imagination, expression and invention. What matters among the New Aesthetic ecology, then, is not the objects, nor humans themselves, but rather the collusions, collaborations, and cooperations that lead to the advent of new techno-human sensibilities—with the larger New Aesthetic ecology drawing these sensibilities to the attention of working creatives, including those of the rhetorical persuasion, in and of everyday culture.

Here one begins to grasp something of the third contour of the New Aesthetic, which is tied to human–technology relationships that allow for a new kind of vision, a new kind of expression, and a new kind of writing/making that results from this collaboration. For not only do human–technology assemblages provide an ability to sense (and make sense of) that which resides beyond the human sensorium alone (gesturing toward one necessity of the human–technology assemblage in today's media-saturated moment) but also, in contemporary acts of making, the technologies involved invite collaboration: the act of production (discursive or otherwise) is not simply an opportunity for a rhetor to dump her mind onto a neutral screen but rather involves playful cooperation between human and technological agencies. And this is not merely an extension of the axiom that "one is only as good as one's tools" but rather prompts consideration of what happens when the "tool" or even Bogost's "object" makes its own design decisions or makes assumptions about what it thinks its collaborators want.

Part of what the New Aesthetic offers, then, is a collection of artifacts that offer moments of intervention into the seamlessness (and assumed relationships) of this partnership. Thus, contour 3 focuses on the varying accretions that give depth to *human–technology making,* with chapter 5 more fully extending its implications into contemporary rhetorical practices.

CONTOURS AND CONCLUSIONS

While contours 1, 2, and 3 have emerged relatively organically, contour 4 is more subtle, lingering within a multitude of circulating intensities in the New

Aesthetic ecology. It begins with the New Aesthetic being something of a network aesthetic that is enacted in its own medium and calling attention to its own medial conditionality. By residing on a Tumblr account, its archive exists in/on/of the very substrate that much of its collection draws to attention. Second, the New Aesthetic features artifacts, like glitch works, that regularly destabilize the illusion of the seamlessness of mediation; in so doing, these interruptions expose both the material conditions of screen mediation and the underlying ailments of computationality. Third, there are many New Aesthetic elements that intervene in the forms and function of media—offering commentary precisely because they create dissonance in one's medial expectation: from the increasing sense that our devices and screen media are aware of us (taking stock of one's presence and actions) to moments in which artifacts overtly demonstrate shifts in human perspective itself. Take artist Aram Bartholl's Map project (Plate C) for example, which has a kind of cultural/critical value because it locates the "digitally ethereal" Google Maps balloons outside the screen, leveraging what the balloon represents as a way to call attention to a contemporary, global positioning system (GPS)[11] constructed sense of space and place.[12]

Together, these three gestures result in a kind of hyperawareness that does not simply exist as a default condition of New Aestheticism but is rather part of the very reconfigurations being introduced by today's assemblages—that a hyperawareness of mediation can be/should be a fundamental part of how artifacts create meaning and communicate value in the digitally saturated, overtly mediated twenty-first century. While something like a pixel aesthetic may seem innocuous on its own, when manifesting in a culture that is past the pixel moment, it operates hyperrhetorically—creating an overt attentiveness to the mediation (and its meanings) and calling attention to one's relationship to the mediation as well as to the pixel itself. Thus, enacting works in their own paradigm creates one layer of awareness, while aesthetic elements that call attention to mediation and the mediating act (and its underlying substrate) create another layer of awareness. Together, along with other considerations that will manifest throughout this work, they result in what I am offering as contour 4, a *hyperawareness of mediation*.

With the four contours now identified, the remainder of this work picks up with these contours, more fully grasping their shape, developing their implications, and then situating their value for rhetorical studies. Chapter 3

11. GPS is a global navigation satellite system that provides geo-based location and time information. It is owned by the US government and made freely available to anyone with a device that has a GPS receiver.

12. Bartholl's installation is more fully addressed in chapter 3.

focuses on *eversion as/of design,* looking specifically at how its dual drives (making digital real, making the real digital) expand the capacities of expression and explanation for rhetoricians. Chapter 4 picks up with *pixel orientations,* exploring what makes the pixel rhetorical and critically examining the implications of the pixel aesthetic becoming a human aesthetic as part of contemporary techno-human conditionalities. Chapter 5 focuses on *human-technology making,* looking at how human–technology assemblages lead to the production of new kinds of artifacts and creations and invite a completely different orientation to the writing/making situation: a shift from a will to mastery toward a willingness to play. And chapter 6 examines *hyperawareness of mediation,* demonstrating how this contour works in the New Aesthetic and/or connects to new media considerations as well as how it helps rhetors better understand a fundamental shift in the medial expectations of contemporary audiences.

PLATE A. *Pixel Pour,* by Kello AKA Leyla Daze (@leylaDaze, kelloworld.com). Photo by Benjamin Norman. Used with permission from Kello Goeller.

PLATE B. Heydar Aliyev Center, in Baku, Azerbaijan, designed by Zaha Hadid and Patrick Shumacher. Photo by Iwan Baan. Used with permission from Iwan Baan.

PLATE C. *MAP, 'Hello World!' Kasseler Kunstverein,* by Aram Bartholl. Photo by Nils Klinger. 2013 © Aram Bartholl. Used with permission from Aram Bartholl.

PLATE D. *Real Life Coin Block,* by Bruno Pasquini. Used with permission from Bruno Pasquini.

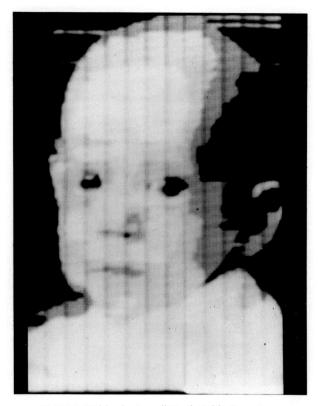

PLATE E. *Walden,* by Russell Kirsch. Public Domain.

PLATE F. Orange River Irrigation (border between Namibia and South Africa). Photo by NASA ALI/EO-1.

PLATE G. Telehouse West Data Center (London Location). Photo by James Bridle. Used with permission from James Bridle.

PLATE H. *Street Eraser* (Brick Lane, London), by Guus ter Beek and Tayfun Sarier. Used with permission from Guus ter Beek and Tayfun Sarier.

PLATE I. *Lounge Spectre, Digital Ethereal,* by Luis Hernan. Used with permission from Luis Hernan.

CHAPTER 3

Eversion as/of Design and the Blurring of Rhetorical Binaries

IN "A MANIFESTO for a Theory of the New Aesthetic," Curt Cloninger suggests that New Aestheticism thrives in documenting the residue of the digital in everyday life (n. pag.). It does this by capturing (and calling to attention) digital irruptions in the physical world and physical irruptions in the digital realm. In so doing, the New Aesthetic not only helps one attune to marked intensities and irruptions (sites for critical and creative inquiry) but also, more significantly, highlights a differently distributed sense of the digital— one where digital mediation and computational possibilities have, as artists Jamie Zigelbaum and Marcelo Coelho indicate in "The Rasterized Snake Eats Its Analog Tail," broken free from the confines of traditional devices (e.g., laptops and mobile phones) and "seep[ed] chaotically into every corner of the world" (n. pag.). But this "seep" involves far more than just the overt infusions of algorithmic media, mobile computing, data sensors, and the like into everyday life (unequally distributed as they may be); it also includes the slow boil of a human–technology perspective that routinely imagines the materialities of the world as being/becoming digitally responsive and that increasingly situates human activity (and human bodies) as things to be tracked, targeted, and tabulated (data streams subject to computational manipulation). Which is to say, while the "seep" most assuredly creates new assemblages, it also, as I expressed in chapters 1 and 2, introduces new configurations for attending to things in the world.

Among these reconfigured attention structures is a far tighter coupling between digital processes/operations and human/nonhuman materiality. Bridle referred to this as the blurring of the digital/real divide, but its larger gesture is that the digital/nondigital dynamic is being reconstituted: the reductive digital–real coupling is understood no longer as a contentious dichotomy but rather, as the rhetorical ecology of the New Aesthetic demonstrates, as competing and complementary orientations for post-digital making practices.

To understand this reconfigured attention structure—and the irruptions and intensities to which it is drawn—one must begin from the premise that the digital is not as separate from the real as popular imaginations might have it. Rather, as many scholars have suggested, the digital and real are increasingly integrated, leading to a kind of hybrid, mediated world. What matters in this kind of hybrid orientation, as N. Katherine Hayles explains in "Cybernetics," is the emergence of a view of the world as composed of digital and physical "realms [that] merge in fluid and seamless ways" (148)[1]—the seamlessness of which stems from a combination of any number of elements: the pervasiveness of networked technology, the insertion of sensors into everyday objects, the ubiquity of screen media, and the depth to which all have seeped into daily human activities (among other considerations). For people now wear "Fit" watches to track steps, monitor heart rates, and measure sleep patterns (turning themselves into data); they take technological devices to bed with them (as alarm clocks, as white-noise makers, even as sexual-fetish objects). In short, they live in an everted world (a concept to which I will return) and have, in turn, adapted their lifestyles (and tastes) in accordance with the affordances and experiences of this eversion.

What is important to understand, then, is that everyday reality is not inherently distinct from the digital. Instead, as digital media scholar Jason Farman has argued in "When Geolocation Meets Visualization," everyday reality may be no more and no less than pervasive computing space, adding the thickness of the digital (an expansive representational dimension) to the physical world. The result of this pervasive condition, as Farman positions it, is that the ways in which one moves through (and makes sense of) the physiological world (including the aesthetic dimension) are beholden to a "constant interplay and permeability" between digital mediations and material reality (and digital realities and material mediations) (180). Therefore,

---

1. Hayles employs the term *mixed reality* to designate this hybrid digital/physical reality, but many other scholars have made similar gestures—see Nathan Jurgenson's notions of "enmeshing," Beth Coleman's "x-reality," and Adam Greenfield's "everyware," to name a few. There are, of course, important nuances within these different terms, but what matters is their collective gesture, which positions the world as fundamentally composed of a blend of digital and nondigital materialities.

what emerges is not simply a digital/real mixed reality but altogether different modes of embodiment, as the aforementioned "thickness" is only perceptible and accessible to particular human–technology assemblages. Moreover, making sense of and enacting change within these hybrid mediascapes requires certain techno-enhanced or techno-altered sensibilities (including the very impulse toward understanding life as being routinely lived in and through digitally layered realities). Thus, in a way that extends Hayles's thinking, what the New Aesthetic brings into view are the remnants and residues of the differently oriented aesthetic sensibilities and attention structures that take shape in and through the different modes of embodiment—with these sensibilities and structures being in no way exclusively (nor exclusive to the) human.

To put this in more expansive terms: if the ways in which one approaches the aesthetic dimension are tied to an everyday, lived conditionality—as suggested in chapter 1 in relation to Dewey's pragmatic aestheticism—then any lived experience linked to a human–technology mode of embodiment also points toward an increasingly human-technology-infused aesthetic (seeing and sensing patterns of perception germane to the assemblage itself). Consequently, new assemblages do not simply extend the human sensorium and introduce new ratios (and related attention structures), as Marshall McLuhan might have it, but rather invite, in the context of this chapter, new concatenations in and across the illusory construction of something like the digital/real divide. And what is of critical interest here is not simply that new linkages emerge as part of new assemblages but rather, in a kind of post-digital Lyotardian[2] condition, that new human–technology configurations introduce an altogether new capacity for linking, for forming different kinds of connections, and for exposing different rhetorical ecologies.

Thus, when the New Aesthetic directs attention to moments, events, and artifacts that reside both between and beyond the digital/real divide, it is calling attention to these different registers (as well as their different linking practices)—not to reinforce the digital or the real as governing conditions, but rather to offer an attunement to the movements and manifestations across these categorical orders. And this movement is the critical focus of this chapter, for it designates what I referred to earlier as eversion: the digital everting into the real and the real everting into the digital.

---

2. In *The Differend,* philosopher Jean-François Lyotard makes the case for paralogical thinking where what matters is not how one links but that one links—or, in more expansive terms, "It is necessary to link, but the mode of linkage is never necessary" (29). This is central to his response to what might be seen as differends, competing positions in need of a third for adjudication; or, in the context here, paralogy readily moves one beyond dichotomous impositions (digital/real binary).

Eversion, as I am using it here, comes from William Gibson, who offered it as a corrective, of sorts, to his better-known concept of cyberspace. In 1984, in his book *Neuromancer,* Gibson introduced the notion of cyberspace to denote the notional spaces or environments that take shape in and through digital mediation and computer networks. The concept (and Gibson's work) was so popular that cyberspace became cultural dogma—understood, in a general sense, as designating something "out there," something removed from physical reality. This orientation had such impact, according to digital humanist Steven E. Jones, that Gibson's cyberspace served for nearly twenty years as the dominant metaphor shaping Western understandings of human relationships with networked technologies (27). But as Jones details, between 2004 and 2008 there was a "cumulative effect of a variety of changes in technology and culture" that "converged and culminated in a *new consensual imagination*" (25; emphasis added)—that is, a set of perspectives in which Gibson's cyberspace ceased to be separate from everyday reality and instead was taking shape through the engineered devices built into the material fabric of the world (22). Gibson himself picked up on these shifts in his novel *Spook Country,* written during that same four-year window, and offered eversion (more specifically, the eversion of cyberspace) as an alternative that understands people as being immersed in digital technologies, as living in, among, and through medial experiences. For example, while many individuals may still be inclined to use a metaphor like "cloud" to refer to online technologies and digital media storage (understanding the network as a kind of ethereal-other rather than the brick-and-mortar monstrosities that are server farms), in an everted culture the network no longer floats in the sky. Instead, it exists down in the muck of everyday life, with people living among Wi-Fi, airplays, Bluetooth connectivity, and so on. In an everted world, the "network" penetrates floors, walls, and bodies; and individuals use handheld devices and dynamic eyewear to access and interact with digitally layered and digitally altered material spaces. What matters with this shift is not any digital/real divide but rather the myriad ways in which people experience different configurations (and saturations) of mediation. Moreover, how individuals make sense of these experiences includes the very reconfigured perspectives and sensibilities that make those things possible in the first place. What the New Aesthetic provides, then, is not some further implication of a digital-other, nor an extension of the effects of the digital/real divide, but rather a different set of orientations that take shape part and parcel with contemporary human–technology assemblages.

Beyond these new modes of embodiment and the different rhetorical orientations they introduce, what is at stake is a fundamental shift in the core metaphor by which human relationships with technology are understood (as well as the kinds of inquiries which that core metaphor facilitates). For the grounding metaphor carries with it a host of assumptions about how individuals envision, engage, and embrace technologies (from methodological practices to artifacts for analyses). Therefore, in shifting from something like cyberspace (and its corollary of a digital/real divide) to eversion (which champions movements across this illusory coupling), what takes center stage is not any categorical division but rather the new consensual imagination that emerges from the circulating intensities manifested within the flows permeating the multiple registers and materialities of post-digital culture.

Jones, of course, turns to the digital humanities as a vehicle for thinking about this new consensual imagination. He begins by remarking how the period 2004–8 included more than just Gibson's eversion; it also marked the critical period in which digital humanities transformed from being primarily oriented around digitization (the digital conversion imperative and the archive drive) toward a perspective of "putting the digital into reciprocal conversation with an array of cultural artifacts" (26). This helped usher in a wave of scholars who sought not to just create additional archives but to link the rhetorical capacities of digital mediation to traditional humanistic objects and modes of inquiry, establishing new, digital-born methods, artifacts, and epistemologies. The collective result was the development of a host of new perspectives that would link humanities' scholarship going forward to digital practices, to being realized in and through digital spaces, and to being uniquely possible because of the affordances of digital mediations. For example, an undertaking like Jasmine Mulliken's The Mapping Dubliners Project,[3] which creates a digital map that layers information from James Joyce's Dubliners over representations of the geographical space of Dublin, Ireland, engages new methods and modes of representation but also quickly makes digital humanities work public-facing and publicly available. The same is true, though in different ways, of Janelle Jenstad's "Agas Map" project (The Map of Early Modern London)[4] and the Folger Digital Text initiatives,[5] as well as the postcritical engagements coming out of Gregory L. Ulmer's EmerAgency Konsult creations.[6] This is not to suggest that earlier formations of digital humanities were not also public-facing but rather to indicate that shifts in practice, in preference, and in perspective

---

3. http://mulliken.okstate.edu

4. https://mapoflondon.uvic.ca/map.htm

5. http://www.folgerdigitaltexts.org

6. See, as two examples, John Craig Freeman's "Minute Man Monument" (https://johncraigfreeman.wordpress.com/2013/10/20/fre-emeragency-konsult-minute-man-monument/) and Sean Morey's "Deepwater Horizon Roadkill Tollbooth (A MEmorial)" (http://kairos.technorhetoric.net/21.2/topoi/morey/index.html).

tied to the "seep" have paralleled an academic and culture movement in which participation begins with production: with *to make* now sitting slightly before *to make sense*. And where the things people produce (whether in progress or finished product, whether popular or academic) are instantly available for others to see, critique, repurpose, and remix—which means *to make* not only comes before *to make sense* but includes the dimension of *to make available,* with that availability increasingly facilitated through digital means and digital representation (if not digital compression).

As such, the dimension of *making available* includes not only the obvious ways in which digital works are disseminated via digital means but also (increasingly so) how nondigital artifacts are digitized, represented through digital means, or (re)made/(re)imagined for digital platforms. This is part of the impact of eversion and part of the reason why Jones sees eversion as offering a "useful master trope" for contemporary digital humanities (and its rhetorical ecologies)—as it provides a conceptual metaphor that accounts for digital-to-real and real-to-digital transformations, better reflects people's everyday experiences (14), "calls attention to the messy and uneven status" by which cyberspace is now deployed into the world (through networks connected to and constructed by everyday objects) (29), and helps create "a set of shared perceptions about the world" (the new consensual imagination) (9). It is through eversion that Jones himself touches on the New Aesthetic—showing how readily New Aestheticism maps onto eversion and his own grand narrative of the digital humanities. But for all his efforts to extol the virtues of the New Aesthetic, Jones ultimately limits New Aestheticism to eversion—no more and no less than being demonstrative of eversion—which ignores the fuller complexities at play, including the nuances among the competing discourses in and around the rhetorical ecology of the New Aesthetic. Although Jones was focused on the metaphor of eversion and the perspectives it offers for digital humanities practices (with New Aestheticism situated firmly within that metaphor), the New Aesthetic, particularly when considered on its own terms, is actually better understood as offering perspectives and practices for the *making of things in a culture of eversion*. It is not that the New Aesthetic is part of Gibson's eversion, as Jones might have it, but rather that New Aestheticism offers an attunement to the making of things in an everted world. As Jonathan Openshaw puts it, in post-digital cultures "the digital world leeches on the physical . . . [and] the physical draw[s] on the language of the digital" (7). What we are dealing with, then, is a differently configured perspective— where human–technology assemblages are equally attuned to the *making real* of the digital and the *making digital* of the real, a dualism at the core of the first contour of the New Aesthetic: *Eversion as/of Design.*

The rest of this chapter explores more fully this contour and its competing trajectories for making things in the world. I first introduce and unpack the considerations of *making real* and *making digital,* respectively, before situating the value of each (as well as the implications of eversion overall) for postdigital rhetorical practice.

MAKING REAL

In Bridle's articulation, the "making real of a digital artifact" deals with creating "in the real" things that previously existed only "in the digital" ("Waving"). For example, instructables.com member Bruno Pasquini (brunoip) created a "real life coin block"—a real, working version of a *Super Mario Bros.* Question Block (Plate D). Using 3mm cardboard, an MP3 player, two springs, an old servomechanism (a device used to control operations through feedback), plastic, coins, and select electronic items (circuit boards, amplifiers, wires, etc.), Pasquini constructed a functioning replication of the coin block in *Super Mario Bros.* Striking the bottom of the coin block, much like Mario in the game, triggers both a sound effect (looped on the MP3 player) and the mechanism that tosses out a coin (launched by one of the springs). This is a colorful example, to be sure, but it readily demonstrates the principle here: Pasquini moved a born-digital artifact—a completely digital object—into the physical world.

Another example of this eversion can be found in the unique creations coming out of the parametric school of architecture—computer-assisted building designs that seem impossible as structures but are quite architecturally sound (see Plate B, as one example). What parametric architecture illuminates, among other considerations, is the various ways in which digital forms transfer into analog design—often doing so, as curator Glenn Adamson demonstrates in "Craft in the Digital Age," in seemingly unconscious ways (288). Further, as Bridle implies in his own commentary, parametric practices, which manipulate algorithms and materialities to create complex structures, have in recent years leveraged digital aesthetics and/or computational sensibilities as part of their geometries of design. But parametricism is not inherently digital; it has been around for well over a century—starting with Antoni Gaudi's Church of Colònia Güell in 1898. What digital technologies have done, however, is open the practice of parametricism to the play space of computer-aided design (CAD) programs, creating an emergent possibility for parametric design and digital aesthetic patterns/values (particularly with things like computer-generated geometrical shapes). With parametric mathematics extended into CAD programs like Autodesk Revit or Catia, architect-plus-CAD assemblages can now work through a series of input parameters, equations, and outputs to model, analyze, test, and optimize even the most unusual of designs. This, in turn, allows for the production of buildings that are unique, imposing, and possessing great presence because they employ computational geometry, multi-angled surfaces, paraboloid perimeters with unexpected curves and bends, and so on. But while parametric architecture is interesting, the question is what it helps one understand about the New Aesthetic and/or rhetoric's interest in New Aestheticism. The answer is that (a) it introduces structural designs and physical artifacts that employ computational aesthetics in such a way and to such a degree that people *look at* parametric buildings as much as *move through* them, and (b) it introduces structures that are rendered digital long before becoming physical, material manifestations.

Surface Tensions

The first raises considerations of artifacts (in this case, buildings) that draw attention to themselves as mediated entities (and to the mediation itself). While Bridle has cautioned against looking only at the surface of New Aesthetic artifacts, parametric architectures seem to exude a kind of self-conscious awareness of their own design—an awareness that passersby (and passers-through) must wrestle with as they experience the structures. And this awareness (or even attentiveness) emerges precisely because the buildings' design features violate expectations: they do not fit with what buildings should look like, nor do they employ shapes/patterns readily located in the natural environment. Thus, to experience parametric architectures, particularly those that manifest uniquely digital aesthetics and computational geometries, can be destabilizing because they invite looking at a building—at its design and component parts (inside and out)—as much as moving through or inhabiting its architecture.

While I pick up with this self-conscious awareness more fully in chapter 6 and, to a certain extent, in chapter 4, I want to briefly situate this digital-to-real destabilization in something of rhetorical parlance (particularly as pertaining to matters of mediation and/or the experiences of media). One way to do that is to suggest that the digital aesthetics employed by parametric architecture and other New Aesthetic artifacts toggle what Richard Lanham denoted as the *at/through* switch.

In his 1993 *The Electronic Word*, Lanham offers this coupling as a way of highlighting a shift in expectations (and experiences) of print-centric mediations to those of an electronic variety. He argued that print media, the primary (if not exclusive) focus for rhetoric and literary studies up until at least the late 1980s, seemed, minus a few anomalies, to be locked into the mode of *through*—"print wants the gaze to remain *through* and unselfconscious all the time" (43), putting readers into direct relation to the author's ideas and removing all barriers to that immediacy. Appropriately, then, much writing instruction (rhetorical or otherwise) focused on the C-B-S system (clarity, brevity, and sincerity), which was designed to reduce the impediments to accessing/understanding an author's ideas. Much like the master oil painters of the Renaissance, good writing effaced itself. It got out of the way. But computational mediation introduced so much more, allowing every element to not only include a self-conscious aesthetic but to also serve as a marker, concept, or function (hypertext). For Lanham, computational mediation (as rhetorical entity) required a kind of perpetual "oscillation between unselfconscious expression and self-conscious design," which, in his view, was "the most powerful aesthetic attribute" of any digital artifact (43). In so doing, computational mediation extended decades of avant-garde art practices and served as the optimal medium for a kind of recovery of rhetoric.

Further, as rhetoric scholar Collin Brooke indicated in *Lingua Fracta: Toward a Rhetoric of New Media*, rhetoric more or less has always concerned itself with "situated responses" to general "cultural imperatives" (43); as such, its practices and purposes have taken shape over the years in relation not only to culture forces but also, as Brooke suggests, to the available representational technologies (and techniques) that were part of those situational affordances (35). Therefore, when a culture experiences shifts in representational technologies, what occurs is not merely the advent of new modes of expression (which alter the parameters of rhetoric) but rather a fundamental transformation in human–technology assemblages, which, in turn, usher in new practices and/or transform the very understandings of what counts as / constitutes a discursive and/or rhetorical act (see also Haas[7]). This is why Lanham argued that the digital was bringing the marrow of rhetoric firmly back into the conversation—not merely expanding the available means but opening up entirely new

---

7. Christina Haas offered an examination of the relations between writing, computer technologies, and the practices of literacy in her 1996 work *Writing Technology: Studies on the Materiality of Literacy*. One of Haas's key considerations, in counterdistinction to many of her contemporary writing scholars, was that technology was anything but an independent agent, for shifts in technology and/or material tools introduced shifts in writing processes. Therefore, it was up to scholars, particularly humanists, to "take an active role in designing and implementing technology" (199), as the technologies were integral to the kinds of writing taking shape and to what would count as writing.

assemblages and perspectives for discursive representations in/of/through computational spaces (*Electronic* 43).

That said, what makes the New Aesthetic of interest to rhetoric—at least in this framework—is that most of its representational artifacts, like parametric architecture, thrive in the liminal space between unselfconscious expression and self-conscious design. They call attention to themselves as representational artifacts and to the very nuances of their own representational practices; and in most cases that attention pushes quickly beyond surface-level considerations to matters of context, computationality, and culture. What the New Aesthetic is doing, then, is not just collecting examples of materialized digital artifacts that flourish in the threshold of an at/through divide, but rather subtly emphasizing the rhetorical significance of maintaining a level of attentiveness to both the *what* and the *how* of particular representations. As the New Aesthetic features artifacts and practices that thrive in the play between unselfconscious expression and self-conscious design, it demonstrates how that kind of play can offer critical value to the rhetorical capacities of different media and materialities.

Born Digital

The second element I want to focus on is the preproduction dimension, as there are clear connections between the "making real of the digital" and the production of everyday things. For CAD is not exclusive to architecture; it is the industry standard for (nearly all) manufacturing. Most products and objects today are born digital and, only later, if ever, are they rendered "in the real." But the making of everyday entities like car bumpers or custom-designed T-shirts is not quite what Bridle's New Aesthetic is pointing to (though, to be sure, these things are related). Rather, Bridle prefers more exotic examples like parametric architecture and Pasquini's Question Block because these objects (1) reflect aesthetics that have previously only seemed possible in digital environments, and (2) call to attention both their unusual aesthetics and the very systems and structures by which people make sense of them as objects (functional or aesthetic).[8] Meaning, unlike the more mundane, everyday objects that use digital design practices to mimic established or expected aesthetics

---

8. In many ways we can see similar gestures in Hayles's works on *Electronic Literature*, which presents all writing as being electronic in the sense that it bears the mark of digital processes; also in the examples of electronic literature accompanying the book, one can see literary-like productions that bear the unmistakable aesthetic and function of digital mediation.

(e.g., using Microsoft Word to write this text), the more exotic materializations give "the real world the grain of the virtual" (Bridle, "Waving" n. pag.). In so doing, they occasion a reconsidering of the thickness between the digital and the real.

Of course, in analyzing the New Aesthetic collection itself, there seems a danger (or at least a necessary hesitation) with Bridle's moving of digital-oriented, materially rendered artifacts back into digital spaces. In *New Aesthetic, New Anxieties*, David M. Berry et al. assert that material-based experiences designed explicitly to call to attention *digital ways of seeing* or *digital ways of representing the world* have the potential to be undercut precisely where they matter most when they are re-presented in/through digital platforms. Meaning, showcasing artifacts that have "manifest in the real" on the New Aesthetic tumblr relocates these "in the real" creations back into the very digital apparatuses to which they call attention. For Berry et al., this kind of movement—a form of digital relocation—can be problematic. To further explore these considerations, they focus on Aram Bartholl's *Map* project (Plate C), which was posted to the New Aesthetic tumblr on June 2, 2011.

From 2006 to 2010, Bartholl created a number of life-sized Google Maps balloons and placed them in public places. Bartholl was "making real" a digital artifact, and so it should seem obvious why Bridle would include it in his collection. But Berry et al. interpreted Bartholl's larger-than-human balloons (placed "in the real") as being primarily about drawing attention to the "awkward relative measurements of digital artefacts" that are "accept[ed] without question in the digital realm" (35). Meaning, for them, what was primarily at stake was the issue of scale that the red balloon on Google Maps seemed to violate. Put simply, Google Maps balloons were (and continue to be) grossly out of proportion with the other elements in/of any Google Maps.

As a point of critique toward New Aestheticism, Berry et al. argued that Bridle's reintroducing *Map* to the digital arena (via the New Aesthetic tumblr) causes Bartholl's project to lose some of its impact because of its being showcased in the very space where issues of scale (or being out of scale) are readily accepted (if not naturalized). But while there may be some cause for hesitation with how digital re-presentation influences the ways in which Bartholl's work is received, Berry et al.'s critique, first and foremost, seems suspiciously devoid of other forms of re-presentation. That is, Bartholl's material-based, experience-oriented artworks, like many artists' works, have been documented and reproduced in any number of venues and event promotions, both print and digital, which manipulate scale in interesting ways as well. While there is a need to consider how being part of a Tumblr collection affects the project's implications, it seems problematic to limit the critique to only one kind of format—particularly when art of all kinds, commissioned and non, gets regularly presented across different materialities and platforms, circulating among various representational and rhetorical registers.

But the real problem of Berry et al.'s critique is that the authors rely on (if not reinforce) a necessary distinction between the digital and the real—between physical and digital realms. The simple reality is that the very movement of the Google Maps balloon from the screen to something like the White House lawn back to the screen changes the balloon marker. As it circulates across ecologies and materialities, it accretes meaning and signification, which necessitate a different understanding as it moves back into the digital/Tumblr mediaverse. This is precisely why Edbauer's rhetorical ecologies orientation is critical to this work, for to privilege the experience of the artifact in any single iteration seems to bear less fruit than tracking (and/or attuning to) how entities and artifacts like Bartholl's balloons flow into, out of, and across the rhetorical ecologies in which they participate.

Thus, in letting go of the very language of the digital/real divide and attuning to the circulating intensities of something like *Map,* one can focus less on Bartholl's and Google's balloon-size considerations and more on thinking about what something like *Map* suggests about how one might come to understand oneself and one's practices in the mediated (and mediating) world. Therefore, when tracking the movement of Bartholl's *Map* in relation to the New Aesthetic rhetorical ecology, what matters is not its commentary on balloon size or scale, as Berry et al. might have it, but rather more *making real* (or manifesting "in the real") what is otherwise a digital orientation to space, place, and information. What makes *Map* so interesting is not that it offers an awareness of any particular cartographic practice (scale) but rather that in moving a digital artifact onto a physical landscape, it makes visible the layering of information that gets placed on top of the GPS-constructed world—a different kind of attentiveness. For no matter what the scale of the representation in a Google Map (and scalability, of course, is one of the defining features of digital maps in general), the balloon is always an extra layer of information. It is a way of bringing noncartographic data into play with cartographic representation. The balloons on the map have "awkwardly relevant measurements" no matter the scale of representation because the balloons are not native to the map itself. Much like in videogames, the balloons serve in a heads-up display (HUD) capacity. And many in today's culture have, to a certain extent, internalized HUDs as somewhat natural to digital environments, particularly those that offer representations of a world (or worlds) in digital spaces. To be fair to Berry et al., Bartholl's project does call attention to the balloons' relative size issues in Google Maps, but when understood in relation to the New Aesthetic rhetorical ecology, it more profoundly calls to attention an internalized Google Maps (human–technology assemblage) understanding of the world. From smartphone apps to in-car navigational systems to Google Earth, nearly every sense of traversing space and place is now tied to these representational practices. Thus, while the larger-than-human balloons may draw attention to scale issues, they also significantly locate the wider culture's own sense of size, involvement, and engagement in a GPS-coordinated world. And most importantly in this ecology, *Map* serves as yet another example of work designed explicitly around bringing digital representational practices and their aesthetics into "real" spaces.

What this project demonstrates is an eversion-attuned approach for giving "the real" the grain of the digital and for calling attention to that granularity—showing how New Aesthetic considerations can be extended to provoke further ideas and thinking. The New Aesthetic is, therefore, far more than just its Tumblr beginning and Tumblr holdings; it introduces a rhetorical ecology that moves away from the digital/real divide toward a focus on the practices of *making* in which digital objects and aesthetics move into material landscapes and/or physiological reality. But it also includes, as kind of a third consideration, manifestations that fold these two registers (digital and nondigital) together. For example, something like interactive print texts (e.g., the very augmented reality of Sean Morey and John Tinnell's edited collection on augmented reality) are situated somewhere between *making real* and *making digital* because they augment the materiality of the page with the expanse and playability of digital mediation. That is to say, augmented reality apps like LAYAR (created by the Dutch company of the same name) and Aurasma (created by the British company Autonomy) give the flat, printed world the thickness and interactivity of the digital. Thus, rhetors can now design rich mediated experiences that combine static and dynamic representation and expression—bringing the affordances of multimedia composition to bear, quite overtly, on traditional textual practices by embedding a "fingerprint" (a particular icon or visual representation) on the page. When app users scan the printed document/object with their phone, the "fingerprint" triggers the associated augmented reality experience. In so doing, LAYAR, Aurasma, and other similar applications imbue nondigital materials with layers of digital mediation. This practice/process is neither fully digital, nor fully material but vibrates across the representational materialities of post-digital practices to bring the qualities of the digital into the realm of the real, and vice versa. But more than that, unlike something like Bartholl's *Map*, which is limited to its own expressive potentiality, augmented reality systems like LAYAR open an entirely new spectrum of possibilities for the tradition (and trajectory) of print, which includes not only the institutions of writing but design as well. Company logos can be the "fingerprint" that triggers promotional videos. Presidential campaign posters can become interactive position statements or be overlaid by a live Twitter feed. And dissertations—the staple of the nineteenth- and twentieth-century academic tradition—can offer an interactive media experience (perhaps foreshadowing what twenty-first-century dissertations should be). The point is that bringing elements, experiences, and even expectations of the digital into the real calls into question the digital/real divide and expands the rhetorical capacities available to everyday people doing everyday things.

MAKING DIGITAL

If the first approach is about giving "the real world the grain of the [digital]," then the second consideration at play is the inverse: preparing "something in the physical world for its entry into the [digital]" (Bridle, "Waving" n. pag.). For more and more of our run-of-the-mill material artifacts are being digitized—both as part of regular life activities (as entities in the background) and as objects unto themselves. From "foodies" who photograph their meals and distribute those visuals via Snapchat, Instagram, or the larger twitterverse, to everyday items, objects, and elements being embedded with various sensors that stream real-time information, what we are undergoing, culturally, is a transformation in which everything is susceptible to participating in/with the digital. The impact of this conditionality is that *working creatives now have to design as much for digital representation as for user experience.* It is that moment when the designers of pastry toasters begin considering how their products will look on Facebook. Or, to use Bridle's example, when Access Agency based their pitch to Virgin Atlantic on designing planes (particularly plane interiors) that people want to take pictures of and share on the web ("Waving"). The agency was attempting to craft real-world things with the express intent of digital (particularly social media) showcasing—meaning form and function has given way to additional rhetorical considerations in post-digital representation.

But commercial enterprise is not the only arena in which this is occurring. Professional artists are dealing with this conditionality perhaps more explicitly than most. As Openshaw argued in *Postdigital Artisans: Craftsmanship with a New Aesthetic in Fashion, Art, Design, and Architecture,* "some of the most successful exhibitions of recent years provide 'Instagram moments,' meaning photo-friendly opportunities for the viewers to insert themselves into the installation, and share the resulting imagery online" (7). This material-to-digital conversion is changing "the way art is now commissioned, conceived, and installed" (138). Artists Rachel De Joode and Michael Staniak have echoed (if not extended) these considerations. In an interview with Openshaw, De Joode tells us that "the look" of the installation, the artifact, the art piece is only "half of the success of art nowadays; it [also] has to look good on a blog" (in Openshaw 138); and Staniak suggests that the importance/impact of having one's work traversing the network in addition to living in studios, galleries, and the like has led to artists "consciously, or even subconsciously" using "materials and colours that will look good online" (in Openshaw 135). The reality is that designed artifacts meant for public consumption or display need to work aesthetically in both digital and nondigital realms (as well as hybrid manifestations). This is a relatively new consideration, one highlighted by the New Aesthetic, but while artists can play somewhat freely with these matters, owing to the different contexts and affordances available to artworks, rhetors and working creatives in industry or the civic sphere have the added rhetorical dimension of ensuring that the explicit and implicit values of the object(s) created also readily transfer with digitization (i.e., do different digital representations of the object carry with them recognizable [and positive] company/product values?). This suggests that the making of material artifacts is no longer just about functional design, or even design theorist Donald A. Norman's emotional design,[9] but also must include critical considerations of other aesthetic dimensions: sound, touch, taste, smell, and so forth—all of which contribute rhetorically, intentionally or otherwise, to how an object or artifact is understood. But perhaps chief among these other considerations is that of image design—and here I do not mean the visual design of the object or artifact itself, but rather what that entity will look like as a flattened, digital image captured in a selfie or as a revisualized Prisma[10] image. Meaning, does it provide the kind of saturated values that become vibrant screen representations or that allow for dynamic algorithmic and/or artificial intelligence manipulations? And here what is most interesting to me is not the algorithmic

---

9. In *Emotional Design: Why We Love (or Hate) Everyday Things*, Norman makes the case that emotions have a critical value to human capacities for understanding the world. In particular, he argues that objects designed to be aesthetically pleasing were often perceived, in turn, to be more effective at the task (whether that was the case or not). For Norman, designers must attune to the emotional dimension of their designs, as better emotional design leads to greater affinity between the user and the design/object, which leads to increased valuation of the object.

10. Prisma is a photo-editing application that augments images by applying algorithms to transform a photo into an artistic effect. It transforms the image not through application of a standard filter but rather by rebuilding the image through algorithmized layers.

affliction but rather the potentiality of visual vibrancy, which is far more suggestive of the flows across ecologies. Vibrancy matters in screen mediation, and as more and more of everyday life becomes facilitated in and through screens, the physical world is adapting itself to the saturated-color expectations of screens (and/or screen-based augmentations). Or, to put it another way, "the real" is being recolored and recast by the affordances (and sensibilities) of "the digital's" visual values, preferences, and available manipulations.

There is, then, more at work here than just an increased degree of visual vibrancy needed for everyday objects. As Sean Morey suggests in "Digital Ecologies," what is being introduced is a new metaphysics not only for digital entities, artifacts, and practices but also for the ways in which digital capacities reshape everyday thinking with, understanding of, and representation through nondigital materialities (112). What begins to manifest, as I have suggested throughout, are differently configured sensibilities that no longer perceive the world as beholden to the silos of the divide, but rather that operate among varying flows and intensities across rhetorical ecologies. And one mode of taking stock of the flows includes, as per the focus of this work, an attunement to how things like the aesthetic affordances and constraints of screen mediation can come to bear quite overtly on the aesthetic dimension of nondigital objects and events. But to glean this movement conditionality—to take stock of the impact of digital ecologies on nondigital manifestations—one need not go to cutting-edge art installations or blockbuster design agencies and Fortune 500 companies. Rather, academics are increasingly exposed to this dynamic. For as the bulk of our work is meant for public consumption (from teaching to giving talks, publishing to giving performances), our words and works are routinely recorded, uploaded, and published (shared publicly) in and through digital venues. What is interesting, however, is not that public intellectuals of all varieties create blogs, make podcasts, or record lectures, but rather that the fluidity with which things move across ecologies is beginning to influence the practices and products produced by these individuals.

Take, as a more tangible example, the relatively stable genre and activity of the conference presentation. Thanks to social media networks and participants who augment conference experiences by tweeting during sessions and talks, presenters are now aware of the value and importance of embedding "tweetables"[11] in their presentations/papers. This is because live-tweeting presentations has become integral to the conference experience—whether dealing with an idiosyncratic academic event or a widely popular program like South-by-Southwest (SXSW), the very forum that helped mainstream the New Aes-

---

11. Tweetables: key images, clips, or 280-character sound bites that audiences can readily reproduce and share via Twitter.

thetic. The live-tweeting aspect of a presentation, panel discussion, presser, and the like allows for a different kind of engagement on the part of presenters as well as audiences (those present and those tele-present); it also alters/augments the presentation itself.

For example, at the 2014 Computers and Writing Conference (C&W14) held at Washington State University, roughly 400 conference participants generated nearly 9,000 "#cwcon" tweets, which collectively populated nearly 3.5 million Twitter timelines.[12] This, of course, is a far cry from SXSW, but it demonstrates the potential reach of event live-tweeting. Speakers, in turn, take stock of this tweetable conditionality and craft/perform talks accordingly. Not only have apps been built that automate tweetables, pushing out preconstructed tweets in a timed fashion (see Hootsuite and Later as two examples), but many speakers (scholarly and non) have figured out ways to orchestrate the tweetables via other avenues. Some go low-tech and provide handouts with tweetables instead of talking points. Others manage to manually tweet during their talk. This is decidedly easier, of course, when one's talk is primarily composed of playing a video creation (like my own presentation at C&W14), but the intent remains the same: to add a digital dimension to an otherwise real-world occurrence, bounded by the limits of embodied materiality.

In my own case, I live-tweeted my tweetables at C&W14 to allow audience members to focus on the video artifact that was my presentation (minimizing the chances of their missing visual/aural elements because of tweeting and/or reading the tweet-stream). Knowing this tweetable condition going in, I thought about my presentation in different terms: crafting key phrases or takeaways that could be readily reproduced in a tweet and structuring key visuals that would reproduce well as an image online. Similar to Openshaw's claims about the conditions of post-digital art (7), the feedback loop provided by digital documentation resulted in a need, or at least a preference on my end, to account for that digitization as part of the crafting process. This necessitated that I envision my work in relation to the larger conference audience— the twitterati who might "experience" my project as part of the conference but not as part of the live audience. Thus, I tried approaching the tweetables as a microcosm of my video project, hoping that conference-wide Twitter readers would be able to take away the larger conceptual arc in addition to key sound bites and visual snippets.

Now, this may seem like a simple thing or an obvious (maybe even obnoxious) kind of practice, but thinking of a presentation as both a live, in-the-real kind of performance and as something meant for digital deployment changes

12. Data from http://www.tweetarchivist.com/cgbrooke/2.

how one approaches issues of design and/or revision. What used to be governed by insightful passages and clearly developed arguments has given way, at least in part, to 280-character snippets meant to intrigue, be retweetable, and serve as signposts for the talk, performance, argument, and so on. It is a metonymic rather than synthetic kind of approach. Of course, designing tweetables in an academic paper/talk is not of the same magnitude as Access's design for Virgin, or, for example, Random International's widely successful *Rain Room* installation,[13] which has been excessively reproduced in digital-visual artifacts, but it nonetheless reflects the same conditionality. What is more, it is not necessarily the big corporate projects or highly acclaimed artworks that best demonstrate the increasingly intertwined digital and real but perhaps the simpler, subtler everyday practices of unknown academics, toiling away over three 30-second passages of a ten-minute talk.

However magnificent or mundane, this is an important shift for rhetoricians and designers alike because one must account for one's creations being/becoming readily available for appropriation and/or serving as "ready-made digital artefacts" (Bridle, "Waving" n. pag.). It is a kind of twenty-first-century inversion of Marcel Duchamp; whereas Duchamp used readily found objects and artifacts to make art and to call attention to particular practices and ideologies of art, museums, and culture, designers now explicitly design artifacts to also act as readymades (as sound bites, objects, and backdrops), which help facilitate the varieties of digital life: tweets and tweet pics, Facebook posts, web design, Instagram images, GIFs, and the like. In fact, Bridle's concept of render ghosts, which denotes those people, or representations of people, who live "in the liminal space between . . . the physical and the digital" (n. pag.)—those manifestations that urban architects use to populate their visions with people—are also part of this conditionality: demonstrating how individual humans are just as digitally representable as any other object (digital and nondigital) and just as available to being a readymade, inserted unknowingly into someone else's design/representation.

This idea of critical and creative works as well as a person's own likeness existing as an always-already-made artifact for representational practice is of slightly more interest than the materialization of *Mario*'s Question Block. The reason is that, from a rhetorical perspective, the more objects and artifacts (assets) one has at one's disposal to create digital representations, the greater potential one has for rhetorical mobility in digital expression. As such, unlike

---

13. I revisit this project more fully later in this work, but for a complete overview of the project, visit https://www.random-international.com/rain-room-2012.

the Question Block example, which calls attention to a very particular kind of digital-to-real movement in relation to a particular cultural phenomenon, material artifacts designed for digital representation do more than just lend themselves to general digital activity; they also serve as metaphors, as ambient signals, and as socio-politico-cultural markers readily leveraged in digital creations. For example, traveling on a Virgin plane, taking pictures of that activity, and uploading images to the web (all while in-flight), says quite a lot about one's status, class, privilege, access, and the like. Making a video and live-tweeting the tweetables points to a different set of markers and ability. In both cases, once these things are uploaded to the network, the rest of the networked world can appropriate them in and out of context and can build from or subvert what the elements of each may signify—much in the way that Jenny Edbauer mapped the mobility of the "Keep Austin Weird" slogan, tracking its intensities across different local, civic, and commercial ecologies; except here the movement in and across ecologies occurs at the speed of light, manifesting and moving in the blink of a fiber-optic moment, with its rhetorical fluidity shaped as much by sociocultural affordances and constraints as by the flow and function of computational networks.

Consequently, in *making digital* what are otherwise nondigital material artifacts, the fuller residues of those artifacts convey with (and within) their digital residencies. The same, of course, is true of the digital-to-real eversion. Which means that there is perpetually an excess with eversion: an array of capacities and intentions, meanings and implications, beyond the given everted creation—an excess in which an original intentionality and an artifact's newfound availability as readymade (to be remixed, remade, repurposed, and the like) are equally present and irreducible to one another. There is, then, not only a rhetorical dimension to eversion as a kind of twenty-first-century maker's guide (critically thinking about how meaning can be made to convey across representational manifestations) but also a question of how one attunes rhetorically to the flows across registers and materialities where different intensities form differently within the excess and often in excess of human sensibilities. Of course, while both of the aforementioned considerations are crucial to this scholarly inquiry—with the latter essentially being this book's performative gesture as it offers one set of attunements to the circulating intensities among the New Aesthetic—it is the former that may have the most practical value for rhetorical studies. For what this text presents is not just a kind of rhetorical analysis of a cultural phenomenon but rather a set of orientations for post-digital rhetorical engagements: the making of rhetoric in a post-digital world.

MAKING RHETORIC

At a very pragmatic level, then, what contour 1 does is introduce a reconfig-ured sensibility to how the leveraging of a digital artifact "in the real" or a material artifact "in the digital" allows for invoking the aesthetic sensibilities, structures, and explanatory values of the one in the other. This further blurs the divide, to be sure, but it also opens a wider array of meaning-making prac-tices. And one way to situate the potential of these practices for rhetoric and composition is to look at the work of multimodal writing scholar Jody Shipka, who has attempted to ground material (and materiality) as a key part of con-temporary composition.

In *Toward a Composition Made Whole,* Shipka argues that the field of writ-ing studies needs to revisit how it thinks about technology (and process) to include both real and digital artifacts and activities. This counters the larger trajectory, which has been to move further and further inside the digital since the early 1980s marriage of computers and composition. But Shipka pushed back against the computer-centric orientations that composition studies had adopted (particularly following the rise of new media). Instead, she picked up with the process orientation of Paul Prior, Geoffrey Sirc's "Happenings" rheto-ric, and the intertextuality suggested by Kathleen Blake Yancey to embrace both digital and nondigital materiality and embodiment in rhetorically sig-nificant ways and to frame writing as a complex, mediated activity (not just something one does on a computer). This, in turn, created opportunities in the composition classroom for including everything from gesture and move-ment to object-oriented activities and expression (with scholars like Jentery Sayers and James Brown Jr., among others, extending Shipka's work, at least pedagogically, to advocate for arduino boards and 3D printers falling within the purview of composition classroom and writing labs).

Outside of returning composition to a focus on materiality, Shipka's work also highlights how writing is something done in direct relation to the con-straints and affordances of the platform(s) involved (some algorithmic, oth-ers material). Thus, whether it means inscribing words on a ballet slipper or typing them in a Word document, writing revolves around a person learning to leverage the complex relations between material and representational affor-dances toward a particular rhetorical (or at least expressive) end. In short, Shipka's work allows for a fluidity of writing across digital and real materiali-ties, situating writing not in a particular medium but as emergent with dif-ferent cultural and material registers. She not only calls for a nondigital turn in current perspectives on multimodal composition but also openly embraces Yancey's perspective that (1) "a composition is an expression of relationships

. . . between human beings" and (2) digital compositions "bring us together in new ways" ("Looking" 100). Given the implications in Shipka's work, along with those of the New Aesthetic, I would argue that scholars and teachers need not divide composition between the digital and nondigital but should rather attune to individuals interacting with mediation, letting the relationships among representational systems and actants take center stage in terms of invention and interpretation. Thus, contour 1 of the New Aesthetic has the potential to thrive as a compositional guide—allowing writers (multimodal or otherwise) to operate with a tint toward eversion (engaging in a practice that intentionally moves across different digital and nondigital materialities) or to simply be more attentive to the particular human–technology assemblages in which they participate (as part of any expressive ecology).

Now, extending this slightly beyond the frame of writing studies, there are also interesting resonances between Shipka's work and that of Maiko Takeda, a post-digital artist, who employs analog processes to create works that could be (or project like) digital artifacts. At the core of Takeda's art is an intention to "undermine a viewer's expectations," which are predominantly screen-centric, and to force viewers to wrestle with digitalesque qualities manifested by material components and analog processes (in Openshaw 92). In her *Atmospheric Reentry* collection, for example, Takeda combines her expertise as a jewelry designer with her interest in ethereality (digital and non) to create body adornments that are suggestive of an extrahuman dimension. There is, simply put, both wonder and disjunction present in her works. And there is something similar in what Shipka is doing: creating artifacts (and designing assignments) that suspend the screen-centric privilege of composition, asking students to write / write with (or at least think critically about) the rhetorical significance of different materialities. These materialities may project something digital or even be taken up in the digital, but the works themselves destabilize the assumptions of what it means to compose and have the potential to point to that which is in excess of the human condition alone. Thus, in both Takeda's and Shipka's cases, much as in the New Aesthetic, what is at stake is creating an awareness of how mediated artifacts sit "*in relation to* the complex processes" by which they are "produced, circulated, and consumed" (Shipka 40).

Therefore, if rhetors operate in relation to the fluidity of materialities rather than to any disciplined practice within a categorical order, they (whether composition student or industry professional) may be better prepared to create artifacts and utterances that circulate within and move across ecologies and do so with greater rhetoricity. What emerges is less a focus on the technicity of things and more an attentiveness to expanding one's rhetorical capacities by bringing together and working across digital aesthetics and material expressions and digital expressions and material aesthetics. In so doing, much as can be seen in both Takeda's and Shipka's works, one can give tangibility to or create authentic mediated experiences for those objects and entities, feelings and forces that reside beyond the human sensorium alone. In this regard, eversion as a guiding orientation is, in short, one manner by which everyday writing and making practices can call forth things from an extrahuman dimension.

CHAPTER 4

Pixel Orientation and the Technologized Human Sensorium

IN 1957 engineer Russell Kirsch and his team at the National Bureau of Standards created the first digital scan of an image, a square-pixel rendering of a picture of Kirsch's son Walden (Plate E), which paved the way for today's pixel-oriented world. But Kirsch's digital scan represents more than just a pixel aesthetic; it, like Joseph Nicéphore Niépce's balcony photograph or Wilhelm Conrad Röntgen's X-ray image, also denotes a significant moment in human history. As Kirsch tells it, that project came in response to the question "What would happen if computers could see the world the way . . . [people] see it?" (qtd. in Ehrenberg). While that initial digital scan was not perfect by any means, nor did it offer a high fidelity to that of human sight, it nonetheless gave computationality access to the visible world.

Sixty years removed from its inception—and unprecedented exponential development since—much of culture now finds itself beholden to the pixel tendencies of the *computational eye* (an amalgamation of technologies by which humans have attuned computers to pay attention for them in particular ways). From network voyeurism to institutional surveillance, from smart gaming systems like Xbox One (and its Kinect device) to smartphones like the iPhone X, everyday reality is now routinely reduced to pixel-oriented data values subject to the processes and procedures of computationality. These systems—attention structures created by a combination of digital cameras, computer hardware, software algorithms, and human interest—track and react to human presence but do so by rendering people (their faces and facial gestures) and their surroundings as visual data streams. In this configuration, people are less bodies-in-space than mobile and motile pixel values, fluctuating in front of a *computational eye* that flattens them into a visual grid (as visual data)—no more and no less significant than cars in the crosswalk caught on a traffic camera.

This sense of computer vision (and its imposition) lingers at the root of the New Aesthetic, as one of the first creations Bridle included in his archive was artist Adam Harvey's *CV Dazzle,* an art project that responds to (and actively resists) computational vision.[1] Harvey used makeup to create contoured shapes (in contrastive colors) on human faces and/or crafted different hairstyles (often with strands of hair interrupting the facial plane) as a means to camouflage individuals from the pixel-vision-plus-facial-recognition-software assemblage that constitutes the *computational eye.* As such, what *CV Dazzle* offered was both an art exhibit that commented on a particular technologized condition and a set of tips / guides for bodily aesthetic augmentations that could allow one to resist the digital algorithmic gaze. This, of course, may seem an issue quite removed from everyday reality for many readers, but for those who live in heavy surveillance cityscapes—metropolitan areas like Beijing, London, or Chicago—Harvey's project provides a set of rhetorical and representational practices that can be adopted to resist (if not reject) the underlying sense of pixelism at the core of computer vision and, in turn, to move relatively unencumbered through an increasingly surveilled environment.

Now, while Harvey's work is meant to subvert computer vision itself, what it does as part of the New Aesthetic is point to a more general shift in human sensibilities. In a fascinating turn of events, part of what the New Aesthetic ecology draws to attention is a cultural moment in which there has been an inversion of Kirsch's team's guiding frame. As the human dimension is increasingly shaped by the flows and functions among its medial ecologies, what is at stake is no longer what it would mean for the computer to see the world the way humans do but rather what it means that humans are beginning to see the world from the perspective (and in the aesthetic) of computational mediation.

It is not simply that computer vision (and the people attached to it) routinely reduces human subjectivities to pixel-based data values, but rather that there is a developing cultural propensity of seeing or sensing pixel aesthetics in all manner of representations in the world, even in those of a nonpixelated variety. For the sheer ubiquity of pixel-based media coupled with something

---

1. For a more complete look at *CV Dazzle,* visit https://cvdazzle.com.

like the increasing presence of computer vision has led to a condition in which people recognize certain patterns and/or representational aesthetics as being either of the pixel or as inherently pixel-like. This suggests that while the pixel may exist as a technical thing in the world—as part of a technological assemblage that "sees" the world in a particular way and, in turn, represents it back to viewers and voyeurs in the same interpretive values—what matters in a work like this is the magnitude by which something like a pixel aesthetic moves into human capacities for making sense of things in the world.

To this end, the historical link to Kirsch is important, as is the clear connection to computational vision, but what is critical in the *pixel orientation* of the New Aesthetic is that it puts into relief certain movements of the pixel across human and nonhuman dimensions. And perhaps the best way this gets demonstrated is in those moments or representative artifacts where people have a tendency to see-pixels-where-they-are-not. Bridle points to this condition with a satellite image of farmland on the border of Namibia and South Africa (Plate F). This New Aesthetic artifact visually captures a series of irrigated fields (all in the shape of a square, all different shades of green—corresponding to different stages of growth) surrounded by rocky terrain and curved waterways. The square fields in the image seem less the result of agricultural practice and more that of monochromatic pixels taking form as part of something like a computer glitch. In *New Aesthetic, New Anxieties,* David M. Berry et al. argue that Bridle selected this image precisely "because its graphics suggest a pixillated [*sic*] version of a landscape" (28). They go on to say that this example is "pure surface image" (29) with no real-world correspondent: it could not be "seen" without digital (satellite) technology. But while Berry et al. are willing to write off this image because "its referent in the real is of no consequence for our aesthetic appreciation of it" (29), they skip by the very underlying technologized condition needed for people to see (or even be inclined to see) pixels there in the first place—a condition Berry would later, in "The Postdigital Constellation," refer to as *digital pareidolia*: "seeing digital causes for things that happen in everyday life" (56). What is valuable in this image, then, is not that it suggests pixels but rather, as Bridle indicates, that people find it difficult *not* to sense a pixel aesthetic in its monochromatic squares in the first place. There is something recognizably "digital" in the image, and that quality is present not because the land has been cultivated in that way but because post-digital culture has grown accustomed to perceiving (if not expecting) digital-pixel patterns of representation, particularly in screen-mediated forms.

In "The Genius and the Algorithm: Reflection on the New Aesthetic as a Computer's Vision," digital culture philosopher Stamatia Portanova refers to this condition of seeing or sensing digital, pixel patterns in the images of the world as "obsessive digital," which she indicates marks "a qualitative rather than simply quantitative modification of the visual style of our age" (97). She argues that the problem is not that "digital images are everywhere all the time," nor that we are inundated with computer vision, but that people now understand visual representations everywhere (especially photographic images) as digital by default, as reflecting digital aesthetics, as being available to digital manipulation, as constructing meaning within the representational affordances of the digital. What has changed is not necessarily the aesthetic patterns/values themselves[2] but rather, as Katja Kwastek suggests in "How to Be Theorized: A Tediously Academic Essay on the *New Aesthetic*," the contexts and ecologies in which people find themselves (the contexts and ecologies that shape human perception) (78). Which is to say, as *to be* becomes *to be mediated,* human perception itself attunes to, reflects, and becomes constituted by the base affordances and constraints of its highest forms of mediation—in this case, the pixel-based, representational qualities of screen mediation and their conditional availability to computational machination.

Now, while Portanova and Berry situate these reconfigured sensibilities in negative terms—with Portanova's "obsessive digital" being linked to a kind of neurosis and Berry turning to *pareidolia* as well as *apophenia* to frame the matter in terms of human error (e.g., the "mistake" of seeing meaningful patterns where there are none)—Kwastek takes a more positive approach. She aligns this *pixel orientation* with what art historian Michael Baxandall refers to as "period eye." In his book *Painting and Experience in 15th Century Italy: A Primer in the Social History of Pictorial Style,* Baxandall offers "period eye" as a way to describe how a particular confluence of factors configures how individuals and cultures look at, understand, and experience different works and objects in a particular epoch, in a particular culture. This confluence not only includes the social relationships that produce particular paintings but, as Baxandall notes, is also composed of commercial, religious, and perceptual institutions and conventions (1). Visual studies scholar Malcolm Barnard allows one to push this further, arguing in *Approaches to Understanding Visual Culture* that media, particularly visual media, depend on the life-worlds of both the general interpretive public and the inventive artist (43). These life-worlds (an echo of Dewey's aesthetics in/of the everyday, discussed in chapter 1) include not only Baxandall's confluence but also the beliefs and knowl-

---

2. The aesthetics being ascribed to computation and screen representation existed long before computational media came into the mix (see, for example, the 1940s work of Swiss artist Richard Paul Lohse or the early work with voxel aesthetics of LEGO Company product designer Dagny Holm Jenson).

edges (and assumptions) that audiences bring to an interpretive act as well as the culturally situated forms and practices that constitute the mediation itself (including everyday expectations of particular medial experiences). Together, then, Baxandall's confluence and Barnard's life-worlds point toward a perspective in which human perception is intertwined with its socially, culturally, and individually situated forms and function of mediation. Or, as Kwastek more pointedly suggests, human perception reflects the medial patterns to which people give primacy (patterns that take shape as part of the ecologies in which people find themselves).

Of course, for those who work at the intersections of rhetoric and technology, this idea is anything but new. Marshall McLuhan, in his collaborative with Quentin Fiore, *The Medium Is the Massage: An Inventory of Effects,* contended that different types of mediation alter both the available representational means and the very ways in which "we perceive the world" (41). Moreover, these shifts in perception transform the core of human sense ratios (the means by which people make sense of the world), and, in so doing, alter what (and how) it means to be human. Thus, while something like the *pixel orientation* of the New Aesthetic may indicate a general pixel ubiquity and may draw attention to the *computational eye,* what it more fundamentally puts into relief are the underlying patterns of perceptual understanding—patterns that not only reflect a digital, pixel aesthetic, but which have become intrinsic to a twenty-first-century human manner of making sense of the world.

Working more directly in relation to rhetoric and the technology of literacy, Walter J. Ong has made similar claims. In his *Orality and Literacy: The Technologizing of the Word,* Ong offers an extended treatise on the shifts in the human condition that accompany a cultural transition from being of a primary oral culture to one of literacy. To this end, he offers many claims about both oral and literate practices of invention, memory/history, reasoning, and the like—all of great value to how one understands the complexities of rhetorical engagement. But one of the critical (and perhaps underlying) implications in Ong's work is that Western culture has been so saturated with the technology of literacy (and its corresponding seep into human ways of being) that even nonliterates in a Western world develop literate habits of mind, literate ways of reasoning, and literate modes of seeing and making sense of the world (76–116). While Ong is focused on technologies of the word in a way that this work is not, what he presents is a view toward understanding the depth and degree to which the infusion of literacy (a technology) has introduced altogether different sensibilities (perceptual and intellectual alike).

In an interesting kind of dynamic, Jonathan Openshaw has essentially recast Ong's position to fit the current post-digital milieu. In *Postdigital Arti-*

sans: Craftsmanship with a New Aesthetic in Fashion, Art, Design and Architecture, Openshaw swaps out Ong's "literacy" for a contemporary sense of "the digital"—writing that the world "has been [so] reformulated by the digital moment" that people have developed a "digital mindset," one "inextricably entangled with existence, whether or not the digital *technology* is actually present" (5; emphasis original). What Openshaw is saying, much like Ong, is that current ways of perceiving, conceiving, and even receiving the world (and things in worlds) have become colored by the premises and practices of pervasive technologies. In a contemporary context, this includes both the pixel as representational unit of computational systems and the pixel as aesthetic entity of ubiquitous screen mediation (in visual and haptic interactions alike).

Therefore, as changes in technological capacities set upon the human-technology assemblage, what manifests in addition to new ecologies and new practices are altogether new sensibilities (and sense ratios) that attune people to different attention structures as part of their making (and understanding) practices. For, as rhetoric scholar Kenneth Burke famously claimed in *Permanence and Change,* a way of seeing is also a way of not seeing (49); to which might be added that a way of seeing also heightens one's attentiveness to (if not preference for) particular patterns, practices, performances, and products. Take, for example, how visual design specialists or graphic artists view magazine covers: these individuals cannot help but see things like kerning, color, stroke effects, drop shadows, and font choice, as well as quick corrections, layering, masking, layout, and so on. In this regard, both the techniques of design and the logics and practices of technological components (specifically computer software like Adobe's triumvirate of InDesign, Illustrator, and Photoshop) have permeated the designers' and artists' worldviews. As Richard Lanham puts it in *The Economics of Attention: Style and Substance in the Age of Information,* individuals develop "stored-up impulse[s] to pay attention to certain kinds of things in certain kinds of ways" (9), and once conditioned to these impulses (like visual designers and the technicity of design), they find it difficult not to do so.

But while "expert" ways of seeing, listening, and/or being attentive are developed in relation to training and exposure—which render elements discernible in certain ways and which can be leveraged for rhetorical purposes (see Ceraso[3])—the same "storing up" of attention structures happens at dif-

---

3. While this section focuses on the pixel and leans inherently toward the visual as a way of thinking through its critical issues, the kind of attentiveness at stake here is available to all sensory modes. Steph Ceraso demonstrates this beautifully in her work, where she turns to the multimodal listening practices of deaf percussionist Dame Evelyn Glennie to demonstrate how an expert way of listening invites certain types of attentiveness, which can then be extrapolated to students to develop more embodied ways of experiencing mediation.

ferent depths, scales, and intensities with a more general condition like being saturated by digital screens and digital scans (all of which bear the mark of the pixel). Hence, the pixel attentiveness operative in the New Aesthetic takes form not as the result of the trained eye of a professional assemblage but rather from an everyday citizenry awash in ubiquitous modes and means of mediation. The situation is far more akin to Baxandall's "period eye"—perhaps here a kind of "post-digital period eye"—than to any gaze of the master class. Thus, the more that everyday producers and consumers experience the artifacts and practices of their primary medial forms, the more they become accustomed to (if not expectant of) those representational affordances and their overt and underlying aesthetic elements—which, in the case of screen media, include an attentiveness to pixelation itself (and its implications).

What matters here is not simply that people have become accustomed to pixelated media, but rather that contemporary human–technology assemblages have made it possible for something like the pixel (as representational unit and aesthetic entity) to transition from the realm of technical mediation into an embodied mode of human understanding. Or, to put it another way, human–technology assemblages seem to intertwine the technicity of digital mediation with human sensibilities—and the New Aesthetic is one entity taking stock of these flows across human and nonhuman registers: capturing (and capitulating on) the ways and means by which mediations (and medial elements, like the pixel) *evert* into the human condition.

One particular apparatus that might help better situate this dynamic for rhetorical studies comes out of new media studies: specifically, Jay David Bolter and Richard Grusin's concept of remediation.[4] In their now iconic work, *Remediation: Understanding New Media*, Bolter and Grusin initially define

---

4. As new media studies has drifted widely across art, aesthetics, and architecture, dipped into and maneuvered through considerations of computational processes, code, culture and convergence, and, in more recent years, ventured across materiality, new materiality, media ecologies, and even actor-network theory, there may be something of a grand narrative wanting as a guiding orientation here—with an extended overview of new media opening its own lines of inquiry as well as providing something of a history against which the New Aesthetic might be set. But I hesitate to turn toward such actions, as attempting to reductively suture together the varied tensions and perspectives that fall under the banner of new media would prove troublesome at best. Rather, this chapter heeds philosopher Jean-François Lyotard's charge for *petit récit*: the call for little narratives. While little narratives may cover less ground than the synthetic perspectives operative at the level of any grand narrative, little narratives do allow one to work in far finer granularities. To this end, I turn to Bolter and Grusin's work because they situate their concept of remediation as the "defining characteristic of new digital media" (45), they offer a trio of concepts that account for media-to-media and human-to-media relations, and Grusin himself has gone so far as to claim (via tweet) that the New Aesthetic is nothing more than "just the latest name for remediation" (qtd. in Kwastek 75). As such, there is perhaps not a better *petit récit* available.

remediation somewhat generically as the "representation of one medium in another" (45). In so doing, they extend McLuhan's foundational principle of media: the content of any medium is always another medium (*Understanding* 8). But they press remediation further—doing so with an eye toward particular experiences of media (described in their subterms of immediacy and hypermediacy) and the specific manipulations by which media come to borrow from other media to create meaning or to have cultural value. They eventually set upon remediation as being the set of practices by which media "appropriate the techniques, forms, and social significance of other media" (65). It is from this more pragmatic orientation that N. Katherine Hayles, in *Writing Machines,* recasts remediation as media-to-media parasitism, with media content and media techné cycling through different types, forms, and materialities of mediation (5)—with mediation itself being of the flows and circulating intensities. And it is here, with Hayles's introduction of parasitism as a way of thinking about remediation, that one begins to see an advantageous crack in the more rigid media-to-media veneer of Bolter and Grusin's remediation. For, being parasitic, the appropriative practices of remediation are, like viruses and infections, of a pathogen not beholden to sequence or system, nor pattern or predictability, but rather are opportunistic and transmittable via varied points of contact. With the screen serving as the primary point of contact between humans and technology, and with the pixel operating as the smallest available unit of interaction and representation within screens, it should not seem so outlandish that screen mediation (and its medial elements) has the capacity to move into and across biological materialities, essentially remediating (infecting) the human condition.

What the *pixel orientation* of New Aestheticism calls to attention, then, is not simply a kind of rampant pixelism, nor merely the presence of computational vision, but rather the manner by which different assemblages adapt, adopt, and acclimate to different medial affordances and cultures at differently situated moments. By focusing on the New Aesthetic's pixel orientation, one not only begins to glimpse the media-to-human infusion operative in postdigital culture but also begins to understand contemporary rhetorical practices in terms of a general shift in human–technology assemblages.

Beyond offering a theoretical orientation to human–technology relationships, however, what the *pixel orientation* also illuminates is something of a pragmatic threefold: first, it demonstrates, in intentional and unintentional ways, how technological shifts (particularly in relation to remediation) render previous media aesthetics salient; second, it points toward the manner by which those media aesthetics can be made to function rhetorically (a kind of rhetorical hypermediacy); and third, it hints at how the very affordances and constraints of a particular mediation can be brought into alignment with (and flow across) perspectives in other registers (like those of methodology or technique). Thus, in the second half of this chapter I turn toward these more pragmatic dimensions, situating them as germane to this *pixel orientation* contour and as part of its contributory value to rhetoric.

MAKING SALIENT

One key element to understand with human–technology assemblages is that the highest form of media available in any age establishes the individual as well as cultural expectations for mediation. As such, any remediation of that "highest" form also remediates human expectations. But among the multiplicity operating in this human-to-media dynamic is a lesser, yet equally significant, development: each evolution in media also shifts the available perspectives by which one is able to discern the previously indiscernible.

Take, for example, what happens when something like a VHS-based audio/visual culture comes into contact with DVD audio/visual media. The DVD representational affordances offer improved picture clarity, improved sound quality, deeper blacks, faster frame rates, and the like. Yet even with a marketing strategy designed to call attention to these qualities, what begins to manifest among a general viewing public is not a direct attentiveness to the qualities themselves (which remain somewhat invisible as part of the default immediacy of the initial DVD experience) but rather a hypermediate awareness of the representational impurities of VHS cassette media. Meaning, when moving from DVD back to VHS one becomes aware, near instantaneously, of the light "fuzz" that lingers in the visual plane of VHS media or the fact that the screenic-blacks are really just shades of darker and darker gray. Such "shortcomings," as Hrag Vartanian suggests in "A Not-So-New Aesthetic, or Another Attempt at Technological Triumphalism," begin to more readily appear in "some machines [and mediations] now that we have better ones" (n. pag.). Of course, the qualitative assessment here should include a degree of hesitation, as the transition to improved forms of mediation does not always mean *better*,[5] but each iteration does provide a new position from which to critique or create with the representational aesthetics of previous mediations.

---

5. For example, the shift from vinyl music records to magnetic tape to digital music files demonstrates, with each transition, the limits to fidelity of the previous mediation (with clearer, cleaner, and crisper productions exposing, by comparison, the snaps, pops, and hiss of previous iterations). But in terms of the listening experience provided, each new material and medial form does not inherently point to a better kind of experience.

And the way it does this is by making hypermediate that which was previously immediate—giving saliency to both certain medial qualities and particular cultural expectations, but doing so only in relation to other (contemporary) mediascapes.

But before I more fully explore the implications of what it means to make a media aesthetic salient, let me turn briefly to Bolter and Grusin's concepts of immediacy and hypermediacy, as they will be helpful in understanding this kind of saliency as well as the rhetorical gestures it opens.

As a quick overview, immediacy and hypermediacy are the two "logics" or competing drives/desires of remediation, and what they describe are the ways in which humans experience media (Bolter and Grusin 71). For example, immediacy is aligned with transparency—the "transparent presentation of the real" (22)—and the experiences to which it gestures are those in which "the medium itself" seems to disappear, leaving an audience "in the presence of the thing represented" (6). Hypermediacy, in contrast, is aligned with "the enjoyment of the opacity of media" (22) and, in all cases, is tied to an experience in which users/viewers are (made) "aware of the medium or media" (34). Bolter and Grusin write, "If the logic of immediacy leads one either to erase or to render automatic the act of representation, the logic of hypermediacy acknowledges multiple acts of representation and makes them visible" (33–34). Immediacy is governed (at least primarily) by a logic of effacement, whereas hypermediacy "multiplies the signs of mediation" (34). But despite their contrastive natures, both are beholden to how media offer claims to (and representations of) an authentic experience (65). It is just that one (immediacy) is associated with an authenticity generated through an increased fidelity of representation, while the other (hypermediacy) employs a saturation of media (and an attentiveness to that mediation) to offer its own rich sensory experience (34).

In borrowing these concepts, one might see an absent awareness of mediation as (by default) immediate and any overt awareness of mediation as hypermediate. Thus, when the DVD representational qualities put into comparative relief those of VHS mediation, what happens is not that one becomes aware of the medial aesthetic of the DVD but rather that the previously immediate qualities of VHS playback become impossibly hypermediate. On its own this is a fairly inconsequential kind of issue. But when this kind of medial saliency gets coupled with algorithmic techniques, what manifests is something like Rarevision's VHS Camcorder app, which allows iPhone users to render digital video with a VHS aesthetic. In so doing, it capitalizes on the "impurities" of VHS not as failures of representation but rather as aesthetic markers of a particular moment, era, culture, technology, practice, ecology, and the like. Once the aesthetic qualities of VHS media have been made salient (become hyper-mediate), they can be subject to algorithmization and, in turn, be available for creative manipulation by an entire generation of iPhone users.

While this VHS aesthetic may be somewhat at a remove for an everyday post-digital citizenry, the same condition applies to something like black-and-white photography. What was once the pinnacle of photographic creation—owing to material and technological limitations of its time—has become a standard filter in nearly all digital photography practices (from digital camera features to smartphone applications). The result is that black-and-white imagery is a design choice, not a default feature. In making black-and-white images (via taps and clicks and such), one employs the technical elements of black-and-white imagery and, in so doing, leverages the "classic" feel that has come to be associated with black-and-white photography (an aesthetic designation owing to the decades of distance between the formative moments of photography and its contemporary digital practices).

In an interesting sort of parallel, this is what is happening to the pixel. In the formative days of 8-bit and 16-bit video games, the pixel was part of a fairly immediate experience, but over the years there has been a concerted effort by industry to obfuscate the pixel: continued evolutions in screen technologies, software, and computational hardware have made pixels smaller and have generated algorithms to dissolve their edges. What was once a clear aesthetic designation between digital video games and broadcast television has given way because (a) broadcast television is now also digital, and (b) the pixel has seemingly been hidden from the vast majority of screen-mediated cultural practices and products—echoing, as Bolter and Grusin might put it, the effacement logic of Renaissance oil painters. Thus, when pixels now appear, they stand out (function as hypermediate); pixelated images are increasingly an exception, not the rule. And much like Generations X and Y, who grew up in a world where black-and-white photography was an aesthetic choice and not a mechanical/chemical limitation, the tablet generations of today will essentially have little to no understanding of pixelated aesthetics (and related 8-bit graphics) outside of their retro (and/or disruptive) sensibilities—the pixel aesthetic will increasingly exist as a design aesthetic and/or available rhetorical choice.

But unlike black-and-white imagery, which is achieved in digital representation by taking away particular values (color saturation), and unlike something like VHS Camcorder, which applies a series of algorithms to a video data file, the pixel of the pixel aesthetic remains materially at the root of all screen-based representation. The pixel is not just hypermediate marker and carrier of a particular aesthetic value; it is a natural marker for computational mediating technologies (even if manifesting in glitches, broken signals, systemic misfires, etc.). Thus, when pixels occur in contemporary mediascapes, they call attention not only to their surface mediations but also to the underlying materialities and assemblages (human and nonhuman) in which they operate and through which they acquire meaning. In so doing, the pixel demonstrates the fluidity with which representational elements circulate among mediating practices, aesthetic values, and human expectations, further affirming the need for new rhetorical ecologies. For what this dynamic underscores is the troubling limits of a categorical order, and what the New Aesthetic is capturing, in turn, is something of the different configurations and sensibilities emergent within post-digital ecologies. In the context of this chapter, this includes the degree to which pixels make themselves available to the rhetorical practices (and implications) of hypermediacy.

PIXELLING RHETORIC

To begin to glean something of the pixel as rhetorical hypermediacy, let me return to a familiarity from chapter 3—the digital irruptions that proliferate the New Aesthetic. But unlike with *eversion,* where these irruptions functioned to draw attention to flows across digital and real ecologies, the *pixel orientation* here homes in on those moments and materializations where pixel aesthetics destabilize (if not altogether disrupt) medial expectations across practices and platforms. Take, for example, Bridle's own muse, the Telehouse West building (Plate G) in London. What makes this artifact of value to New Aestheticism is not simply that it captures a digital, pixel aesthetic rendered in material, architectural space, but rather that the pseudo-camouflaged, pixelated exterior of the building's design—what architects refer to as a disruptive pattern—operates as hypermediate. The hypermediacy occurs from (a) the pixel itself being of a hypermediate quality in contemporary culture (again, the result of the technological improvements that have seemingly moved screens beyond pixel aesthetics), and (b) its employment as an exterior building design, which, as suggested in chapter 1, destabilizes aesthetic expectations for those still operating with sensibilities that reflect the digital/real divide. But no matter how the hypermediacy occurs, what it accomplishes is to direct attention to Telehouse West as a particular kind of building (what it is, what it does, what it houses, what it represents, etc.). To understand the implications of this awareness, it helps to know that Telehouse West is a major data/server storehouse for Telehouse Europe, one of the largest global data-center providers in the world, and the employment of a disruptive, pixel pattern renders the building visibly distinct from its surroundings—directing attention in one kind of way. But this exterior aesthetic also separates Telehouse West from most other buildings of its kind as data centers or server farms tend to be nondescript, large sheds—having more in common, appearance-wise, with livestock confinement buildings or shipping warehouses than with any technological avant-garde—directing attention in another kind of way. Therefore, the pixel-camouflaged quality of Telehouse West not only fails to obscure the building but has the exact opposite effect: creating a hypermediacy in which the building's aesthetic works counter to its representational expectations (geographically, categorically, and the like), and, at a very base level, calls attention to its own mediation.

Now, Bridle goes so far as to claim that the mediation of Telehouse West involves the building wearing "the skin of the network"—with its exterior gesturing toward both the building's own digitality and its participation in some larger, more significant cultural complexity ("Waving" n. pag.). But not everyone agrees with Bridle's reading. Kyle McDonald, whose own works involve the manipulation of code and algorithms to subvert network culture and communication, has countered in "Personifying Machines, Machining Persons" that examples like Telehouse West are nothing more than just another iteration of functional design (in the sense of hardware/software modularity and in terms of the applied arts). The pixel aesthetic that marks Telehouse West is, in McDonald's view, just another leveraging of an aesthetic pattern from a functional (in this case, computational) system. And, if true, this position could be applied to most artifacts and objects that employ a pixel aesthetic—just more and more adaptations of the principles of functional design. But even if McDonald's reductive assessment holds, the leveraging at stake here is not the same old "form follows function" of modernism, nor the postmodern rejection of such. Rather, what makes the exterior design of Telehouse West of interest, particularly in this work, is that its hypermediate aesthetic quality operates rhetorically—capitalizing on the tropes connected to (and slightly adjacent to) its function: it employs the pixel as its primary aesthetic element rather than the 1s and 0s that reside at the core of a data center or server farm; or, as another example, it features a pixel-patterned exterior rather than being shaped like actual servers (perhaps too obvious a gesture). Given, then, that Telehouse West primarily deals in the storing and transmitting of data or the archiving and relaying of information, not pixels, its exterior design is far more metonymic than a reflection of its function. Pixels are simply part of the technological as well as ideological and ontological world that Telehouse West inhabits, and in leveraging a pixel aesthetic the building's design participates in the identity of the company itself (and, in many ways, enacts something of its own paradigm). In this regard, the pixelated exterior is not simply a matter of function, nor of disruptive architecture, but rather is meant to serve as a relay across the rhetorical ecologies in which the building and passersby participate.

One can see a similar rhetorical capacity at work in the *Street Eraser* project of artists Tayfun Sarier and Guus ter Beek, who use stickers to create the appearance of real-world images and artifacts being "erased" in Adobe Photoshop (Plate H). Initially the "sticker erasures" (which leverage the empty background layer in Photoshop as visual aesthetic) targeted print advertisements, which are frequently created via some combination of Adobe products (InDesign and Photoshop, for example). The pixel aesthetic of the background layer was meant, therefore, to call attention to the fabricated quality of the advertisements themselves. But *Street Eraser* extended these considerations beyond the print advertisement world to graffiti art, road signs, business marquees, and the like, bringing the metaphors, methods, and models of digital production (encapsulated in a hypermediate, pixel aesthetic) to bear on the artifice of everyday reality (harking back to the near ubiquitous "born digital" quality of all manufacturing discussed in chapter 3).

But more than this, the "erased portion" (the sticker itself) created the illusion of layers, which adds what digital compositionists Daniel Anderson and Jentery Sayers would call a sense of verticality to mediation itself (80). *Street Eraser* artifacts deploy the rhetoricity of layers and, in so doing, ask viewers to be attentive to the production processes that proliferate digital culture as well as to the vertical thickness of mediation associated with digital making. Sarier and ter Beek distribute the techné of digital layering into spaces (and onto objects) of general public activity.[6] In so doing, they leverage the pixelated representation that underlies the Photoshop "canvas" as a means to capitalize on the verticality of layers (a core digital affordance[7]) and to expose the overlapping layers among digital and real ecologies. Simply put, the pixel aesthetic of *Street Eraser* forces viewers into a hypermediate position, one where they have to reconcile the dissonance that emerges when the vertical thickness of the digital is put into a mediascape governed by the thinness of material reality.

The pixel elements of *Street Eraser*'s stickers vibrate, then, between being an aesthetic value and a systemic marker. It is not that one is unable to make sense of these works in digital and nondigital ways; rather, it is that the meanings available perpetually migrate across the different registers. This suggests

---

6. See http://streeteraser.com for more images.

7. See Manovich, *The Language of New Media* 229.

that the pixel aesthetic of the *Street Eraser* project operates as a rhetorical multitude—calling attention to the very ecologies in which these artifacts and their audiences participate. Understanding the pixel's value, then, as a single piece; its relation to a larger set of pixels (as visual and haptic formations, like the background layer); the underlying systems and structures to which pixels are connected (technically, socially, politically); and the possibilities of their perpetual manipulations (via algorithmization, hardware changes, and even flows across ecologies) is critical for the ways in which post-digital rhetoricians might augment, alter, or even authenticate digital and nondigital artifacts.

That said, in the next section I want to shift the scale at which this examination operates. For while the considerations to this point have focused on a fairly granular engagement of the pixel—with particular attention to how it manifests across key New Aesthetic examples—the next section is designed to maneuver somewhat abstractly with the implications of a pixel orientation (leveraging the very affordances of seeing the pixel as a way to think about rhetorical inquiry itself).

ANAMORPHOSIS

With this last gesture within this *pixel orientation,* I want to return (at least somewhat adjacently) to the earlier consideration of seeing-pixels-where-they-are-not. This is not to rehash a tendency among a twenty-first-century remediated condition—such as noticing pixel aesthetics in nonpixel patterns—but to point to a technique and/or representational affordance that allows the pixels (and related representations) to participate in yet other registers as well. Thus, the movement being illuminated by this section is not of a surface matter but is rather more attuned to the potential rhetorical ecologies in which pixel aspects can be understood to participate.

Let me begin, then, by turning to a nondigital, nonsatellite example demonstrative of the pixel orientation: Salvador Dali's *Gala contemplating the Mediterranean Sea which at a distance of 20 meters is transformed into the portrait of Abraham Lincoln (Homage to Rothko) (Second Version).*[8] Aside from its unusually long title (which became *Lincoln in Dalivision* as a lithograph), this 1977 painting plays with perception itself, as up close it is a portrait of a nude female staring at a sunset over the ocean, surrounded by a series of multicolored squares (a technique of photomosaic art) that bear the style mark-

8. This image can be viewed online at the website for the Dali Museum (http://archive.thedali.org/mwebcgi/mweb.exe?request=record;id=152;type=101) or on Wikipedia: Lincoln in Dalivision (https://en.wikipedia.org/wiki/Lincoln_in_Dalivision).

ers now commonly associated with pixels. But as one moves away from the image, what comes into view (in an abstracted way) is a portrait of Abraham Lincoln. What is interesting here, in addition to the brilliant play of perspective, is that even when one is aware that the techniques employed are not that of a pixel aesthetic, one still wrestles with the pixel allusions of the aesthetic. Even the slightest sense of Dali's squares being pixelesque hints at this remediated human condition.

But perhaps more interesting to this conversation is how Dali's *Lincoln* taps into a fundamental representational technique associated with the effacement of the pixel. That is, when one views the work from the twenty-meter perspective (as suggested in the original title), the square aesthetic elements seem to fade away and an abstracted representation of Abraham Lincoln comes to presence. What is happening is that the aesthetic elements of the painting, much like the pixel, are subject to anamorphic play. Anamorphosis is an art technique in which a work (painting, sculpture, etc.) is rendered so as to need either a specific device (reflective cone, cylindrical mirror, etc.) or a specific vantage point (e.g., twenty meters) to reconstitute the image as it is intended. Absent device or vantage point, what one sees is a distorted projection—just a series of pixel squares—and not the larger representation in which the elements, marks, or materials participate.

One of the better-known works to include anamorphosis as representational technique is Hans Holbein the Younger's painting *The Ambassadors.*[9] The skull in the foreground of the painting is skewed to such a degree as to introduce the necessity for two (if not more) perspectives for viewing the work: the front view, which allows patrons to visibly engage most of the details in the painting, and the skewed perspective, which allows them to see the skull. There are any number of theories about why Holbein the Younger painted the skull in this work, and why he did so with an anamorphic technique, but one in particular suggests that this work was meant to be hung in a stairway so that viewers approaching or descending from the work could be startled by the sudden visibility and presence of the skull—a kind of painter's attention to viewers' experiencing the work.

But anamorphic perspective with regard to this *pixel orientation* is more than just a practice of distorted representation; it has multiple layers of significance because screen representations are themselves inherently anamor-

---

9. This painting features two male figures, presumably travelers, from the 1530s who are standing against a tall desk or shelving upon which several objects reside (from a globe to a polyhedral sundial). In the foreground, however, is a skewed figure of white and gray, which, upon closer inspection, reveals a skull notably out of perspective with the rest of the painting. To see the image, visit https://en.wikipedia.org/wiki/The_Ambassadors_(Holbein).

phic. Take this text as example, which was written using Microsoft Word. The anti-aliasing of alphabetic text is fundamentally a kind of perspective (or oblique) anamorphosis. Zooming in to the pixel level would reveal the jagged and multi-shaded squares that compose each letter. But at the right level of scale: nothing but smooth-edged letters. Meaning, that with the proper play of perspective (e.g., the zoom-in/zoom-out affordances of screen media), one can see past (or perhaps through) the pixels to the larger representation(s) in which they participate—essentially rendering the pixel tree invisible in order to see the visual forest. But screen-mediating technologies have improved to such a degree that they have essentially placed the viewing public perpetually in front of the visual forest. Thus, there is often a need to manipulate scale and perspective to see pixels in the first place—one must "zoom in" closer to the visual forest to see the pixel trees.

Of course, this particular pixel/screen orientation is perhaps not the exact use to which anamorphic perspective normally applies, but it nonetheless remains true: pixels, much like the dots in pointillism, operate at multiple levels of scale, requiring different perspectives for them to function as part of a larger graphical representation. But what the zoom-in/zoom-out capacity points to at a more fundamental level is the rhetorical value of scalability itself, with manipulations of scale allowing one to both defamiliarize an audience and construct altogether different ecologies. Lanham went so far as to suggest that manipulating scale was "one of the truly enzymatic powers of electronic text"—foregrounding the capacity of digital and computational mediations to allow one to decide upon "the central decorum of a human event" by establishing "the boundary-conditions [set by perspective] within which that event is to be staged" (*Electronic* 41). So, while the play of perspective operative at the level of the pixel may seem innocuous enough, it points to a larger set of rhetorical concerns for a post-digital era.

As Elizabeth Losh argued in "Nowcasting/Futurecasting: Big Data, Prognostication, and the Rhetorics of Scale," the play of perspective (via scalability) operates not only as rhetorical and representational tool but also as a method for inquiry and analysis: changing the scale sets the "boundary-conditions" of an engagement and determines, in many ways, the granularity of the inquiry as well as the available manipulations. For example, digital humanist Franco Moretti's well-known practice of "distant reading" demonstrates this rhetorical capacity, situating critics (particularly literary critics) at an altogether different distance from their usual relationship with texts in order to illuminate (and/or manipulate) different considerations. For changing the scale (and perspective) by which one approaches an artifact (or data set) changes the very depths and degree of the engagement as well as the very manner in which (and language

in which) the artifact is understood. In Moretti's case, this includes a rhetorical shift in which the words of a book come to be understood as "data" as
much as elements of a literary narrative. Granted, this kind of rhetorical shift
is not specific to digital ecologies, for Freudian psychology long transformed
what a word or absence of a word could signify (introducing a different kind
of multiplicity), but what Moretti demonstrates is that the play of perspective
and scalability afforded by digital ecologies necessitates, as Losh suggests, that
one "adapt to making sense of content at new orders of magnitude" (286).
However, it is not just that new orders of magnitude are being introduced;
rather, it is that different orders of magnitude move more and less fluidly
among different rhetorical registers. This suggests that whether the pixel is
situated as computer-vision data point, representational unit, retro-present
aesthetic marker, or other, its scalability and hypermediacy qualities allow for
altogether different configurations by which to make meaning, manipulate
representations, move across registers, and maneuver among a given ecology.

Thus, whether considering Dali's *Lincoln,* the general play of perspective
and perception central to all screen representations, or the possibility of anamorphosis informing critical inquiry practices, the *pixel orientation* (like with
most aesthetic movements) is an attempt by the New Aesthetic, as Bruce Sterling might put it, to acknowledge "a new way of perceiving reality" (n. pag.).
In this case, the New Aesthetic taps into the temporality of a cultural moment
(e.g., a "post-digital period eye"), but does so with attentiveness to the relationships between humans and mediation and how artifacts call to attention
different ways of experiencing and understanding mediation. The more one
becomes involved with technologies, the easier it is to naturalize the practices, preferences, materialities, and operative logics of those technologies as
part of a worldview. What makes the New Aesthetic of value, then, is that it
makes salient some potential naturalizations (and their underlying artificial-
ity)—helping people attune to the proclivities of living in, with, and through
digital devices (and the pixel markers they bear).

THE PIXEL RHETORICIAN

The issue for rhetoric, then, is not "why" people adapt to technological ways
of seeing and sensing the world, nor how to better delineate between categorical orders like the digital, the mechanical, the real, and so on, but rather how
to adjust the practices of rhetoric to account for the ripples of a remediated
human condition and the medial, material, and methodological capacities it
exposes. Meaning, if the pixel functions as a representational unit, a hyperme-

diate aesthetic, a model of scalable affordances, and a meaning-making pattern routinely employed by post-digital audiences, then rhetoricians crafting artifacts in/for a post-digital culture need to consider these matters. To this end, I want to conclude this chapter with a few implications of the quartet of considerations raised above, as they provide pragmatic avenues by which this New Aesthetic contour may be brought into rhetoric.

First, what this contour allows post-digital rhetoricians to grasp is that the pixel is the smallest available unit of rhetorical engagement and representation in screen mediation. While screen essentialism is problematic in its own right, to ignore the fundamental role that screens play in today's digital mediascapes would be foolhardy. Further, if one is attempting to craft a digital artifact to be distributed by computational networks and displayed on screens, then failing to recognize the representative potential of the pixel would be disadvantageous as well. For the individual pixel, and/or its mutability to be grouped and perpetually regrouped with other pixels, establishes the very point of contact between human participants and screen media. Even in a fairly simple construction such as turning *The Ambassadors* painting into a webtext where the skewed skull is rendered as a clickable sprite,[10] pixels would still be that which displays and marks the sprite as a trigger point for users. Of course, in scrolling settings, the trigger function itself would flow across pixels as the corresponding sprite relocates on the pixel grid, but whether that sprite links to the Wikipedia page on anamorphosis or launches a video overlay of dancing sharks, the unit of value (and functionality) of the pixel remains rhetorically stable. Thus, while rhetoricians would be well served to attune to a variety of representational scales in digital mediation, they should never lose site of the pixel level and the granularity it offers.

Second, because the pixel functions as hypermediate, it can be deployed rhetorically in a multitude of ways. On the surface, it can be used to signal the aesthetics of error—computational misfires and glitch practices—in order to draw attention to particular technical shortcomings (or to reflect a computational shortcoming in a noncomputational representation). It can also be employed to leverage retro-present sensibilities (harking back to the 8-bit graphics of yore)—using cultural icons and entities from the dominant media artifacts of that era (e.g., Pasquini's coin block). But neither of these move the needle in terms of the fuller set of rhetorical complexities occasioned by the pixel aesthetic. Rather, what is the more significant value in this consideration

---

10. *Sprite* is a term used in computer graphics, particularly in video game design and construction. It designates two-dimensional bitmaps that are integrated into a larger scene (a composite of digital artifacts). Thus, a composite image created in Photoshop that places a basketball, a buffalo, and a bugle all on a white background would be composed of three sprites.

is that by using a pixel aesthetic, one can seemingly fold together different registers of meaning and mediation—bringing the metaphors, models, and metonymic dimensions of the digital to bear on the nondigital, and vice versa.

This "coming to bear" is relatively easy to see in the key examples in this chapter—Telehouse West and *Street Eraser*—as both leverage a digital aesthetic and deploy it in a material space. But in so doing, they simultaneously point toward the fundamental relationality between the material, physiological world and that of the digital. And this relational dynamic is often overlooked. After all, the visual metaphors employed in the dominant computational operating systems come from the physical world (computer "desktop," "trashcan" for deleting "files," "folders" for holding "files," "files," and so on). What this suggests, to return to the new media vocabulary introduced earlier, is that what can be remediated is not just media and human conditions but the metaphorical functions and capacities of everyday objects—understood in particular ways, in relation to particular cultures. Thus, when folding these competing and complementary registers together, the elements and artifacts and rhetorics and aesthetics of each become suspect to drifting in and out of one another—circulating among the ecologies in which they participate and which they help constitute. In terms of the hypermediate qualities of the pixel, this allows one to call attention to mediation in particular ways. But in terms of the remediation of visual and operative metaphors from the material world into that of pixel-based representation, what manifests is the ability to both expand and delimit digital and nondigital rhetorical capacities.

Third, what the anamorphic quality of the pixel provides is a model of scalable affordances. By changing the perspective at which one operates, one can fundamentally change one's relationship with the object of inquiry. In some cases, this allows one to see patterns and predilections otherwise blurred (much like Lincoln in Dali's *Lincoln*). In others, it allows one to work either with a finer granularity or with a greater degree of abstraction. In either case, what something like the pixel orientation demonstrates is the value in shifting perspective—a necessity, in most cases, to even be able to see pixels in the first place. This strangely parallels the objectivist impulse, which sought to efface the researcher/rhetorician from critical inquiry and the production of knowledge: the appeal to objectivity, much like industry's drive to obfuscate the pixel, essentially moved us past the intimate considerations of an individual's relation to an object of inquiry—projecting (in both language and practice) the necessity of distance. But, as so many works have shown—particularly those pulling from the feminist perspectives of Luce Irigaray and the call to write one's body, or the work of Gregory L. Ulmer and his rhetorical play of the *mystory*—moving closer to an object of inquiry and acknowledging one's closeness can reveal new considerations and capacities as well. To echo a line from Sean Morey's "Digital Ecologies," individuals both participate in and help constitute the ecologies themselves (119). Which is to point out that people are shapers of and beings shaped by the ecologies in which they participate. Thus, while there is a value in zooming out to "big data" levels so as to discern forest-level patterns and practices, there is equal capacity and value to zoom in and dance among the trees. The *pixel orientation* of the New Aesthetic, then, should push rhetoricians to at least be attentive to the distance they adopt in their engagements and to consider what playing with the orders of magnitude might yield.

Fourth, if the primary gesture of the *pixel orientation* includes a remediated condition by which something of a digital, pixel aesthetic has moved into human sensibilities (and is understood as being somewhat natural to the world), then what is taking shape is the emergence of rhetoricians and rhetorical audiences that are of a techno-human hybridity—and a hybridity that takes form in the confluence of mechanical equipment / materiality, digital software / algorithmization, and human actants, all situated in a particular environment, of a particular moment, and in relation to other human and nonhuman entities. While I more fully explore the implications of this dynamic in chapter 5—focusing explicitly on human–technology making—what the hybridity (and its corresponding *pixel orientation*) allow for are digital ways of seeing, sensing, and selecting, while maintaining human ways of feeling, forming, and fathoming—with both sets of sensibilities emergent from life as it is lived and transformative of one another. What matters for post-digital rhetoricians is not that there is a tendency to see pixel patterns in the world but that as part of a techno-human assemblage, technological aesthetics evoke new orientations to rhetorical constructs, including things like pathos, logos, and ethos.

Now, while I would like to have ended this chapter "George Costanza" style—walking out following the mention of the classical rhetorical appeals— I would be remiss to not include one additional consideration in adopting a pixel focus as a way of exploring a technological condition: the seeming impartiality of the pixel. As Carla Gannis argues, the tint toward the pixel as orienting marker suggests that there may be "something more humanizing than dehumanizing in the endeavors of the New Aesthetic" (n. pag.). For pixels are "ubiquitous and functional patterns embedded in the operations" of people's everyday lives, and yet they are, in many ways, relatively "dislocated from culture, gender, and race" (n. pag.). This means, according to Gannis, that pixels offer a kind of neutrality—being somewhat removed from a presupposition toward a particular subjectivity. For what the pixel offers is less a matter of subjectivity and more that of a technical consideration—a technicity to which all people are exposed and to which all screen mediations are subject. Further, what the New Aesthetic points to, even in its most pixelated of examples, is not any particular human subjectivity over another, nor even the human over the technological, nor any particular technology (or material-technological element, pixels included) over the human condition, but rather that human relationships with technologies come to color the very ways in which individuals see, act, and understand their worlds (and vice versa)—not only seeing pixels in places they are not, but designing programs, procedures, and even policies based on the (inventive/interpretive) possibilities of the world rendered through a pixel grid (the post-digital equivalent of Plato's *liknon*).

Interestingly enough, one of the few subjectivity concerns to emerge with the pixel stem from the practices and preferences of the *computational eye*—a practice in which a computational voyeur/viewer interprets the visual world through a pixel-as-data orientation. With most facial recognition software operating on contrast values and disparities between recognizable features, those who possess darker skin tones and/or more uniformity in their key points of analysis (cheekbones, eyes, lip form/color) are less likely to be "recognized" by the computational-machinic assemblage. In operations where this *computational eye* is linked to policing practices, there are instances in which many people of color may (finally) hold advantage, as their faces can be harder to decipher when "understood" (rendered) as pixel-data values. This is by no means to suggest that they are less likely to be tracked or targeted by these systems—as the systemic assemblage is increasingly tied to policies and policing institutions that have historically been linked to a variety of racial bias. But when operating at the level of pixels and using the "pixel-captured" points of human faces as patterns for recognition, those faces that offer less contrast reduce the success rate of recognition by the *computational eye*. To be sure, this opens far greater cultural considerations than can adequately be explored in this text, particularly given the undercurrent with policing practices and people of color, but what this points to is that despite there being some validity to Gannis's claim that the pixel (in a technical sense) remains somewhat "dislocated" from these matters, there are, nonetheless, layered concerns of subjectivity. For any system using a pixel attunement is doing so inherently as part of an assemblage that includes humans, and the "neutral" pixel functions, by default, as the very representational value upon which human-built programs and assemblages act or to which they respond.

Thus, while the pixel remains somewhat dislocated from issues of subjectivity on its own, it nonetheless is part of an increasingly subjective set of practices—and matters of subjectivity that swing in multiple directions. For when individuals bring *computational-eye* devices into their homes, the potential recognition/nonrecognition advantage reaffirms the sense that computational technologies have been increasingly built for audiences of a particular race and/or class. But the success or failure of recognition when deploying one's Xbox One-plus-Kinect device or home security system seems to pale dramatically compared with the larger surveillance-plus-policy issues operating in this country. Although I do agree with Gannis that the pixel is far more neutral than many other technological entities (and/or the related perspectives they introduce), it seems important to also recognize that the pixel is rarely deployed on its own. Meaning, the pixel is not immune to the intrusions (and potentially even atrocities) of identity politics and computationality, because it always functions as part of an ongoing human–technology assemblage. It possesses the potential of representational neutrality but in practice becomes ensconced in all manner of bias that lingers within human perspectives and procedures.

What this pixel focus gestures toward, then, across the quartet of considerations indicated above as well as this subjectivity/neutrality dynamic, is that what resides in the undergirding of this *pixel orientation* contour remains fundamentally a matter of assemblages—with those assemblages themselves taking shape via an unevenly distributed reciprocity: with humans (in varying depths and degrees) setting upon the technological, and with technologies (of varying capacities and kinds) setting upon the human condition. Therefore, though the pixel is a medial and material element distinct from human physiology, it is increasingly (if not intrinsically) located at the base of contemporary understandings of human–technology dynamics. It operates as the smallest available unit of most post-digital rhetoric, reflects the techno-infused human sensibilities by which individuals see and (make) sense of their worlds, and captures, in one and the same moment, the technicity and the rhetoricity of screen-based technologies.

CHAPTER 5

Human–Technology Making and a Willingness to Play

WHILE THE NEW AESTHETIC may have emerged (conceptually, at least) with a small group of artists (the digital futurists) operating out of London, its manifestations pervade a much wider range of commercial and creative practices—finding "voice" through architectural structures, art installations, and techno-accidents alike. For the reality is that a far larger collective of working creatives have attuned their own design practices to the manner in which technologies set upon the human condition—with evidence of this dispersion manifest throughout the New Aesthetic archive. Consequently, New Aestheticism seems less a matter of an avant-garde imposing a new perspective on reality and more a matter of a collective attunement to a perspective that has been in play for some time (for one generation at least). That attunement involves an awareness of representation, an orientation toward screen-media aesthetics, and an attempt to call attention to the already present (and often hidden) techno-human practices, preferences, and protocols that produce particular artifacts.

Thus, while the New Aesthetic may seem, on the surface, somewhat removed from the field of rhetoric, what it does at its core is direct attention to matters critical to the knowing, doing, and making of rhetoric in the twenty-first century. This includes demonstrations of pragmatic considerations like techno-aesthetic values and/or how different representational aspects move across different registers (digital and real alike) as well as matters more aligned with epistemological and ontological implications. In other words, as Bridle suggests, the root of New Aestheticism is not a pixel aesthetic but rather a fundamental attempt to "explore, catalogue, categorise, connect and interrogate" the underlying systems and interactions *between* humans and networked technologies—exposing, as part of its plight, the socio-culturo-politico-rhetorical implications of these interactions ("New Aesthetic" n. pag.). Key among New Aesthetic considerations, then, are the manner in which (and degree to which) technologies accommodate and respond to human habits, methods, procedures, schemas, and so on for being in the world, and, of equal magnitude, how humans accommodate and respond to technologies (and accommodate and respond to the habits that technologies form in relation to specific individual human engagements). Which is to suggest that at the base of New Aestheticism resides critical attunements to both technological and human agency—with the coming together of the two allowing for new kinds of vision, new means of expression, and new capacities for writing and representation otherwise not possible.

With this in mind, in this chapter I focus on both the pragmatic and the theoretical implications of New Aestheticism, with specific attention focused on how the New Aesthetic ecology illuminates relations (and rhetorical considerations) central to *human–technology making*. I do so through three primary frames of inquiry, with the first dealing with the formations of new subjectivities, the second taking up with the development of new capacities for (rhetorical) action, and the third attuning to the underlying manner of engagement in human–technology *making* practices.

EMERGENT SUBJECTIVE CONFIGURATIONS

Joanne McNeil, editor of *Rhizome* and one of the four panelists Bridle put together for the 2012 South-by-Southwest (SXSW) New Aesthetic catalyst event, argued that while the New Aesthetic may offer new ways of seeing and perceiving the world, it does so not in relation to any particular machinic vision but rather as the result of collaborations between humans and technologies ("New Aesthetic" n. pag.). To demonstrate her point, McNeil draws an analogy with photographer Dziga Vertov, who famously claimed that his camera did the seeing for him and he for his camera. Through the analogy, what McNeil suggests is that the coming together of the two (human and technology / Vertov and camera) allows for some vision, some representation, some "thing" otherwise not possible. One can hear echoes of this dynamic from rhetoric scholar Victor J. Vitanza, who, in a remixed (and animated) conversation with filmmaker and media studies scholar Anthony Collamati, says, "Now, you know, you've got a camera. You pick up the camera, you push the button. Who's in control? For the most part, when I push the button, I find out the camera is in charge of me. I think I'm shooting something, and something else comes out. The camera has produced something else" (Hodgson et al., Act VIII, 1:24). Similarly, artist Eno Henze, whose work regularly translates the digital into the physical, says, "I approach a computer with a certain idea, [but] what I get back from the machine is something else" (in Openshaw 43). What Vertov, Vitanza, and Henze all point to is an awareness of the ways in which their technologies (camera or computer) set upon them and upon their acts of making. In so doing, they gesture toward a hybrid way of seeing/making, where the results, as Henze says, are of both "human and machine origin" (43). This reflects emergent representational practices, where locating the agency of the action (human vs. machine) is secondary to the mediation itself. For, to pull a thread from Bridle, no amount of machinic vision can exclude the human viewpoints necessary for making sense of those representational practices (and vice versa). The point here is not that technologies "see" and "capture" in ways that humans do not comprehend but rather, as Jamie Zigelbaum and Marcelo Coelho put it, that "humans and computers are combining agencies," creating new artifacts, and dissolving the "dichotomy between human and machine, analog and digital" (n. pag.). Therefore, part of what makes the New Aesthetic viable, visible, and valuable for rhetoric is that it attunes itself to the hybrid flows among these registers—situating its artifacts and arguments in a kind of third space (neither exclusively human nor exclusively technological). In more expansive terms: the New Aesthetic's emergence out of a technological history and an overtechnologized present does not mean that it privileges the technological; rather, the New Aesthetic is concerned with how humans and technology come together to allow for new ways of making (and making sense of) mediations in the world.

One can hear echoes of these considerations in the scholarship of John Tinnell, whose "Post-Media Occupations for Writing Theory: From Augmentation to Autopoiesis" argued that writing studies needed an altogether different orientation to the relationships between technologies and human subjectivities. He showed how writing studies has traditionally adapted itself to the language of technologies and digital mediation as *tools*, which, in turn, positions writers and rhetors as *users*—orienting the conversation, by default, toward matters of instrumentalism. But the instrumentalist perspective, as Tinnell argues, is "incapable of registering the dissolving border that (supposedly) once separated humans and technology" (125), preventing one from taking up positions in which technologies and humans are parts (co-productive parts) of the relational complexities that compose digital writing systems.[1] Instead, Tinnell advocates for an ecological orientation that situates the act of human–technology making as *autopoietic*—as being emergent not from any individual human subjectivity but through a distributed set of relations of human and nonhuman capacities of engagement. These capacities include the heuristic impulses and procedural proclivities of people (individual and collective), computationality, and the mechanical—all setting upon one another in the very moments of making, which points not only to a new paradigm for human–computer considerations (each part of the complexity infecting the other in irreducible ways) but also to new kinds of writing and/or making that result from the merging (or hybridity) of agencies.

Of course, having an interest in the impact of technologies on writing clearly makes sense for those in rhetorical studies, but, interestingly enough, it was also very much a matter at the core of the New Aesthetic catalyst SXSW moment. For, in addition to McNeil raising concerns about the implications of the New Aesthetic leading to new considerations for writing (within a larger scope of digital making), the combining of human and technological agencies as having major influence on the practices of writing (and reading) was also what was most exciting for author, creative director, and former communication strategist Russell Davies. Specifically, Davies argued in his SXSW presentation that the New Aesthetic (and even the larger gestures of post-digital art practices) necessitates a critical attentiveness to the nonhuman and/or technological third parties (machines, software, bots) that are routinely introduced into the reader/writer dynamic—as these assemblages point to a different kind of writerly subjectivity (or at least a shift in traditional understandings of such). To be fair, Davies himself would go on to focus on something more akin to human–robot writing collaborations, where programmed "bots" contributed snippets of bad prose to the writing mix (a kind of algorithmic manifestation of William Burroughs), but I think the co-agential implications to which he calls attention can be seen more tangibly in the subtleties of everyday writing/making engagements—via things like autocorrect or the variety of filters in video- and audio-editing platforms. That is, one need not go to cutting-edge creations like Davies did with Allison Parrish's Autonomous Parapoetic Device (APxD mkII)—a self-contained, portable, poetry-generating device—or her more recently published *Articulations* (a book of computer-generated poetry) to highlight the importance (or future) of the human–technology writing collaboration, where a given technology is as prominent in the making/shaping of a rhetorical mediation as the human

---

1. For Tinnell, digital writing systems are the confluence of human and nonhuman materialities and mediations that make up the act of writing in and through digital technologies.

rhetor. Of course, the more mundane, accessible engagements of daily writing/making activities may not possess the same kind of curb appeal as the APxD mkII or the "bad prose machine" described by Davies (a practice routinely displayed by any number of Twitter bots); they nonetheless point to this increasingly collaborative process (and do so in a way that helps to emphasize its ubiquity in post-digital culture).

At the core of all these considerations, then, is not simply an attunement to the rhetorical implications of something like autocorrect, but rather a fundamental shift in how one approaches the human–technology relationship. Meaning, what is at stake is, in many ways, a matter of prepositional concern: for people write not *on* computers but rather *with* computers—with computational technologies shaping the writing/making process as a kind of collaborative, co-agential entity, and doing so by taking on more and more of the labor burden of the actual writing/making practices (alphabetic, visual, interactive, etc.). Therefore, writers and working creatives alike have to learn to adjust to these shifts in labor and to how technologies set upon them during the making process, developing new approaches for accommodating and responding to the contributions of the software-plus-hardware affordances and constraints of a technological co-agency.

Casey Boyle also picks up with this turn to *with* and to the ways in which rhetors learn to accommodate and respond to technology in his "Writing and Rhetoric and/as Posthuman Practice." There Boyle uses the 2011 *Framework for Success in Postsecondary Writing* report[2] as exigency for a posthumanist reorientation to rhetoric. The *Framework* encourages educators to focus on cultivating habits of mind that foster intellectual and practical ways of learning, which Boyle claims invites rhetoricians to move on from traditional habits of practice and/or orientations to subjectivity and instead better connect "rhetoric to emerging appreciations for materiality and mediality" (533). Boyle furthers this position by following the work of composition scholar Laura R. Micciche, situating rhetorical practices as being intimately "codependent *with* things" (533)—a relational orientation that echoes Tinnell's position, where any subjectivity to emerge necessarily does so through the relations between humans and technologies that are part of any given rhetorical complexity, not in spite of them.

To demonstrate his point, Boyle argues that by embracing the prepositional orientation of *with* (rather than Lanham's dichotomy of *at/through,* or even Collin G. Brooke's *from*[3]), one can situate writing (and even the rhetor) as

---

2. The Council of Writing Program Administrators, National Council of Teachers of English, and the National Writing Project developed this report.

3. In *Lingua Fracta: Toward a Rhetoric of New Media,* Brooke argues that Lanham's *at/through* distinction implies an all-important third prepositional orientation: *from,* which adds

something inherently more posthuman—as a practice that "unfolds . . . as an ongoing series of mediated encounters" (534). The value of this, in Boyle's perspective, is that each encounter, each mediated iteration, each practice (and practical engagement) *with* a technological or nonhuman other establishes and re-establishes human–nonhuman relations (and the capacities one has to act within the ecologies in which those entities participate). For Boyle, writing *with* new media, networked expression, computationally infused rhetorical practices, and the like necessarily transform an individual's habits of mind (as well as the individual herself) and foreground the very interconnectedness between human and nonhuman entities—with any subjectivity that may take form doing so from a constellation of relations. What Boyle's argument points toward (and what gets demonstrated through the New Aesthetic) is the manner in which human–technology assemblages activate (through practice) new relations within the ecologies in which they reside.

At a pragmatic level, this points to technologies as being far more than inert objects or neutral tools to be mastered in any writing/making undertaking; rather, as Tinnell and Boyle both suggest, and as implicated in the New Aesthetic, technologies should be situated as increasingly collaborative entities (with varying degrees of agency) that set upon people as much as people set upon them. And in the age of smart technologies, where technologies themselves have the power to learn and/or adapt to human collaborators as well as situations, this reciprocity of "setting upon" includes not only the cultivation of human habits of mind or practice but also considerations of technologies cultivating their own habits in relation to specific individual partners—which, in so doing, activate yet other relational configurations in the given ecologies of practice.

As a kind of quick example, one might look at the functions of most word-processing programs, which have a tremendous impact on how people produce traditional, alphabetic text. Microsoft Word, to target one specific example, does not just present a set of blank pages waiting to be filled with text.[4] Rather, Word is a collaborative writing partner, one that increasingly assists with grammar and spelling issues—not only providing autocorrection features (e.g., transforming "teh" into "the" as one types) but also developing habits of practice in relation to its human interlocutor (from autofill functions to adapting to linguistic and/or stylistic preferences). But more than that, Word makes default choices at the very outset about format and layout, and

---

position or perspective to the set of considerations. That is, to look *at* or *through* is always an act done *from* a particular perspective and/or subject position.

4. In fact, the "page" itself may be a bad metaphor, as (a) the screen is not the page, no matter how mimetic it may appear; and (b) the page limitation already orients working creatives to Word in particularly reductive ways.

includes autoformatting features that often have to be hacked to create nonde-fault representations. Additionally, with the litany of templates available, Word also operates heuristically, co-shaping content through aesthetic and infor-mational architectural choices. While this kind of techno-collaborator may not be the same as a human partner in the way that one traditionally thinks of collaboration, the program itself nonetheless influences the look, feel, and development of what gets created. Further, writing an essay with Google Docs or Scrivener in lieu of Microsoft Word may offer an uncanny familiarity, but each program will feel (and produce something) different. This is not simply because the default fonts and formats are different but because as collabora-tors they possess different affordances and constraints, and accommodate and respond to human collaborators in different ways. It is correlative to some-thing like co-writing with a psychologist versus an architect; they have differ-ent expertise and experiences, different preferences, ideologies, and purposes, and so the collaborative process and idea development is simply different.

Of course, writing has always been grounded in this kind of relational ecology—as a collaborative act between humans and technologies, with paper quality, ink type, writing surface, and the like influencing and shaping for centuries the kinds of writing that people do. For example, holding a cal-ligraphy pen or a writing quill both invokes a particular kind of feeling and invites one to write in particular ways (and to develop techniques of writing in relation to those material affordances). But the degree of agency associ-ated with the materiality of writing changes dramatically when it includes the software-plus-hardware combination central to writing *with* computers and any/all digital media production, for "the machine" and its expanded media ecologies do something notably different from the pen.

To explore this condition further, I want to turn focus to the smartphone photography application Hipstamatic, which not only will pull this conver-sation back toward matters of subjectivity but which also explicitly demon-strates the collaborative dynamic under consideration here: where the coming together of the technological and the human produces something otherwise not possible and, in so doing, invites the cultivation of different habits of prac-tice (for both).

Hipstamatic and Post-Digital Subjectivity

Photo apps like Hipstamatic are quite prolific for smartphone and tablet own-ers. They not only allow for taking pictures that directly connect to social media networks but have added levels of sophistication to the camera-phone assemblage by pairing the mechanical, camera eye with digital, algorithmic filters. These filters often work to mimic standard camera functions: on the production end, the algorithms allow users to adjust focus, alter exposure, manipulate shutter speed, and so forth; on the postproduction end, they offer a wide range of image effects, from creating black-and-white photos, sepia images, and pictures with vignettes, to altering saturation levels, augmenting hues and color tones, and adjusting contrast effects. Hipstamatic's filters even offer nonstandard camera manipulations through effects like "x-ray" or "infrared," among others. But what makes Hipstamatic different is that it essentially combines these activities into one productive moment. Hipstamatic uses algorithms to mimic the visual production (and aesthetics) of several plastic/toy cameras of the 1980s. Users select different lenses, film, and flashes, and then push a "yellow button" (a group of pixels on the screen of the phone) to capture a picture. The app then renders a square photograph (an image with a 1:1 aspect ratio as opposed to the 4:3 ratio of standard phone cameras), to which it applies a number of algorithmic filters to mimic the aesthetics that correlate with the particular lens, film, and flash choices. What gets produced through the Hipstamatic app is something different from what the human eye sees on the precapture screen and different from what the camera eye captures. It is the result of an entangled activity between mechanical camera device, software application, and human.

What makes Hipstamatic of particular interest here, as opposed to any number of other human–technology assemblages (including the multitude of other smartphone photography applications), is a trio of considerations, really. First, Hipstamatic's moment, like that of the New Aesthetic, has essentially come and gone—providing a kind of critical distance that allows one to better understand the app as a relatively stable part of a techno-cultural history. Along these lines, it seems relevant to know that the app launched in 2009, won Apple's first App of the Year award, in 2010, and, though it still operates successfully today, reached its peak popularity during the period 2011–12. Which suggests that although the New Aesthetic and Hipstamatic were not explicitly connected, they operated in the same media-saturated waters.

Second, Hipstamatic resides precisely in the tensions of the digital/real divide, with one of its co-founders, Ryan Dorshorst, claiming it to be "the app you use when you want your photos to feel less digital and more real" (in Downs, n. pag.). With mobile devices becoming more sophisticated every day and offering increasing levels of fidelity, Hipstamatic thrived by offering an aesthetic of the materialities of yore: as co-founder Lucas Buick suggested, Hipstamatic is "Kodak for the digital era" (in Downs, n. pag.). Further, as Dorshorst suggests, what made Hipstamatic a success and what continues to sustain it today is its focus on the experience of photography—"of taking a photo and having it turn out even more beautiful than your memory of the moment" (in Downs, n. pag.). In short, Hipstamatic has always been more about the process of photography than about any algorithmic imperative. However, the result of this orientation meant that it was never well suited to be adapted to social media culture. But while it may have been left behind by more social-media-friendly photography apps, Hipstamatic's representational techniques did inspire a plethora of practices in many other apps, including more than a few elements in the now-behemoth, Instagram. In a historical sense, then, it functions as a kind of precursor to the more widespread, social media, photography apps today.

Third, in November 2010, a few months before Bridle would make the New Aesthetic recognizably a thing, four Hipstamatic images by photographer Damon Winter graced the front page of the *New York Times*.[5] Winter had gone to Afghanistan that year to capture images of the First Battalion, 87th Infantry of the 10th Mountain Division. He took all the normal bells and whistles needed for cutting-edge photojournalism—he was, after all, a photographer for the *New York Times*. But he also used Hipstamatic on his iPhone to capture a number of stills, and those pictures captured something unique—scenes of war as seen through a human–technology collaboration in which the technology had equal agency in the rendering. In one moment, the Winter–Hipstamatic assemblage had both captured and crafted reality. Thus, while considerations one and two above are of value in establishing the importance of Hipstamatic to this conversation, they pale in comparison to this third element, to Winter's work with the app.

The reason for this distinction is that one of Winter's Hipstamatic images went on to be awarded third place in the 2011 Pictures of the Year International. This put the photo purists in an uproar. The problem was not the subject of the photo but rather the technology used to create it. What had occurred, as Collamati argued in his dissertation, *Camera Creatures: Rhetorics of Light and Emerging Media,* is that the Hipstamatic photos "unsettle[d] the camera's journalist credentials as a fact-based observer" (99). It replaced the ideology of "mechanical objectivity"—an "ideology that maintains that machines, when unimpeded, yield direct evidence of the material world" (100)—with an emerging "machine subjectivity," which forces a recognition of the collab-

---

5. These images were part of a series by Winter called *A Grunt's Life,* with selections from that series being featured, initially, in James Dao's "Firefights, Jokes, Sweat, and Tedium" article. However, a more targeted engagement can be found in James Estrin's "Finding the Right Tool to Tell a War Story" article (https://lens.blogs.nytimes.com/2010/11/21/finding-the-right-tool-to-tell-a-war-story/?ref=asia).

orative nature of the human–technology relationship. But Collamati's idea of machine subjectivity emphasizes the agency of the camera, remaining inexplicably tied to the mechanical, to the nonhuman. This is not to suggest that the camera does not have a degree of agency but rather that the focus should be on the *with*—the particular set of relations by which the mechanical equipment (iPhone and camera), digital software (algorithmic processes and culture), and human being (Winter) play *with* one another in the act of making. It is not just that Winter took the photo or that the phone's camera produced the image or that the software rendered/recolored the mechanical eye anew, but that any subjectivity to emerge in that situation results explicitly from the relations among the assemblage.

What is taking shape in this ecology of practice, then, is an increased attentiveness to the fact that the mechanism (camera) and software (Hipstamatic) alone could not produce what their partnering with each other and with Winter allowed. And the human component is vital, for it was not just anyone taking those pictures and playing with Hipstamatic. Winter is a trained professional, possessing expert knowledge: understanding things like shading and contrast, angles and framing, not to mention the likely aesthetic outputs of the simulated lenses, film types, and toy cameras. He is, in short, an expert in writing/making with light (for photography is an art of capturing and/or manipulating different exposures of light). Therefore, what he produces with his engagement is not just happenstance, nor just the result of playful clicking and toggling through effects/option; rather, it is an informed, crafted engagement. And this is crucial in understanding the rhetorical capacities available in any post-digital making: for producing a text, video, image, and the like today involves both the affordances and constraints of particular technologies and, as with Winter, the affordances and constraints of the specific human collaborator(s) involved. As such, any subjectivity to emerge (posthuman or otherwise), while not fully accountable in this example to Winter alone, is in no way absent of Winter and/or his capacities through the assemblage.

What was produced in Winter's images, then, was not an objective capture of the world as it was ("mechanical objectivity") but a subjective production of the world as it was wanting to be envisioned by the confluence of human, machine, and software. And what emerged in the images was only possible through the function of the device plus the artistic/mechanical filters of Hipstamatic plus the photographer's knowledge and ability—in other words, through what might be situated as a post-digital subjectivity. While the images may not be New Aesthetic proper, as they predate the launch of Bridle's Tumblr archive, the reaction to the images more than aligns them with New Aestheticism. That is, Winter's images revealed an increasing sense of technology as an agential mediator, ushering in an awareness of the mediating act and its intrinsic human–technology partnership.

Of course, this sense of individualism tied to Winter may seem too easy. For what Winter creates with something like Hipstamatic is bound to be different from what the average Jasmine or Jalen produces. But in the formation of any post-digital subjectivity—the subjectivity that emerges from the confluence of mechanical equipment plus digital software (algorithmic processes and culture) plus human being—one cannot elide the human dimension any more than one should privilege the technological at the expense of the human, as humans are, to spin a phrase from Marshall McLuhan, the life source of established and emerging mediating technologies. Now, I recognize that any movement toward the recovery of the human triggers Cartesian antibodies and imbalances the scale of what is often (mistakenly) situated as a zero-sum game with humans and technologies (i.e., focusing more on one comes at the expense of the other), but this work is operating in a different ecology, drawing attention not to humans and technologies as isolated dimensions but rather to the very flows by which they set upon one another, accommodate and respond to one another, and come together to produce new platforms, perspectives, and preferences for making sense of the world.

Further, I would argue that what the photo purists were most upset about with Winter's Hipstamatic images was not the technology itself—for photography as a practice does not exist without technological equipment. Rather, most disconcerting was the fact that the digital-camera-plus-application had automated not just mechanical reproduction but the techniques (and techné) of the master class. Saturation values, contrast, exposure, cropping, focus. All done inside the box. All before the digital/mechanical blink. In short, what Hipstamatic had done (like most contemporary photo apps currently do, with Prisma being a prime example) was remediate the techniques and artistic capacities of the master class—reducing sophisticated techné to filters and effects subject to the production whims of anyone who can tap, toggle, swipe, and send.

Now, the point in all of this for rhetoric is not to champion any particular humanistic or computational agency but to draw attention to flows among the assemblages and the corresponding shifts in labor (and the rhetorical dimensions to which they grant access). For what is emerging in the post-digital moment (as demonstrated through the New Aesthetic) is that the labor-intensive efforts of any master artisan or technological evolution are, in their very moment of coming-to-be, subject to the impulses of algorithmization; and, in turn, made available to the play space of today's click-and-pick or drag-and-drop post-digital rhetoricians. Moreover, everyday people have a corresponding sense of how easy it is to manipulate these filters in order to apply the stylistic qualities of the master artisans and to generate, in turn, multiple iterations of the same artifact featuring distinct aesthetic markers. Spending even two minutes with a photo-plus-social-network app like Prisma or Instagram allows most users the opportunity to toggle through all the filters for a single image creation. Which is to suggest that if technologies like these make it possible for any Jeff or Janice to create artistically savvy photographs using professional-level techniques, then the artist can be (perhaps has been) replaced by the novice, and the trained gaze and technical abilities of the master class are giving way to the frivolous glance and (playful) finger tapping of the noob.

What this points to, then, is not only the emergence of what I see as a post-digital subjectivity (with human and technological and material agencies all setting upon one another in a moment of creation) but also, as Boyle suggested, the cultivation of different habits of practice, distributed across different rhetorical abilities and/or levels of technological access/acumen. The challenge, however, is in figuring out the actual habits being formed and/or engagements being undertaken when the novice taps through seven filters and adjusts the saturation values four times before deciding on the right fit or look or appeal of an image artifact or when she plays with distortion and reverb filters in sound editing to produce the "right" sound or audial quality. And, just as importantly, what those practices or habits look like when being done by someone like Winter. Or, to go back to Steph Ceraso's work, when done by someone like Glennie. Do the expert and novice engagements have affinities that not only are reflected in the New Aesthetic but that might be distilled into techno-rhetorical frameworks?

For his part, Boyle locates these pragmatic considerations under the concept of *serial practice,* where one forms habits of practice not through the long-standing (and long-championed) practice of reflection (making something and then reflecting, often in writing, back upon that process) but rather through serial medial perceptions. Consequently, his *serial practice* indicates something more akin to the formation of styles of engagement (tied to specific medial perceptions), with each *practice* (whether a specific technical undertaking, like Winter's, or an abstract value of engagement) activating the relations in a given ecology in new ways, offering new configurations, and contributing (in cumulative fashion) to the adopting of (or adapting to) a set of behaviors and orientations to different techno-rhetorical situations. On the one hand, then, Boyle's *serial practice* has the ability "to produce greater capacities within any given ecology" (547), as each iteration introduces difference by adding another version of engagement, experience, or expression, which, in turn, reconfigures the intensities and connections among ecological relations. On the other hand, *serial practice* allows individuals to develop, in embodied capacities, certain tendencies and techniques in relation to a given ecology. But while Boyle uses these abstracted considerations to signal an ethic of post-human practice—one in which a rhetor might "compose new capacities for conducting . . . [herself] within expanded media ecologies" (549)—what feels wanting is something of a description of the ways in which people—expert to novice—actually work *with* technologies to produce post-digital artifacts. To this end, while Boyle's *serial practice* points the conversation in the right direction—attuning a rhetorical readership, much in the way the New Aesthetic ecology does a more general public, to how both humans and technologies develop habits of practice in relation to one another—I think there is still yet a dimension or two to be articulated.

One of these dimensions (picked up in the next section) includes the specific ways in which technologies and humans come together to make that which is otherwise not possible—focusing on the different magnitudes by which new configurations can be introduced, along with the particular relations that particular humans foster in particular ecologies. The particularity of the "comings together" is critical, as there are many rhetorical practices that take place in post-digital culture in ways regularly removed from human access and/or the human sensorium alone. Additionally, there are many relational considerations that particular humans bring to the assemblage—with the human particularity central to the rhetorical capacity of the assemblage as well. Therefore, the different assemblages open up access in particular ways: from breathing new life into established techné to making visible that which is otherwise non-sensible.

The second of these other dimensions deals with the underlying orientation that governs how everyday rhetors interact (in terms of *making*) with co-agential mediating technologies. To this end, in the final section of this chapter I focus on a condition of play (and a willingness to play) as the basis for the cultivation of ludic habits of practice in contemporary human–technology assemblages.

ENHANCEMENT OF POST-DIGITAL CAPACITIES

Human relations to mediating technologies run a bit of the conceptual gamut. There are, to put it mildly, a wide range of ways in which one relates to a given technology. But what I am concerned with in this section are the particular ways in which specific technologies and humans come together to grant access to rhetorical capacities of expression and representation otherwise removed from the human sensorium alone. On one end of the spectrum resides something of a traditional perspective: technologies-as-prostheses—which I situate here not as an extension of a human subjectivity but rather as a form of human–technology symbiosis. For even if a technology is augmenting a bodily limitation, it is not making a human subject whole but rather introducing different potential relations among the ecologies in which both already participate. To this end, I will pick up with graphic designer and artist Hal Lasko as a representative figure, for his artworks (which possess a rich pixel aesthetic) result from this conditional sense of human–technology symbiosis.

On the other end of this spectrum are relational ecologies that allow humans to sense / make sense of all manner of entities otherwise invisible to the human sensorium. In a mechanical sense, the microscope stands as one example, which when partnered with individuals introduces altogether new configurations among the rhetorical ecologies in which both participate by making visible to human sensibilities a dimension of everyday reality that is otherwise impossible to know/access. But beyond the magnification mechanisms of the microscope, there are numerous considerations and configurations in (and of) the technological realm that reside beyond the sensible limits of the human condition. From radio waves to Wi-Fi signals to algorithmic processes operating at the speed of light, every day people are saturated by information-rich, quasi-ethereal signals and intensities that are only discernible (and only decipherable) with corresponding (or enabled) technological devices. Once partnered with an enabled device, however, people are able to determine presence/absence conditions of these etherealities and, in some cases, render them visible, tangible, malleable—in other words, draw attention to their conditional presence and representational possibilities in exacting ways. To this end, design scholar Luis Hernan will serve as the primary figure, for his work demonstrates both how one can take stock of that which is beyond the human sensorium alone and how doing so introduces altogether different configurations to the rhetorical ecologies by which and through which one understands (and represents) the world.

Symbiotic Capacities

In the technology-as-prosthesis orientation, even in its most positive of renditions, there is a fundamental kind of tension, if not altogether resistance, that needs to be acknowledged. This tension, as Tinnell argued in his essay, stems from prosthetic orientations situating technologies as extensions of some human condition or capacity. These perspectives traditionally end up privileging the human in specific ways or they assume the human (and/or any human subjectivity) to be a relatively stable category. But if posthumanism and/or new materialism has taught us anything, it is that the categories of human and technology are anything but stable. This is why Tinnell argues for something more emergent—for an *autopoietic* quality in which subjectivity takes form in relation to and through mediation. Or why Boyle calls for an altogether posthuman reorientation, where technologies are situated not as prosthetic attachments to an individual human capacity but rather, along with the human, as a component among a complexity in which each assemblage, practice, or iteration reconfigures the relations within and among ecologies.

Of course, part of what amplifies the troublesome qualities of these prosthetic/extension orientations is that they reside at the foundations of media studies—stemming from McLuhan's situating of all media as "extensions of man." Further, they proliferate what Tinnell refers to as the various formations of "augmentation-oriented rhetorics," which present technologies as augmenting human capabilities and, in so doing, serve to once again rhetorically "reaffirm the centrality of the . . . writing subject" (123). And while there is something of a wanting posthumanist rejection to these (and related) orientations to human–technology assemblages, the New Aesthetic (as part of a postdigital conditionality) seems to be pointing toward something else. For even in these necessary "turnings-away" from any sense of a stable human subjectivity, one cannot ignore the fact that in some assemblages technologies and humans do in fact function in prosthetic ways. The reality is that the condition of prosthesis itself is not the problem, but rather the ways in which it has been cast (rhetorically, among others) by previous relational ecologies. To this end, I turn to Lasko here because his work demonstrates a set of relations in which the prosthetic orientation is not only present but central to what might be understood as a human–technology symbiosis—highlighting a relational ecology in which any sense of subjectivity is tied to prosthetic symbiosis and yet taking form, as Tinnell would say, via a conditional *autopoiesis*.

Lasko, the representative figure of this section, spent his entire post–World War II working life as a graphic designer and dabbling artist. He had a fairly expansive career in which he produced a number of artifacts and designs for a multitude of corporations, with his work being used by major companies like Goodyear or the Cleveland Browns; he even finished his career as a typographer for American Greetings. But beyond his graphic design work, Lasko also produced a number of noncommercial artworks that displayed a wide array of artistic techniques, from drip paintings to abstract designs. Although he continued to make creative pieces into his late nineties, his work never really garnered much commercial or noncommercial success. Given that lack of prominence, it may seem odd to include Lasko in this work (or any academic work on the aesthetic), as he does not carry the usual weight associated with an art (or aesthetic) figure. But what makes him of interest here is his specific relationship with the artistic medium (a kind of prosthetic symbiosis) and the style of artistic representation (pixelism-as-pointillism) featured in his final works.

With this in mind, it is important to know that Lasko suffered from wet macular degeneration. This condition creates an increasing blurriness (if not blind spot) in the center of a person's vision, which can be completely debilitating for a practicing visual artist. But once his grandchildren introduced him to MS Paint, Lasko was once again able to create rich, visual works (see specifically his work *Looking Up*[6]). The partnership between Lasko and MS Paint was at least partially prosthetic—with the "zoom" affordances (i.e., manipulation of scale) and square-by-square representation of MS Paint reanimating Lasko's capacities of expression. But what matters here are not simply the technological affordances of MS Paint, nor the ways in which it (as part of the larger computational assemblage) compensated for Lasko's differently abled sense of vision. Rather, much like in the Winter example above, what matters is that what was produced was emergent from the amalgamation of Lasko (his abilities/experiences), algorithmic processes (software), and computational materialities (hardware)—a post-digital subjectivity whose stability, if necessary, results from the specific points of intersection, influence, and intensities among these multiple registers and their relations.

While Lasko's *Looking Up* was created using MS Paint—and the program's square-pixel style is prominent in the work—the artifact itself is not intentionally part of pixel art, nor even the arena of pixel aesthetics; rather, it is Lasko the artist, the human element of the assemblage, who reimagined pixels as the dots in the art technique of pointillism. The particular style of representation to emerge, of course, was always available in the aesthetic possibilities of pixel designs, but its manifestation in this context was not simply the result of the basic mediated unit of MS Paint—the square pixel (e.g., aliased visual

---

6. While one can find a series of Lasko's art pieces at hallasko.com, *Looking Up* (https://www.hallasko.com/products/looking-up) offers a forest-scene representation that is most demonstrative of the technique and engagement central to Lasko's creations.

data, presented on grid)—but was the result of Lasko's specific artistic training and background coming into contact with the affordances and constraints of MS Paint. On the one hand, MS Paint operates as prosthesis; on the other, it operates as co-producer of these images. But while MS Paint certainly helps facilitate the emergence of this artisanesque expressivity, the style/practice itself of pixelism-as-pointillism is as much ensconced in Lasko's individual engagement with the program (human element) as it is owing to any natural affordances of the program itself (technological element). For the reality is that the vast majority of people in today's digitally saturated mediascapes would find the pixelism of MS Paint to leave much to be desired, aesthetically speaking at least. But Lasko saw and embraced the pixel as something else, with its expressive value corresponding not to a technological nostalgia but rather to its parallelism with an established representational technique. In this assemblage, then, part of what gets reconfigured among the relations in and around the participating ecologies is the pixel itself.

What Lasko's work does is not just create attentiveness to a kind of pointillism-cum-pixelism aesthetic style; it also functions as relay (as much New Aesthetic art does) to the particular ways in which human–technology assemblages enable different relations that allow for different capacities for action. The affordances of the technological apparatus may have allowed Lasko to once again *see* (and manipulate) the artist's "canvas," even if only at the periphery of his vision, but it did not simply re-enable a previous subjectivity. Rather, in addition to its prosthetic qualities, MS Paint served as collaborative partner, helping reconfigure the relations among the ecologies in which Lasko participated, allowing him to work, pixel by pixel, to inhabit a new space of representational possibilities.

Working pixel by pixel is, of course, not specific to MS Paint, nor is Lasko's approach the singular result of an artistic imperative (Lasko-the-artist wanting to control the finer details of the representation). Rather, in this case, the pixel-by-pixel operations are an emergent possibility among the assemblage— the result of a symbiotic dynamic. What takes form is not so much artwork that bears an intentional computational aesthetic but rather the creation of an object whose existence designates the folding together of human–technology co-agencies: in other words, *Looking Up* reflects the condition in which humans (e.g., Lasko) and technologies (e.g., MS Paint) inform and influence the possibilities of one another in the act of *making*—coming together to allow for an expression/representation otherwise not possible and, in so doing, demonstratively point to the reconfigured intensities among the relational ecologies in which both participate.

The Otherwise Indiscernible

On the other end of the spectrum resides the work of Luis Hernan, particularly his *Digital Ethereal* project, which offers visual representations of Wi-Fi (Plate I). Although Hernan's project may seem quite removed from Lasko's MS Paint pixelism, they remain connected in that both offer visualizations through computational means that are simply not possible outside of their particular human–technology collaborations.

As a doctoral researcher at ArchaID, Newcastle University, Hernan developed a project of *research through design*, with the intent of offering a design discourse on digital technologies. The project began with his view that much in the digital realm, particularly less-tangible elements like a Wi-Fi signal, shares affinities with the figures of the ghost or spectre—each having, as Hernan puts it, this "untypical substance [that] allows them to be an invisible presence" (n. pag.). Yet, unlike the ghost or spectre, through various forms of substantiation, particularly through the technological sensoria that people carry with them, the digital ethereal routinely "become[s] temporarily available to [human] perception" (n. pag.). But Hernan wanted to further translate this ethereality into a more tangible modality (e.g., visualization)—offering something beyond its mere acknowledgments of presence versus absence.

His project begins, then, with an understanding of digital signals as being part of Hertzian space, a concept that emerges in relation to the nineteenth-century German physicist Heinrich Hertz. Hertz proved that electromagnetic waves existed and that everything that requires electricity emits these waves, which includes everything from radio and television signals to visible light. At the end of the twentieth century, design theorist Anthony Dunne argued in *Hertzian Tales: Electronic Products, Aesthetic Experience, and Critical Design* that understanding space as Hertzian space—as an electro-climate equally inhabited by humans and machines alike—would necessitate an increasing interest in the intersections of electromagnetic waves and human experience (how humans encounter/undergo mediated technologies). Moreover, operating with an awareness of Hertzian space would, in Dunne's view, become central for future design practices: that is, the future of design work would involve a critical attunement to electromagnetic devices and their cultural interactions. Designers would necessarily need to operate with a critical understanding of technologies, which includes an awareness of how practices, ideologies, and so on come to be encoded in technological objects as well as, more generally, an attentiveness to how electromagnetic waves, light values, digital impulses, and the like come to bear on human experience.

Hernan picks up with Dunne's orientation and advocates for a creative (rather than critical) approach that produces new artifacts "indexed to hertz-ian space" and that captures "the cultural and social complexity imbued in the use of such [ethereal] technologies" (n. pag.). To do this, Hernan modeled his work on Timo Arnall, Jørn Knutsen, and Einar Sneve Martinussen's method[7] of using "long-exposure photography and RSSI sensors to visualize and spa-tialise WiFi networks" (Hernan n. pag.). He then built an Android app version of a Kirlian Device (KD Mobile), which gathers information from the Wi-Fi manager of the phone or tablet and turns the Wi-Fi signals into colors (based on strength of signal: reds for high intensity, blues for low intensity). What this allows, in Hernan's view, is a mapping of the wireless spectre that inhabits Hertzian space. On the one hand, Hernan's work acknowledges the material qualities of even the most ethereal of digital culture—Wi-Fi signals, like all other electronic entities, give off electromagnetic waves. On the other hand, his work begins from a position that recognizes that much in the digital world is simply un-sensible to the human sensorium alone. And to make those invis-ible presences visible (and visual) requires a particular kind of human–tech-nology assemblage. The smartphone detects a Wi-Fi signal, which humans then recognize as present/not-present through onscreen icons. But Hernan takes this one step further and translates the ethereality into its spatial quali-ties. He uses technological processes, a techno-sensorium, and a color-trans-lation algorithm to turn Wi-Fi into a photographic object.

While Lasko's work demonstrates how individual technologies enhance human capacity for action by enabling new modes and means of practical engagement, Hernan's work offers an enhancement of a different magnitude. What matters here is not simply that Hernan translates an invisible presence, nor that he color-captures something of Hertzian space, but rather that he plays with technologies (and produces technologies) that allow one to take up with (and make with) materialities that reside beyond the human sensorium alone—rendering the pseudo-etherealities of post-digital culture available to rhetorical practices and interpretations.

In truth, as I suggested above, there are many rhetorical practices that take place in post-digital culture in ways regularly removed from human (senso-rial) access. This includes, of course, not only the experience of something like Wi-Fi but also the various levels of code and engagement intentionally hidden by corporate (and/or government) interests; and, more and more, the layers of digital representation and augmentation that reside among and on

---

7. See Arnall, Knutsen, and Martinussen's Touch Research Project, particularly *Light Painting WiFi*.

top of nondigital materialities (from QR codes on store windows to Aurasma's augmented reality triggers in print books) as well as the technological signals and streams that saturate bodily existence. In this regard, Hernan is something of a metonymic figure, representing a creative orientation to thinking with and making in response to a digital realm that includes human bodies as data generators, as electromagnetic feeds and fields to be captured and cataloged by machines and devices designed toward different ends. While Hernan, like the other figures in this chapter, may not be part of the New Aesthetic proper (i.e., not featured in Bridle's tumblr), his use of new techno-materialities to find ways to make machinic and algorithmic sensoriums available to human capacities for action and understanding situates his work firmly within the purview of New Aestheticism and aligns it with the impulses of rhetoric. For Hernan demonstrates the necessity of adopting alternative perspectives in a post-digital realm (attuning to something like a Hertzian view of the world) as a way of taking stock of a wider array of forces and figures that set upon the human condition. While his coloration of Wi-Fi spectres are themselves beautiful creations, they more importantly introduce new relations among different ecologies—from reshaping how individuals understand space in post-digital culture (as inherently Hertzian) to the necessity of finding ways to access (and/or visualize) that which remains hidden from the capacities of everyday human practices.

WILLINGNESS TO PLAY

While Hernan, Lasko, and Winter serve as interesting figures for unpacking certain aspects of the human–technology assemblage, because they are expert practitioners their accomplishments seemingly elide a fundamental shift in how a more general post-digital public engages with new mediating technologies. That is, at this point in human history there has never been a greater supply of new mediating technologies—and what makes these "new" is not just their date of emergence but also their date of exposure, as various cultures and subcultures encounter different mediating technologies at different moments and in different orders. There is something of a general ubiquity of "new" mediating practices (facilitated by perpetually ever newer forms of mediation), which necessitates something of a shift in one's primary orientation to *making* (and learning to *make*) with screen-mediated technologies. For the dynamic is no longer a matter of mastery (an impossible position in any initial ["new"] engagement) but rather is rooted in play: to play with the interface; to play with the affordances and constraints of the software; to play with the forms, formats, and platforms; to play with, against, and across the aesthetics of a technological collaborator; to learn by playing in/with the unfamiliar, and so on. Moreover, as the techniques of the master class continually get algorithmized—made available as part of the agential capacities of a technological playmate—it no longer takes mastery or the same kind of expertise to create with the aesthetics (and epistemes) of the master artisans; rather, the everyday Jeri and Julian can now playfully tap, swipe, click, type their way toward something of significance. Further, as suggested earlier, as more and more of the labor burden gets taken up by the "machine"—and taken up in increasingly obscure ways—one must be willing to engage in more (and deeper) forms of play to produce (or to learn to produce) just about anything. These deeper forms of play (sustained playful engagements) include both a willingness to play and an accompanying willingness to fail (with failure often being just as productive, and often leading to [mis]steps that expose the mediation itself— including things like glitch). Consequently, contemporary human–technology relationships sit somewhat counter to the traditions of the *paideia*, championing play over mastery and embracing failure not as shortcoming but as rhetorical necessity in an orientation to play. Thus, turning to play as a critical dynamic in human–technology assemblages may help rhetors discover, uncover, or recover new capacities for expression, representation, action, and the like by leveraging play as mode of invention.

In many ways, the turning to play here is as much aligned with Vitanza's second counterthesis to composition theory and pedagogy as it is with any technological imperative. For in the early 1990s, Vitanza's "Three Countertheses: or, A Critical In(ter)vention into Composition Theories and Pedagogies" leveraged the critical structures and insights from both Jean-François Lyotard's philosophies of the postmodern condition and sophist Gorgias's negative trilemma to challenge long-standing approaches (or assumptions) in the field of rhetoric and composition. First, Vitanza pushed against the field's definitional imperative (and what he situated as the will to systematize language); second, he called into question the role of mastery (and the will to be the authority of language); and third, he advocated for resisting the theory-to-practice pedagogical impulse of the field and, in its stead, called for creating the conditions by which to rethink pedagogical desire (from a will to teach toward a willingness to learn). While this work shares resonances with all three, the second offers the clearest correlation with twenty-first-century human–technology *making*—a shift from the will to mastery (of a technological *logos*) toward a willingness to play (with/in technology itself).

One of Vitanza's favorite examples of this conditional *play* (and its impact on the knowing/doing/making of being) is the game Tegwar, which comes from the 1973 film *Bang the Drum*.[8] In the film, Bruce Pearson (played by Robert De Niro) engages in a card game where the players make up the rules to the game as they go, relying on a kind of aggregation of conventions (of play) they have learned across other registers and relational ecologies (sports, card games, school, etc.). The single driving play feature of Tegwar is that the rules cannot be determined in advance but rather must emerge with the game play. The game unfolds, then, not from any predetermined win-state but from the act of playing—an act in which players have immense capacity to shift the conditions of the game (and/or play) itself. In many ways, this is akin to the relational dynamic at play in human–technology making today. For how each plays with the other (in initial moments and in recurrent engagements) is based on habits of practices (conventions and rules of engagement) brought to the table in the moment of play. Further, what gets produced in the moment of creation, much like in the Winter example above, is not the result of any predetermined outcome (or win-state) but rather depends on the particular kinds (and depths) of play among the elements in the ecology. And, perhaps just as importantly, like Tegwar players, both humans and technologies have great capacities to shift the conditions of play (and the output likely to be produced).

Now, given the drifting that has occurred in this chapter, and specifically in this section, it seems that something of a recap may be in order to help pull the critical elements of this section back in focus. To this end, what has been suggested to this point is that once representational practices and emergent patterns of human experience undergo mediation, they cease to be obstacles to representation and become part of the base condition of mediated (and mediating) beings. Which is to suggest that as more and more of life is subjected to 1s-and-0s reductionism, and as more and more maneuvers of the master class get simulated via algorithmic practices, working creatives find themselves in an inventive space that allows them to play with all sorts of mediations and with all manner of life reconstituted as data, as emblem, as relay point to some other moment and mantra of mediation. But how one creates (and creates with) these new possibilities is tied up not with a will to mastery but rather with a fundamental willingness to play (and be played). This "willingness" necessitates not a better theory of rhetoric for New Aesthetic considerations

---

8. In the courses I completed with Vitanza at both Clemson University and the European Graduate School, he regularly used the Tegwar example to demonstrate this counterposition as well as what one might imagine as a type of play built on the very impulse of rhetorical invention. Additionally, this example has been deployed in Sarah Arroyo's *Participatory Composition: Video Culture, Writing, and Electracy,* where she adapts Vitanza's construction of the listening game (in relation to Tegwar) to apply to the theorization of and practices for video composing (chapter 4; specifically pp. 83–85).

but a guiding theory of play for post-digital rhetorical *making*—a set of orientations, habits, and perspectives by which to situate what a willingness to play looks like in current mediascapes and cultural configurations (New Aestheticism included). To this end, in the remaining pages of this chapter I offer two potential frameworks for thinking about this "willingness to play"—moving it simply out of Vitanza's counterimpulse to rhetoric and composition and extending it into a pragmatic orientation for rhetorical making at the intersections of humans and technology. The first of these play orientations comes from Miguel Sicart's *Play Matters,* which situates play as an ontological condition; the second comes from Jan Holmevik's *Inter/vention: Free Play in the Age of Electracy,* which uses play as an undergirding for all digital rhetorical activities (doing so in relation to Gregory L. Ulmer's *electracy*).

Playing Sicart

To begin, Sicart argues that computation is "not a technology but a modality of being, a form of expression" (99); and the result of this computational condition is that "there is more than the world to playfully take over now: there's the world, the machines, and the way the machines make the world exist" (100). As such, in Sicart's view, play and digital technologies "need to help each other imagine new ways of being in the world" (98), and it is the "helping each other" that remains key in this passage because for Sicart computers "play *with* us—not for us, not against us, but together with us" (99; emphasis added). This echoes the symbiotic orientations of this work, where technologies are not things separate from or knowable in the absence of the human condition but rather are key figures in the human–technology assemblages central to mediated being. The way forward for imagining new ways of being in the world, then, as Sicart suggests (and as Vitanza implied), depends on the play between the human and the technological nonhuman (not on the mastery of one over the other).

Sicart goes on to offer something of a rhetoric of play—situating play as a way of engaging with things in the world and, more fundamentally, as itself an act of creation and "a form of understanding" that allows individuals to make sense of themselves and that which surrounds them (1). In this regard, the New Aesthetic can be seen as a form of play (an expressive play), as it helps a post-digital public make sense of the conditions they have already undergone. For in playing with New Aesthetic artifacts (as scrolling observers or as post-digital artisans), rhetors are overtly presented with a human condition that has been (or is being) (re)mediated—with everything from one's actions to one's likeness being/becoming available to the masses of techno-culture.

Sicart also argues that play is not only a way of engaging with (others in) the world (human and nonhuman alike) but is itself contextual, by which he means that it takes place "in a tangled world of people, things, spaces, and cultures" (6). When one engages in play, then, one must take into consideration the environments of play, the technologies of play, and the potential companions with whom one might play—the latter two categories, I argue, being increasingly one and the same (7).[9] Now, while this orientation toward context is important for Sicart (and reflects the ecological tint of this work), he also sees play as appropriative, which means it readily "takes over the context in which it exists" (dominating the orientations to a given relational ecology) and yet "cannot be totally predetermined by such context" (11). This locates play in the interspaces and intersections of humans and nonhumans, while possessing a capacity to be in excess of those contextual boundaries, which suggests that while the wider complexities of "context" may be key to understanding play (and perhaps rhetoric, as Lloyd Bitzer suggested many moons ago), the contextual elements are themselves "not sufficient for play [or rhetoric] to exist" (8). For play itself, as Sicart tells us, "is not tied to objects but *brought by people* to the complex interrelations with and between things that form daily life" (2; emphasis added). As such, play shares further affinities with New Aestheticism in that it is fundamentally tied to people, to humans, to human conditionalities (however technologically saturated or infused).

While the conceptual projections of play help add a richness to thinking about New Aestheticism, there are also more practical considerations of Sicart's rhetoric of play, which include (a) play being creative, (b) the practice of developing tactics (ludic habits) for play activities, and (c) play being personal. As a creative act, for example, play is a way of "mak[ing] a world, through objects [and discourse], with others, for others, and for us" (17). This includes not only "creatively engaging" with "technologies, contexts, and objects," in ways akin to Hernan's work, but also grounding that engagement in what Sicart calls "ludic interaction" (17)—a willingly playful exchange between human and nonhuman interrelations toward the experience (and possibly understanding) of the interaction itself (chiefly oriented toward audience; a matter I return to in the next chapter).

The second element here, tactics or ludic habits, refers to the strategies and "on-the-fly creative interpretation[s]" one develops in relation to specific play activities (17). And here one might see how something like play adds a dimension to the habits of mind and/or *serial practice* considerations raised by Boyle

---

9. There are echoes here with Thomas Rickert's work on ambient rhetoric, where play, much like rhetoric, much like sound (and much like the human condition, as I have argued), takes on the tenor of the environment and things in the environments: for example, bellowing into a coffee cup and then into a bucket produces notably different sounds.

earlier. For ludic habits form in serial engagements too, but also in relation to the particular contexts in which the play is occurring (gaming environments, material conditions, play partners [human and nonhuman alike], and so on), as well as in relation to previously established and emerging habits. Playful engagements lead, therefore, to the development and/or refinement of *ludic habits of practice*: the formation of strategies for overcoming a challenge or for creating particular kinds of representation or for relating to/engaging with particular kinds of technology. Further, as a player/rhetor moves across contexts/ecologies, she often builds from and builds upon these habits in both reflective and nonreflective ways—critically reflecting on her play practices to think through new solutions, while developing something like bodily memory (something related to, yet more than, "muscle memory") for things like performance movements or maneuvers of particular actions (from quick-key functions to conceptual architectonic tendencies). Of course, it is not just the human element that develops these ludic habits of practice, as increasingly smart technologies adjust their own parameters and practices in relation to particular play partners. This can be seen in competitive game algorithms in something like the *Mario Kart* series, where the competition of the computer players adjusts to the performance of individual racers. But it also works in relation to more *making-* or production-oriented technologies; Adobe Premiere, for example, adjusts its settings to individual collaborators by adopting a different interface configuration based on the "logged in" player/rhetor.

While the deployment of ludic habits of practice is perhaps easiest to grasp in games themselves—for example, transferring boss battle techniques across different gaming contexts—it is also excessively the case when working with new mediating technologies. For example, working creatives (novice and professional) develop ludic habits of practice for making visuals (still and moving alike), and these habits transfer, with varying degrees of success, to other visual technological settings. But while some redeployments work fairly well (e.g., cutting a video clip in iMovie versus cutting a video clip in Adobe Premiere), other habits require continual play with new contexts (and new collaborative partners) to successfully create new expressions. Take the filter manipulations in Snapchat as one example: these can help human participants develop a particularly playful mindset for remaking digital images (tap, toggle, select, save, and share), but those ludic habits of practice do not convey explicitly to working with visual media in something like Adobe Photoshop, which operates in terms of layers and not simply digital augmentations.

All of which is to suggest that working creatives develop ludic habits of practice in relation to the fuller complexities of the contexts in which they operate, which include environmental and technological considerations along with sociopersonal exigencies and individual intentions. Moreover, as demonstrated with Lasko, these ludic habits also develop, explicitly so, in relation to individuals themselves (to each person's own embodied understandings of the world) as actants in and constituted by different play contexts and experiences. Which means that each person's ludic habits of practice develop (and/or get remade) in relation to her own previous knowledges and habits, established practices and purposes, and emerging (and unanticipated) capacities for action.

The last practical element for Sicart's rhetoric of play—that play is personal—argues that "play is a singularly individual experience—shared, yes, but meaningful only in the way it scaffolds an individual experience of the world" (18). What this means is that while there may be a lingering desire for a general theory of New Aestheticism—one applicable across contexts and persons—what is needed, particularly for working creatives operating at varying levels of post-digital artisanship, is an approach to knowing, doing, and making that is grounded in rhetorical play. And it is here that I turn to Holmevik's work, which, in building upon Ulmer, offers an approach to digital rhetorical capacities tied directly to play and emergent from the technological apparatus itself.

Ulmer–Holmevik Line

Ulmer sets out to invent what he sees as the new apparatus for an electric and/or digital age, with the goal being not to adapt emerging technologies and digital practices to the scriptures of literacy (which he sees as happening as a matter of course anyway) but "to discover and create an institution and its practices capable of supporting the full potential of the new technology" (*Internet Invention* 29). In this regard, he and I begin from a shared position—attuning to technologies and their related phenomena to see what they might offer on their own accord. Ulmer, however, is working on a much larger scale: in the ways that literacy functioned as a new instauration for oral cultures, Ulmer claims electracy as the new instauration for literate cultures. This includes shifts in both practices and institutions: for example, oral cultures were rooted in the institution of religion (and practices of worship), whereas literate cultures are rooted in the institution of the academy (and practices of science), whereas the institution of electracy is the internet (and related practices of entertainment). What this sets up, then, is the ability for Ulmer to create parallels (see Table 1) between orality, literacy, and electracy—with electracy being situated by Ulmer as the third great epoch of human history.

TABLE 1. Sample of Gregory L. Ulmer's Apparatus Theory*

Apparatus	Orality	Literacy	Electracy
Practice	Religion	Science	Entertainment
Procedure	Ritual	Method	Style
Behavior	Worship	Experiment	Play
Philosophy	Mythology	Epistemology	Aesthetics
Ground	God	Reason	Body
Mode	Totem	Category	Chora

*Ulmer's apparatus table has appeared in many locations, from Ulmer's own work (specifically his networked book website [www.ulmer.networkedbook.org]) to that of Arroyo, among others. But the table here is a specific modification of the one Holmevik provides in *Inter/vention: Free Play in the Age of Electracy.*

As one can see from the table, the procedure of the digital age for Ulmer is that of style—ushering in a new set of practices and considerations tied explicitly to the arts, and belonging to the domain of aesthetics—with style itself "marking the aesthetic quality of thinking" (Ulmer interview, in Weishaus n. pag.). This offers a certain resonance with the New Aesthetic, which also uses style markers, but does so as inventive relays to shifts in the human condition. But Ulmer pushes the matter further, calling for a return to embodied ways of knowing, similar to Dewey's recovery of the aesthetic. Here, Ulmer explicitly foregrounds the individual body (as sensorium) and the self (as an amalgamation of experiences) as filters by which one makes / makes sense of the world (an orientation echoed in Ceraso's work). In so doing, Ulmer returns the technological conversation to the embodied conditionalities and individual attunements central to how one makes sense of the raw, unfiltered world (digital or otherwise). This works in contrast to those theories, frames, and perspectives that have continued to push away from the anthropocene—with Ulmer dramatically pushing back toward the embodied experiences of the individual. (He even invents strategies and genres for individuals to discover their own attunements, orientations, and chorographical starting points—see *Teletheory* and *Internet Invention*.) Ulmer does not overlook, discount, or ignore the experiences and knowledges that a person brings to any discursive moment, especially those intertwined with mediating technologies, but rather, much like this work, he understands that the human shapes human–technology symbiosis as much as any material affordances or algorithmic practice.

Now, what Holmevik does is extend Ulmer's apparatus across a play dimension—turning to play because it (a) emerges from an "artistic/creative impulse" tied to style and the aesthetic (20) and (b) functions as a transversal: a line of intersection that moves in, across, and through media and cultural systems. What Holmevik adds is the impulse to play (and play as an intervention) to the embodied experiences of the individual centricity of Ulmer's electrate writing/making practices.

But there is more to this dimension of play than just a name for what one does when working "electrately." For the Ulmer–Holmevik position presents play as being tied to affect and experience. That is, Ulmer argues that oral cultures took shape along an axis of right and wrong, and literate cultures on an axis of true and false, but electrate cultures operate on a Nietzschean axis of pleasure and pain—with the latter tied not to a moral condition, nor to a reasoned imposition, but rather to a life-aesthetic and experientiality. Holmevik argues that it is the very experiences of affect that electracy and the larger considerations of digital rhetoric attempt to augment (and/or invent with). This is why turning to play is essential for Holmevik, because play has long been grounded in affect.

This affectability (particularly in relation to the pleasure–pain axis) is perhaps most identifiable in games with clear win-states: those in which players experience joy or sorrow with winning and losing, with overcoming or failing to overcome obstacles (and with failure not always resulting in negative affect[10]). But in more open play experiences (like Tegwar), the affect results not from predetermined win-states but rather is an emergent quality manifested from the deep play of/through the ludic experience itself (Holmevik 13). To play, then, is to participate in, initiate, and even *undergo* an experience. In more open play activities, however, playing is an experience that both shapes one's ludic habits of practice and is specific to individual humans (see Sicart's "play is personal" position). For how one plays and what one plays with—particularly in playing *with* mediating technologies as a way of being—are not universal conditions; rather, play is tied to individual humans (in specific cultures), individual choices, and individual attunements. While one can, in some capacity, account for general practices and potentialities of mediating technologies, one cannot fully account for the humanistic elements central to the productive acts of engagement with mediating technologies.

In an interesting sort of counterorientation, there seems an underlying drive (if not expectation)—particularly for those who teach things like writing with technologies—to develop in students and in faculty individual levels of expertise in (if not mastery of) different mediating practices. Meaning, since at least Stuart Selber's 2004 *Multiliteracies for a Digital Age*, scholars have correlated an increase in functional ability or technical acumen with a given

10. For example, in *Reality Is Broken*, Jane McGonigal details the concept of fun failure in games, where spectacular failures are experienced as positive values to the play experience and where failure is fundamentally a necessity to the playability (and overall value) of a game.

mediating technology as having the potential to lead to greater capacities for action and expression. But there may be something inherently wrong, or at least worthy of hesitation, with this kind of tint toward "expertise." First, the ever-changing mediascapes of post-digital culture prevent expertise in exacting ways; and, in some cases, the advanced complexities of computational processes render expertise ineffectual (even when composed of the highest human–technology assemblage available in a given area) (see Golumbia 126[11]). Further, educators, particularly rhetoric and writing pedagogues, are seemingly perpetually behind the curve—forever retrofitting the mediating practices of yesterday into/for today's rhetorical situations. This is not meant as an indictment of the field but rather as descriptive—for mediating technologies (and computational operations) simply change and evolve faster than one can learn and teach them. Moreover, the rhetorical and medial conditions in which post-digital natives find themselves shift just as rapidly.

One condition of this technological shift is, as I suggested earlier, that computational mediation has, in effect, led to a kind of "outsourcing" of much of the labor of digital rhetoric: algorithms, processors, and rendering programs work together to mime the productive practices and representational techniques of previous media-writing devices and previous media-writing experts. And this offers a key distinction for screen-mediated, post-digital culture, as what is being made available to current rhetorical practices are both the acts of machinic (re)production (e.g., taking a photo) and, as argued throughout, the representational techniques of post-digital artisans, the avant-garde of twenty-first-century aesthetics. The result is that digitization and algorithmization allow everyone—from expert to novice—to not only *create with the processes of mechanical reproduction* but to also do so *with the aesthetic techniques of the master craftsmen and craftswomen*. Pastiche, located in the click of a mouse. Glitch at the tap of a button. Pointillism, rendered digitally anew through pixelism.

If what is at stake here is a practice of play that includes the materialities of post-digital culture as well as the current and emergent aesthetic practices of the post-digital artisans (commercial creatives included), then what is needed is not only a reorientation toward a willingness to play but also something of

---

11. David Golumbia has explored the implications of advanced computationality in a number of works. As one example, in "Judging Like a Machine," he details how the micro transactions that undergird most of digital culture, including those that compose the backbone of our financial institutions (e.g., stock exchange), can be illegally and unethically manipulated by other machines in ways that are invisible to us. For the machines that have been built to make these practices possible and to transmit their information interact with other machines and algorithms at rates and in ways that are not only not visible to us but are often not even comprehensible to the most expert of experts working with the highest technologies available.

a new figure for the activities of knowing, doing, and making—a figure amenable to the contours (and play possibilities) of the New Aesthetic. To this end, I conclude this chapter by presenting two viable figural considerations that, when considered together, represent something akin to the post-digital practitioner. One of the figures comes from Holmevik, whose hacker-bricoleur functions in direct relation to his construction of play. The other, and the one I pick up with first, is Jenny Edbauer Rice's mechanic.

Potential Figuration

Edbauer Rice, like Ulmer, begins overtly from the personal. Edbauer Rice's father was a mechanic, and he did far more than just fix things: he imagined solutions among materialities and did so through embodied practices. His understanding of the mechanical allowed him to enact new possibilities and interact with the world in ways attentive to relationships among things. Edbauer Rice sees her father's inventive and dynamic complexity as a mechanic as offering a richer vision for the connections between mechanics and digital rhetoric. For Edbauer Rice, "embracing the role of technology's mechanics" is critical to those "who want to serve as rhetorical producers and teachers of production in the twenty-first century" ("Rhetoric's" 368) because an understanding of digital mechanics allows one "to operate a wider range of tools" and, in turn, "to imagine and enact what was not possible (or 'working') before" (373). Therefore, mechanics (as figures) are not simply individuals who do repair work but rather are individuals who engage in manual (embodied) activities, who can improvise relationships and enact unexpected solutions, and who can "help others imagine what they need in order to create, repair, or refit almost anything that has parts" (372).

Edbauer Rice's rhetorical mechanic, then, is one who engages in "material practice(s) of enactment," and one who does so through inventive "deployments of meaning" ("Rhetoric's" 372). With emerging media platforms and materialities offering all manner of new modes of deployment, the mechanic is one well suited to tinker with these platforms and materialities as a way to imagine new modes of representation, new forms of expression, and new enactments of experience. Further, Edbauer Rice argues that as "rhetorical mechanics" become "digital rhetoric mechanics," they develop "a greater potential set of tools for rhetorical production" (374). But the "tools" developed are not just external objects to and interfaces for the mechanic: rather, as indicated with Sicart and Holmevik and the formation of ludic habits of practice, they include internalized capacities of action and deployment (in relation to new platforms and materialities). In talking about how new mediating technologies expand the available means of production, the expansion of one's rhetorical capacities includes, then, not just a consideration of the mediating technologies themselves but the particular ways in which the "digital rhetoric mechanic" internalizes and then redeploys those meaning-making dynamics in other (non)related situations. Or, to say this another way, the expansion of one's capacities for action depend on the relationships of the mechanic (human) and technology. For to be a digital rhetoric mechanic in Edbauer Rice's sense is not simply to possess the ability to use a particular technology (one kind of relationship) but rather to be able to imagine and enact new orientations and solutions within (and beyond) a given technology's deployment. And, for the purposes of this work, these new deployments include the possibility of subversion, of intervention, of working against the grain so as to expose the overt qualities of the mediation itself along with the computational underbelly of the digital/networked world.

But what interests me most in Edbauer Rice's "digital rhetoric mechanic" is the recurrent focus she places on tinkering with available materialities, modes, and tools as an operative form of engaging and addressing an exigency. That is, the kind of "caring for" and "cultivation of self" to which she gestures is rooted in a willingness to play with the available materialities, mediations, and mechanisms (379). And to do this, to help more traditional rhetoricians develop the mechanical-technological abilities to teach and do digital rhetoric, she advocates for the personal—for playing with different platforms in relation to personal projects. In fact, through her interest in personal projects and in tinkering as a mode of material and medial engagement, Edbauer Rice situates a kind of willingness to play as a "bridge [between] the tensions . . . [of] theory and practice that continue to pull [rhetorical studies] in different directions" (385). Play, in this regard, not only may be a key mode of rhetorical engagement in a digital/post-digital culture but may itself better situate how one *makes* in relation to the contours of the New Aesthetic—doing so through personal projects, engagements, and investments that allow for fluid movement between the theoretical orientations and practical guides of the contours themselves. What Edbauer Rice's "digital rhetoric mechanic" gestures toward, then, is not just a kind of repair person but rather a play-figure—a tinkerer extraordinaire—who develops capacities for action through personal projects and who improvises material and medial deployments that allow for new possibilities, whether in accord with representational expectations or as intervention in a driving order.

Given the ties to tinkering (and to play more generally), Edbauer Rice's mechanic has interesting resonance with Holmevik's hacker-bricoleur. Both operate in relation to the ability to improvise and intervene, to repair and remake as a mode of offering different kinds of experiences, and, in many cases, both are rooted in the personal—from personal projects to the personal connections one finds with the available means of expression. But I get ahead of myself; before offering something of a synthesis of these figures, I need to first unpack Holmevik's hacker-bricoleur a bit more systematically.

The hacker is, of course, something of a cult figure—coming to mainstream culture through literature and cinema narratives over the past thirty to forty years that position her as a subversive, as one who can intervene in various technological systems to make them better suit particular needs and/or represent a different vision. The hacker is often understood as anti-establishment, as dangerous, as loner and/or outcast, but in truth the hacker (as person and practice) has brought much in the way of modern technological developments—from cyber security to Facebook. Moreover, the hacker is one who possesses the ability to expose (and, in turn, make a post-digital public aware of) that which is routinely hidden by black-boxed computationality.

The bricoleur, as second component of Holmevik's construction, comes from French anthropologist Claude Levi-Strauss, who situates the bricoleur as a do-it-yourself (DIY) practitioner. Derived from the French word *bricoler*, which means to tinker, the bricoleur is an individual who improvises with the material and nonmaterial possibilities at hand. Unlike that of the craftsperson, who selects specific tools and materialities to best suit the precise needs of the job, task, or purpose, the bricoleur's work is emergent and responsive to the material and nonmaterial conditions available to the productive situation.

Bricolage, the practice of the bricoleur, was fairly popular in postmodern art—denoting a practice of improvisation that brings together varying objects and aesthetics. The tensions created by the juxtaposed elements, in turn, create attentiveness to the surface (a hypermediacy) because the deployment of meaning in these works necessarily takes shape through intertextuality—through the relational intensities among elements as they move across and/or offer touchstones among different registers (forming a rhetorical ecology). If moving one abstraction out from the specific material practices of art or the stylistic assemblages of bricoleur architecture, one might situate the bricoleur as an assembler—the figure who does assemblage. In this regard, bricolage is not only a product and mode of production but could be seen as the very tapestry created by works that stem from and reflect the principles and interests of multiple fields, multiple perspectives, and often-incongruent frameworks. In many ways, Bridle's New Aesthetic is itself a bricolage, and this book is an attempt to put into words its intertextuality.

Now, before moving more fully back into Holmevik's hacker-bricoleur, there are a couple of additional elements to consider. First, if the bricoleur is tied to the tinkerer and to DIY culture, then this component of the figuration has never been more important, as there is (and continues to be) a growing DIY orientation as part of the current cultural mediascapes.[12] Second, while the bricoleur of postmodern art has worked primarily with materialities and objects, today's bricoleur (including Holmevik's hacker-bricoleur) works with the algorithmized techniques of the master class. For example, one need not have available black-and-white imagery, as one can now render any visual in black and white. Moreover, one can add vignette effects with the click of a mouse, add decorative text with the tap of a button, and even reproduce the very objects desired with 3D printing. Put simply, the bricoleur is now limited not as much by materialities as by her abilities to imitate, simulate, replicate, and leverage aesthetics, objects, and artifacts in and through computational systems. If the bricoleur is one who must be adept at a wide array of *making* tasks and abilities, then these must include, in the current context, a variety of ludic habits of technological engagement.

To bring this back to Holmevik: the hacker-bricoleur is a highly capable individual who "works with what is available to create new and exciting possibilities" because this allows for offering new representations of the world and things in the world along with the possibility of intervening into other socio-culturo-political orders (44). Moreover, the hacker-bricoleur is limited no longer by the physical materialities at hand but, when engaged in screen-mediated bricolage, by her ludic habits of practice that allow for accessing and deploying a wider array of digital and nondigital capacities for action. And, perhaps most fundamental, what drives this kind of hacker-bricoleur figure is that creating and recreating in this fashion is fun and entertaining (28)—this kind of making is enjoyable and, in many cases, empowering.

When the hacker-bricoleur is combined with Edbauer Rice's mechanic, one might get something resembling the *post-digital practitioner*: an individual who plays with the material deployments of meaning and mediation to intervene in various technological systems so as to cultivate a different sense of self and to imagine (if not improvise) new representations of the world. The potentialities of deployment, the intervention, the cultivation, and the like are not general conditions of engagement but instead specific to the individuals and individual technologies involved. For, to return to the three examples from this chapter, Winter's, Lasko's, and Hernan's capacities for engagement

---

12. This DIY presence may be a kind of cultural response to an industrial/corporate complex that now is built on a model of planned obsolescence.

(and even the ways in which all three play with technology) are unique to them, owing to their experiences and expertise, and manifested in the unique and rhetorical artifacts they co-produce with technological collaborators.

That said, the contours emerging among the New Aesthetic may serve as a loose set of guides for post-digital practitioners—from novice to expert— who embody the values of this hybrid figuration and who orient to *knowing, doing,* and *making* in ways more amenable to a post-digital posthumanism. While the contours are, by no means, a perfect solution, they can provide something of an operative orientation for those who play with new mediating technologies to imagine new worlds, improvise new possibilities, and enact unexpected solutions.

To support this kind of practice, in this chapter I introduced the third contour of the New Aesthetic ecology and attempted to extrapolate its practical (and figural) implications for post-digital rhetoricians. In so doing, I focused primarily on the rhetor (and/or her partnership with technology). In the next (and final) chapter, however, I push a bit more outwards toward considerations of audience—primarily taking into account the very expectations that rhetors and audiences bring to medial experiences. For shifts in medial expectations necessitate corresponding shifts in the underlying practices of rhetoric.

CHAPTER 6

Hyperawareness of Mediation and the Shift to Medial Experience

IN CONTOUR 1, this work picked up with the notion of eversion as a way of challenging the conceptual coupling of the digital/real divide—calling into question the very premise of the division so as to expand the rhetorical capacities of rhetors and materialities alike. Then, with contour 2, it highlighted both how mimetic patterns central to screen and computational media take on multiple layers of cultural meaning and rhetorical value and how technological materialities transition into human aesthetic sensibilities and (re)color individual ways of seeing the world (and things in the world). Following that, contour 3 focused on how New Aestheticism orients rhetors to the actual practices of *making* in twenty-first-century mediascapes—giving saliency to the ways in which humans and technologies come together to develop ludic habits of practice for working *with* one another. What has been presented to this point, then, is a set of reorientations that move from (a) destabilizing a conceptual coupling to (b) exposing something of the post-digital human condition to (c) realigning the practices of (and preferences of engagement with) techno-human assemblages, with each contour expanding, in its own way, the capacities and concerns of post-digital rhetoric, and doing so primarily from the perspective of the rhetor. With this final chapter, however, I want to push beyond a primary focus on the rhetor and better attune to audience-based considerations, as the fourth contour of the New Aesthetic is oriented around the experiencing of mediation as much as it is around any construction of post-digital artifacts. To this end, this chapter picks up with a conditional hyperawareness central to the New Aesthetic—returning to Jay David Bolter and Richard Grusin's remediation (specifically their concepts of immediacy and hypermediacy) as one framework for situating this hyperawareness and its related connections to a shift in medial expectations.

That said, what I have attempted to present in the arc of this work is that New Aestheticism (whether movement or not) operates as an awareness aesthetic—one as much rhetorically inclined as it is toward any specific aesthetic sensibility. However, while the previous chapters used the tenets and tendencies of the New Aesthetic to raise awareness about digital/real ecologies, about pixels as human aesthetic values, and about the depths and degrees to which technologies might be understood as collaborative partners in digital making practices, there are at least two other medial awareness considerations operative within New Aestheticism. First, New Aestheticism plays on, in, and across the fringes of the fourth wall—the illusionary divide between viewers/users and media/mediated content. While it may not possess the traditional "fourth wall" mediated presence of the box theater, it nonetheless invites both an explicit and implicit sense of the "box" (screen-mediated, computational technologies) looking out, staring back, reading and reacting to human counterparts, and creating a concatenation of awareness of a human-other who knows that the "box" knows that the human knows that the "box" is aware of her presence. Second, as implicated in chapter 1, the New Aesthetic is a kind of network aesthetic enacted in/on the network itself: it performs its own paradigm, folding back on itself as a way of offering critical insight and calling attention to its own assumptions and operations (as well as those of network technologies more generally). This kind of paradigmatic enactment (which uses the hyperawareness of fourth-wall disruptions) situates the New Aesthetic as being hyperrhetorical (a matter I more fully explore toward the end of this chapter). To better explicate these two additional awareness considerations, the following sections pick up with each and situate how they can contribute to the practices of rhetoric.

FOURTH-WALL MEDIATIONS

Western culture has long been wed to the illusion of narrative immediacy (and to a preference for media that require a suspension of disbelief—plays, film, books, videogames, etc.). Therefore, when something (or someone) calls into question (if not shatters) the illusory division between subject and object, performance and audience, representation and viewer, an immediacy-oriented culture experiences something of a destabilization. This disruption is commonly referred to as *breaking the fourth wall*.

The breaking of the fourth wall stems from the theatrical arts, particularly from nineteenth-century theater and the advent of theatrical realism. The "fourth wall" itself refers to the four walls of boxed set theater, which is composed of three physical walls (stage left, stage right, and the backdrop) and one imaginary wall, the opening to the stage (the space between stage and audience). This imaginary fourth wall keeps the performance and the viewers in their respective planes—acting as both an opening and a divider. Of course, it is not surprising how easily this concept maps onto television and film (with the screen serving as the "opening to the stage"). But toward the latter half of the twentieth century, there was an increased amount of breaking the fourth wall in television and film, and this, I believe, was an early gesture toward shifts in cultural expectations of media—for breaking the fourth wall puts viewers/participants into a hypermediate, rather than immediate, relationship with particular media.[1]

One of the most well-known examples of breaking the fourth wall comes from filmmaker Woody Allen's 1977 film *Annie Hall*. There is a scene in the film where Allen, waiting in a queue, is arguing with another man in line about Marshall McLuhan's work. Growing frustrated, Allen goes off "stage left" (breaking the filmic illusion) and pulls McLuhan into the shot/conversation (McLuhan just "happened" to be standing there). Of course, given McLuhan's impact on media studies and his "the medium is the message" mantra, the fact that it is McLuhan whom Allen pulls into the scene is itself significant, which only adds to the genius that is Woody Allen and the *détournement* of disrupting the filmic (and narrative) immediacy.

A decade after *Annie Hall*, John Hughes's 1986 film *Ferris Bueller's Day Off* built this fourth-wall play directly into the fabric of the film narrative, with Bueller (played by Matthew Broderick) regularly talking to the audience. Viewers were both separate from and yet part of Ferris's "day off." Move forward another decade, and video games took this to another level. In Konami's 1998 *Metal Gear Solid* for PlayStation, the character Psycho Mantis could cause a player's controller to rumble, could read the memory card on game consoles in order to reference other games a player had been playing, and

---

1. Immediacy, as a quick reminder, "dictates that the medium itself should disappear" and leave an audience "in the presence of the thing represented" (Bolter and Grusin 6). Hypermediacy, in contrast, "multiplies the signs [and streams] of mediation" (34). The former achieves its goal through fidelity of representation and an effacement of the techné and technological dimensions; the latter by foregrounding the mediation and, in many cases, using the mediation as central to the experience (and representation) itself.

could even change the input signal on a player's television (or so it seemed). In order to negate Mantis's "mind reading" (a major strategy in the battle with Mantis), the player had to unplug her controller from port 1 in the gaming console and back into port 2—a physical, mechanical, and counterintuitive action that sat well outside the bounded walls of traditional gameplay. Then, in 2002, Silicon Knights' *Eternal Darkness: Sanity's Requiem* for Nintendo GameCube employed "sanity effects," a game mechanic that turned down the volume on the game, produced (virtual) bugs crawling on the screen, and even sent out fake notifications that the game had deleted all of a player's saved data for the other GameCube games she was playing. These examples not only breached the fourth wall but also overtly blurred the boundaries of the digital/real divide.

In another media ecology, television programs have increased their breaking of the fourth wall over the past two decades. From Nickelodeon's *Dora the Explorer* to NBC's *The Voice,* television shows regularly engage with, speak to, and ask for interaction from viewers. *Dora the Explorer,* which launched in 2000, has the animated character Dora routinely asking for help from her "friends" (viewers); from calling out the Map (a character in the show) to making decisions in the story, viewers get to "participate" in the show's storyline. These viewer-aided "decisions" are often completed/enacted by a blue mouse cursor moving across the screen and "clicking" the selection/answer. In borrowing visual and narrative metaphors from the computer world (from hardware to video games), *Dora* puts viewers in a default position somewhere between operating a computer and watching a television show. In contrast to *Dora,* whose "interactive" blue cursor always moves in a predetermined fashion, NBC's reality singing competition, *The Voice,* allows for real-time interactions from viewers to help determine particular (though limited) outcomes. Not only does it crown a winner based on viewer votes (and/or song downloads) like many similar shows, but in the later stages of the competition viewers can tweet during the episode to save one of two or three contestants. This breaks the fourth wall through both a TV host talking directly to at-home viewers and in allowing those at-home viewers to become participants in the game (determining particular outcomes).

Further, shows like *Dora* not only entertain and educate (in limited ways) but also offer a kind of media indoctrination: the *Dora the Explorer, Mickey Mouse Clubhouse,* and *Team Umizoomi* toddlers of today will grow up to be the media-savvy (if not media-expectant) teenagers of tomorrow. If my generation grew up in a world firmly grounded in the suspension of disbelief and the upholding of the fourth wall that dominated popular, narrative media of the twentieth century, today's generations are being grounded in something different—and at least one element of that difference includes an affinity for medial awareness resulting from regular disregard (or manipulation) of the fourth wall.

Now, readers may be asking at this point, what does all this "fourth wall" talk have to do with the New Aesthetic? As Rahel Aima, co-editor of *The State* (Dubai), has argued in "Breaking the Fourth Wall: Duende and the New Aesthetic," the New Aesthetic is tied explicitly to the breaking of the fourth wall because "machines and other unknown objects are . . . shattering the artifice, . . . turning to face us, and making pidgin efforts to communicate" (n. pag.). For Aima, the "machines" that constitute a significant portion of today's world are becoming performers who routinely break the fourth wall by looking back at human interactants, and who, in so doing, also ask people to "reevaluate [their] tenuous relations" with screens and the screens' "cast" of characters and performers (n. pag.). Much like my Sims character in Will Wright's *The Sims*— an avatar who frequently looks out to me when he is unhappy or frustrated (pleading with me to do something, *anything*)—many of the digital objects in everyday life have an awareness (or so it seems) of human roles in human-technology relationships. To bring this back to one of the examples from earlier (e.g., word processing), in the late 1990s to early 2000s, the Microsoft Office Assistant (the little animated paperclip[2]) seemed to stare at users, often impatiently, waiting for an opportunity to help. The paperclip's presence was unsettling for some, both because it felt like an intrusion in the writing process and because it seemed to have a significant awareness of one's presence on the other end. In those formative stages of the new media era, one where Western culture was still grounded in a preference for immediacy, some users had a negative response to "Clippy's" hypermediate presence. But what things like the paperclip assistant suggested, and things like Siri and Alexa are reinscribing in the post-digital mediascape, is that as medial objects and artifacts continue to turn to face their flesh-and-blood collaborators, individuals will have to confront (and reconsider) the assumptions guiding their relationships with particular media.

New Aesthetic artifacts, then, have the potential to create effects and/or experiences similar to those that break the fourth wall: they make viewers aware of specific mediations and illuminate particular human relationships (or nonrelationships) with those processes. The problem, as Aima suggests, is that Woody Allen (and Ferris Bueller) are persons with whom individuals can empathize, but the drones and chatbots (nonhuman machines) that seem

---

2. From 1997 to roughly 2004, Microsoft Office included an intelligent user interface that functioned as an "Office Assistant." This assistant, named Clippit or Clippy, was an animated paperclip that interfaced with Office's help content.

significant to Bridle's New Aesthetic are "performers" that "produce an uneasy discomfort in many" people (n. pag.). Unlike with Allen and Bueller, when the fourth wall is broken by objects and artifacts whose "inner lives are inaccessible" to humans—objects and artifacts that are "cold, alien, inhuman"—then not only do people have to deal with the mediating act and their own place within the meaning-making apparatus, they also face an incredibly present sense of irreconcilable agency (Aima n. pag.). The irony is that despite the cold, distant, "never our friends" quality that Bruce Sterling wants to ascribe to technologies, people still feel increasingly bonded to them. Many individuals keep their primary technological devices close to them, next to them, in their pockets, on their persons, in their beds, in their bathrooms. In some cases, technologies are often more intimately connected to people than their human friends (often more responsive, too).

Now, the distrust and/or disdain of technology (and its potential Big Brother qualities) may simply be an orientation stemming from life in a pre-digital moment. For in the current culture, one may be better served to view the possibility of sentient machines more like Number 5 from John Badham's 1986 film *Short Circuit* than Mr. Smith from the Wachowski brothers' 1999 film *The Matrix*. The point is that while the machines may never be "our friends," that does not mean they are inherently evildoers out to destroy or control humankind (with both of these positions already assuming a kind of machinic agency one can recognize). If, however, one continues to operate under this condition of uneasiness toward technologies rather than embrace the kind of *with* partnerships suggested in the previous chapter, then what will emerge through the very rhetoric employed to describe and delineate technological conditions is a worldview that only furthers a kind of techno-psychosis (built upon an underlying condition of techno-paranoia).

To be fair, techno-paranoia is not without grounds. For one, it is not just technologies looking at people; humans (as part of the human–technology assemblage) are looking as well (using the myriad forms of digital representation facilitated by technologies). In this sense, part of what the New Aesthetic is drawing attention to is the fact that everyone is, in many ways, "becoming the object of the gaze" (Aima n. pag.). That is, when technologies begin looking back and when humans partner with those technologies for voyeuristic ends, people move, even if only in brief, as Aima has argued, into a "(conventionally) feminised subjectivity" (n. pag.). For people are increasingly surveilled, tracked, tagged, monitored, followed (by both technological and human actants), which creates a default condition in which individuals are always on display and, perhaps just as importantly for this chapter's consideration of hyperawareness, increasingly aware (or being made aware) of this being "on display" conditionality. The challenge, however, is not to destroy the gazing of a hybrid techno-human agency (or its related post-digital cultures), nor to move "off grid," but rather to adapt to this awareness and to how these technological systems (coupled with particular human actants/voyeurs) come to bear on everyday activities—and, in turn, to leverage those considerations for post-digital rhetorical practices.

In this frame, then, the New Aesthetic might be seen as both a validation and an invalidation of techno-psychosis. It validates the condition by making visible the modes, methods, and mechanisms of surveillance technologies (thus, Bridle's interest in drones, bots, and facial recognition programs). It invalidates the condition by better attuning individuals, as Carla Gannis argues, to the creation of and experiencing of "a hybrid world of novel experience" (n. pag.), suggesting not simply a surveillance culture but an emergent coming-to-be at the intersections of digital and nondigital processes and materialities. By drawing attention to hybrid and novel experiences, as well as to the practices, performances, and platitudes of mediated conditionalities, the New Aesthetic locates people in a world where the fourth wall does not exist— or exists differently. Or, to pick up with the eversion from chapter 3, individuals are no longer separate from their media, from their narratives, from their representations, from their ordering mechanisms. They are of them, produced by them, and that which calls them forth—a Möbius strip of a relationship.

The "validation" dimension of the New Aesthetic and techno-psychosis are important for a whole host of conversations (and chock-full of political, ethical, and cultural considerations), but my interests lie in the latter, the invalidation, which turns the conversation toward the experientiality of mediation and better lends itself to the *making* aspects of New Aestheticism. In this sense, the New Aesthetic is not only illuminating the digital layers saturating (and observing) the everyday world; it also reveals the necessity of a *mediated being* in a world that requires both human and computational ways of seeing, sensing, sorting, and sharing. For example, people may not be able to identify with the human eye alone what a QR code points to, but many recognize that it points to something (or should, in theory). Nor can most "read" a barcode. Nor can they account for the number of steps they take in a given day (a more embodied quality). But in conjunction with a technological device like a QR code reader, barcode scanner, or Nike+ FuelBand (i.e., as part of an assemblage), people become increasingly aware of these other modes of mediation (and learn how to make sense of them) and can, in turn, deploy them (through their assemblages) to particular ends, for particular purposes, directed toward particular achievements/outcomes for an audience who also shares in (and/or who can make sense of) these hybrid perspectives. Which is to suggest that with certain human–technology assemblages, one can leverage digital and material capacities for rhetorical desires and directives, capitalize on their experiential dimensions, and present them to an audience who participates in similar hybrid "ways of seeing" and/or adopts (and adapts to) analogous techno-human perspectives. Or, more pragmatically, working creatives can now design a QR code that both links to a company webpage and has the company logo embedded inside the block-pattern—both a human and machinic kind of "reading." Or, as another possibility, one might use a Nike+ FuelBand to engage in "draw running," as artist Claire Wyckoff does—a process that traces one's run path onto a map. In Wyckoff's case, she draw-runs penises,[3] but others tend to spell out names or to make hearts or other rudimentary shapes.

Artists routinely find a way to intervene in human–technology assemblages in order to create new kinds of expression—using the rhetorical possibilities of hypermediation not to reinscribe a political order but to invite awareness (of subject matter, of condition, of a set of relations, of the self, of culture, and the like). What these hypermediate works suggest, particularly those featured in the New Aesthetic, is a kind of crossroads moment that necessitates a bit of a shift from the analytical to the inventive. Or, as Kyle Chayka puts it, the hypermediate mediascapes of contemporary culture invite people (rhetoricians included) "to go native," to "stop gathering data points and start making things in the intrinsic language of the New Aesthetic" (n. pag.). The contours introduced so far include gestures toward these making practices—from considerations of eversion and design to pixel aesthetics to human–technology collaborations—and hyperawareness of mediation is no different, as it leverages the ethereality of the fourth wall toward rhetorical ends (using an artifact's own mediation as a rhetorical device) while grounding New Aestheticism in matters of engagement and, as I explore in the next section, hyperrhetorical enactment.

ENACTING THE (HYPERRHETORICAL) PARADIGM

The hyperawareness under consideration in this section begins with the idea that New Aestheticism is, as Bridle has argued, "an attempt to 'write' critically about the network in the vernacular of the network itself" ("New Aesthetic" n. pag.). That is, as a movement (or even pseudo-movement), the New

---

3. Wyckoff, of course, has made a number of nonpenis shapes as well, like an image of a dog or of the middle finger, but her penis maps still generate the most web traffic.

Aesthetic is a phenomenon "undertaken [and recapitulated] within its own medium" (n. pag.). It is what Victor J. Vitanza would call a writing or enacting of the paradigm, which might be better understood as an entity that performs its thinking, value, contribution, or purpose within (and as reflective of) the very paradigm it espouses ("Writing"). Thus, what the fourth contour is drawing attention to is not merely that the New Aesthetic participates in the operative practices of the network but that the very acts (and vehicles) of mediation in New Aesthetic artifacts offer comment on themselves (and their own conditions of existence) in their process of becoming. It is not just that New Aesthetic artifacts point toward critical techno-human conditionalities but that their very mediations carry a dimensional awareness that invites one to consider the rhetorical and medial ecologies through which the artifacts take on particular kinds of meaning.

To demonstrate something of this condition, let me return briefly to a key example from chapter 4, the Telehouse West (Plate G) building. While the pixelated exterior of the building calls attention to the building itself, its metonymic qualities, as I argued earlier, call attention to it being a certain kind of building that houses certain kinds of things. Thus, as Bridle suggested, the building's design makes it stand out from its surroundings as well as gives it a sense of belonging to "the digital" ("Waving" n. pag.). This kind of design or even methodological approach is what Gregory L. Ulmer has referred to as *hyperrhetorical practice,* where the impact and/or critical value of the design/ creation stems, at least in part, from its ability to leverage its own privileged logics, practices, ethics, aesthetics, and the like toward rhetorical ends that speak to the creation itself and its relation to the ecologies in which it participates. Ulmer demonstrates this hyperrhetorical practice in his monograph *Heuretics: The Logic of Invention,* which is a project on method and rhetorical invention where he employs the very method he is inventing while he is inventing it (17). As a result, Ulmer's method, inventing, and artifact (e.g., print text) place readers into a critically aware relationality with the text, its contents, and its implications. In certain ways, the same is true of viewers of Telehouse West: by leveraging a pixel aesthetic, the building enfolds into its aesthetic its own implications within the technological, ideological, and ontological ecologies it inhabits—creating, for some passersby, a hyperrhetorical condition.

Hyperrhetorical works do more, then, than just direct attention to the methodology and/or mediating act itself; they also, as a matter of course, make viewers/readers/interlocutors complicit in their enactment.[4] That is, for

---

4. In many ways, this "complicitness" echoes the conditional orientations central to Bolter and Grusin's remediation. In their formative introduction of remediation, they actually

there to be any sense of hyperrhetoricity in something like Telehouse West, not only does the artifact need to employ particular representational (and rhetorical) triggers but also there must be an audience who completes the feedback loop—individuals who bring (or have the capacity to possess) an awareness to the design/creation that includes a sensibility (if not sensitivity) to the logics, cultures, and practices associated with the design. Meaning, for someone without a penchant for seeing pixels in nonpixel spaces, or without an understanding of what a server farm is or does, Telehouse West's metonymic possibilities are seemingly irrelevant and the building sits there as just another building—albeit one with multicolored, square windows. However, for an audience with contextual and digital sensibilities, Telehouse West functions hyperrhetorically because it embodies something of its own logics and aesthetics: it calls to its viewers, making certain passersby aware of its own awareness of its role in the larger complexity that is post-digital culture.

Now, given the feedback loop required for hyperrhetorical entities to function as such, whether in the New Aesthetic or not, there is a necessary interest in accounting for the qualities and capacities of audience. For the rhetor can use hyperawareness in a multitude of ways, but without a corresponding audience capable of attuning to the hyperconditionality or without an ability to play within and against certain audience expectations, the artifact is just another thing in the world, awash amidst the milieu. And it is here that the connective tissue between hyperrhetoricity and hypermediacy begins to take more concrete form. For one of the critical conditions underlying Bolter and

---

begin with an act of negation, separating remediation from Hollywood's practices of content repurposing (the borrowing of filmic content, literary/filmic narratives, and the like). While Hollywood-style repurposing does often necessitate a redefinition of content in ways similar to the tenets of remediation (adapting a book to film, for example, always includes certain recolorations), there is often "no conscious interplay between media" in those acts of repurposing (45). Or, if there is, that interplay occurs nearly exclusively at the level of the individual "who happens to know both versions and can compare them" (45). Meaning, the "interplay" or awareness associated with content repurposing is viewer-specific, not media-specific. The implied counterclaim, then, suggests that remediation (unlike Hollywood's repurposing) must include an awareness of the redefinition or the interplay of media and that this "awareness" must be present (or made present) in the media itself. This is, in many ways, the specific definition of new media offered by Anne Wysocki, who argued that what made new media new was not the technologies themselves but a kind of critical awareness on the part of artists and produced artifacts with regard to the available materialities, the techniques of representation, and the mediation presented/assumed in the artifacts themselves. For Wysocki, the "newness" of new media, then, was not tied to computational underpinnings but rather was linked to this conditionality of a hyperrhetorical capacity, with the artifacts themselves carrying this potential hyperrhetoricity and with the experience of the mediation inviting an audience to multiple levels of awareness (some of which complete the hyperrhetorical feedback loops). The New Aesthetic seems to extend these considerations into a post-digital era, capitalizing on a sense of hyperawareness of mediation as aesthetic and rhetorical values.

Grusin's hypermediacy is that it (as well as its counterpart, immediacy) is culturally and temporarily (and potentially individually) situated. Put another way, the two operative logics of remediation—immediacy and hypermediacy—designate countering orientations by which people *experience* media, and mark, to a certain extent, the expectations of media that people carry with them into different medial registers. Thus, it is important to recognize that what may be a hypermediate medial experience for one person in one culture at one moment in time (inviting a certain kind of awareness, hyperrhetorical or otherwise) may very well be an immediate experience for others in other cultures and times as well as immediate for that same individual in the near future. The reality is that one's medial expectations change with medial experience. Which is to say, if practice becomes perception, as Casey Boyle suggested in his work on *serial practice* (and which I explored in chapter 5), then one might extend that logic to suggest that *experience becomes expectation*. Put simply, the more one experiences hypermediacy, the more one becomes accustomed to (and/or expectant of) hypermediate representational affordances. Hence, for an individual to experience Telehouse West as *hypermediate* requires at least one sense of medial awareness (connected, in part, to a greater sense of medial expectation); further, to experience Telehouse West as *hyperrhetorical* requires another sense of medial awareness (one that involves a kind of a hypermediate awareness that can be situated or read in rhetorically meaningful ways). Of course, both "hyper" conditions are always already located within the representation itself (as part of the possibility space by which different ecologies and their human and nonhuman entities establish relational connections to the design), but they only take on these conditions if certain experiences and expectations are present in (or potentially available within) participant ecologies.

To better explain this dynamic, let me work backward a bit in order to move forward—drawing on new media (in Bolter and Grusin's orientation) and its potential parallels (and distinctions) with the New Aesthetic. The point here, however, is not to impose an unnecessary division or to create a false coupling with new media and the New Aesthetic, but to use these two orientations to highlight something of a shift in cultural expectations of mediation. For example, part of what made new media "new" was the fact that computational modes of representation and expression introduced in the last half of the twentieth century offered a notably different orientation to the experience of media than that of print media or mainstream film and television artifacts of the time—with the far majority of those types of mediations championing immediacy as the driving orientation to the experience being offered. Thus, what mattered for medial practices leading up to at least Bolter and Grusin's "new media" moment was both the fidelity of the representation offered and the corresponding effacement of the techné and technological dimensions that might impugn the illusion of representational purity. But the new media era of the 1990s began something of a transition in cultural, medial preferences—moving the techno-public of the Western world away from the centrality of immediacy toward a penchant for hypermediacy (or at least something oriented toward a bit more balance). For the advent of computers and computational media created widespread opportunity, particularly in the US, for the hypermediate to be present; in so doing, there were increased opportunities for the hypermediate to become valued in representation, critical in the crafting of meaning, and fundamental to the experience being offered—doing so in ways simply not possible before (or at least not to the same extent). Meaning, from the advent and uptake of video games and heads-up displays (HUDs) to multiwindowed desktops and interfaces to multimediated webtexts, computational, screen media have thrived in the very multiplication of "the signs [and streams] of mediation" central to hypermediacy (Bolter and Grusin 34). Thus, much of the turn-of-the-century scholarship on new media—from Bolter and Grusin to Lisa Gitelman, from Lev Manovich to Anne Wysocki—was about accounting for this shift and its impact on contemporary artists, cinematic practices, materialities and methodologies, student compositions, and the like. But while both new media studies and the New Aesthetic seem tied to hypermediate conditionalities—and a corresponding preference for experiencing mediation itself—Bolter and Grusin's *petit récit* was working in relation to an emerging sense of hypermediacy for a culture unquestionably grounded in immediacy. The New Aesthetic, in contrast, involves accounting for a conditional hypermediacy in a culture that has already undergone this hypermediate transition (or, again, an undergoing in which hypermediacy is at least equally viable as an experiential, medial orientation).

Whereas Bolter and Grusin's new media was content with focusing on the hypermediacy of the screen itself, much in the post-digital present, including elements of the New Aesthetic, has to generate the hypermediate condition (and corresponding hyperawareness) through different means. Because of this, there has been an increasing push by working creatives (and by some scholars) to move *inside* "the digital" (or to move computationality's "insides" outward to the aesthetic dimension) as a mode of hypermediate expression—directing attention and awareness in particular ways. Or, put another way, Western culture has become more accustomed to the hypermediate qualities of screen media, undergoing something of a naturalization of hypermediate medial experiences and turning the previous hypermediate elements into somewhat immediate sensibilities (see chapter 4 and the pixel orientation).

Consequently, general mediated publics now expect multiple media streams (and competing representations and sensory inputs/outputs) in most (if not all) of their mediating devices. Therefore, to make something hypermediate and/or to use that hypermediacy in hyperrhetorical ways, post-digital artisans (including post-digital rhetoricians) have begun to draw attention to what it is like to be *in, of,* or even *among* computationality. This is, to a certain extent, what is occurring in Telehouse West, as its design attempts to locate passersby within the pixel aesthetic at the root of computational, screen-based representation—not fully inside the box, but definitely closer in proximity than what the seamlessness of techno-progression narratives might suggest. However, this sense of evolving computational hypermediacy may be more readily grasped in the artworks of Dutch designer Bart Hess, whose *Digital Artifacts* installation attempts to express what glitch feels like on the skin. Hess is trying not to represent glitch as such but to ask what it is like to be part of the computational process/mishap that results in glitch and then to find a way to express that disruption in embodied (if not rhetorical) forms through simulation or representation that call attention to the condition itself. Of course, Hess's work eventually gets rendered as a digital-visual artifact that can be distributed across various networked streams—participating in a multitude of circulating rhetorical ecologies—but as an artistic act and object it raises different questions from those pursued by the new media–era avant-garde. In fact, the distinction between the new media avant-garde and New Aesthetic tendencies provides a revealing dimension to hypermediate/hyperrhetorical orientations.

For example, as Bolter and Diane Gromala explored in their *Windows and Mirrors: Interaction Design, Digital Art, and the Myth of Transparency*— where they looked at the representational, rhetorical, and aesthetic implications of digital art featured in the SIGGRAPH 2000 Art Gallery—new media artists, particularly those playing with digital technologies in the late 1990s and early 2000s, began to approach digital art as "experiments in interaction design" (24). By manipulating the expectations of mediation as part of their very design, emergent digital artifacts were able to offer something of an authentic medial experience that took shape in the very interaction between the designed elements and the (hypermediated) engagements of the participant (25). One can see these considerations in the widely popular *Text Rain,* created by Romy Achituv and Camille Utterback in 1999, where participants used their bodies to interact with virtual letters raining down on a screen.[5] This installation, which was dependent on the play between digital artifacts

---

5. For a deeper look at the project, visit http://camilleutterback.com/projects/text-rain/.

and real, human participants, foregrounded the experience of the mediation. What a work like *Text Rain* accomplished was to remind participants to "appreciate the ways in which . . . [a particular artifact] shapes . . . [human] experience" by framing screens as both mirrors and windows—things not only that people look through but that reflect something of their own conditionality in their very mediation (Bolter and Gromala 27). New Aestheticism, while turning toward ecologies rather than couplings, has retained gestures of the windows-and-mirrors dynamic (particularly with regard to hypermediation). However, New Aestheticism has also pushed further, not just foregrounding the mediated interaction but attempting to represent and/ or let individuals experience both the computationality at the root of various mediations as well as the underlying human registers through which those mediations have meaning—folding layers upon layers of awareness into the mix (and thus inviting a sense of hypermediacy along with the potential of a hyperrhetoricity). In other words, *Text Rain* in a New Aesthetic moment would simply work differently: it might expose the operative mechanics of the installation to participants or sync the letter fall and letter placement with heart monitors on participant smartphones, smartwatches, or smartbands. Or it might push beyond the embodied interaction with falling digital letters and employ real-time sensors with humans functioning as data source (influencing the letter choice, letter flow, and the like), where the screen mediations call to human participants in particular ways (offering facial recognition mapping and pulling up corresponding Google images that share those pixel-map features). Or, as a third example, a New Aesthetic *Text Rain* might expand the interaction space of the installation and allow participants to manipulate the coding or algorithms operative at the core of the interaction (with those manipulations live-streamed in addition to their corresponding shifts in screen representation/experience). Or, as yet another possibility, a New Aesthetic *Text Rain* might introduce glitch into the process altogether, with images, letters, sounds, and all manner of visual disruptions taking place on the screen—all superimposed on the mirrored screen-projections of the real-time human participants. All of which is to say, a New Aesthetic *Text Rain* would be notably different (a) because of changes in technological affordances and aesthetic preferences and (b) because the cultural expectations of mediation (from immediate to hypermediate) and of human-to-media influence have shifted as well—a transition that includes not only ubiquitous computing and a naturalization of certain screen-media-to-human interactions but also an undergoing of a computational orientation that renders humans-as-data and, in turn, seeks to leverage human data streams toward critical and creative (and sometimes controlling) ends.

This, of course, introduces yet another rhetorical consideration in this conversation, which is the degree to which hypermediate, computationally oriented, mediated experiences increasingly invite techno-human assemblages into a humans-as-data worldview. And this is important because how one enacts one's rhetorical capacities is notably different if people are understood less as mediated beings (capable of experiencing mediations in particular ways and serving as mediators of change in a mediated world) and more as aggregates of data streams, responsive and reactive to changes in data-generating activities. The focus in dealing with the former remains a matter of shifting an audience's identities or identifications—a matter rich in the rhetorical tradition—while the latter pushes the conversation necessarily toward the depths and degrees to which one can introduce mediations that manipulate the output values (and intensities) of data streams.

Thus, while new media artists and theorists asked audiences to consider the expressive potential of new forms of representation and their interactions with those elements, highlighting mediation through competing representational practices and other forms of hypermediacy, New Aesthetic working creatives invite hypermediacy-oriented audiences to play with the hypermediacy itself (as expectant value and as interactive possibility) and, in many cases, to experience the computationality connected to the mediation—encouraging an attentiveness to how the experiential artifact participates in computational mediation as well as to how the artifact and its experience invite audiences to adopt particular medial orientations (i.e., to bring together technological and biological desires for understanding the world).

To further situate this orientation, I turn to Random International's 2012 work *Rain Room*[6]—offered here as a comparative, of sorts, to *Text Rain*. *Rain Room* is an installation that allows participants to walk through an environment of falling water droplets and yet remain completely dry. This process involves an incredibly complex set of interactions between 3D tracking cameras, water, solenoid valves, pressure regulators, molded tiles, a grated floor, steel beams, and a water management system (fully dependent on computational procedures). As a participant enters the rain room, the sound of water and the suggestion of moisture remain, but the water stops flowing in the space the participant occupies. Her body (rendered as interpretable data stream for specific computational processes) becomes a negative space in the water flow as the downpour ceases and resumes in response to her move-

---

6. For a more detailed look at *Rain Room,* visit the Museum of Modern Arts webpage on the installation (https://www.moma.org/calendar/exhibitions/1352) or view any number of videos available about the project online—specifically the *Guardian*'s video at https://www.youtube.com/watch?v=EkvazIZx-Fo.

ment and presence. What is interesting is not how the installation speaks to the control that humans may exert over natural forces and phenomena, but the ways in which the water (more precisely its negation) gives a thickness to what is otherwise an invisible computational space—the water, or its absence thereof, makes one hyperaware of the thickness of computational space, and, if extended far enough, of one's body as data stream occupying (or negating) a corresponding set of computational values. Further, as Jonathan Openshaw has suggested, when participants experience *Rain Room,* its complexity is so seamless and yet so pervasive that they cannot help but contemplate its computationality. For in the current epoch of a hypermediate and/or hyperaware culture, one's "first instinct upon seeing a complex form [like *Rain Room*] is to look for signs of the digital technology that made it" (Openshaw 228). While this instinctual move may both contribute to and reflect David M. Berry's condition of *digital pareidolia* (referenced earlier in this work), it nonetheless foregrounds the very experience of something like *Rain Room,* which offers an embodied experience of space while also inviting participants to ask after, experience, look for, and even expect the computationality of the project.

Thus, while there may be something of an operative continuum of hyper-mediate considerations, as Western culture transitions from an era of new media (a becoming hypermediate) to one of the post-digital (leveraging hypermediacy for a hypermediate culture), there is also a necessary overlap: new media hypermediacy foregrounded the experience of screen mediation as a way of talking about hypermediacy, whereas the New Aesthetic leverages the hypermediate qualities (and expectations) of screen mediation in/of/for a post-digital culture to help expose rhetorical and medial ecologies (par-ticular computational considerations, medial conditions, human–technology relations, and the like). One might see the New Aesthetic as the very thing being *occasioned* by the larger orientations of post-digital culture (see Kwastek 78–79). Additionally, by operationalizing hypermediacy for an increasingly hypermediate-oriented audience, the New Aesthetic is able to call attention to a set of sensibilities (and implications) that vibrate between the rhetorical and aesthetic preferences of biological and technological desires. And this refers not only to those moments where artifacts and objects draw incredibly rich parallels between things like biological cells and technological pixels—as in the works of Japanese artist Kōhei Nawa, whose *PIXCELL* sculptures actively "question the line between living being[s] and digital technology" (Openshaw 180)—but also to the fact that mediated beings increasingly see the world in (technologically) mediated ways, while technological improvements (in software, hardware, and techniques) simultaneously render "the everyday" as "increasingly machine readable" (Kwastek 73). Consequently, any hyperawareness that takes form does so in relation to counterpointing forces: a mediated condition that perpetually invites mediated ways of seeing/sensing the world (as well as a preference for particular types of medial experience) and a technological orientation that increasingly reduces the world to interpretable data values (whether as pixels, GPS locations, electric impulses, or the like).

Although these are each critical considerations for contemporary rhetorical practice, it is harder and harder for rhetoricians to intervene directly in the "data streams" themselves, as much of those generative outputs reside beyond the physical and conceptual grasp of the human bodies that produce them (whether via technical complexity, black-boxing practices, or yet other constraints). But one can attune to the medial orientations and experiences themselves, as rhetors and audiences often have (greater) access to those mediations and their potential interventions. Therefore, one can work with different mediating practices (and aesthetic representations) to find ways to extend or counter particular mediated perspectives by producing artifacts and expressions that work within the expectations that an audience brings to particular medial experiences. This, of course, is not only a way to foster rhetorical awareness of mediation (and to use that awareness for rhetorical ends) but, in many ways, often the only recourse one has to exposing, with any impact, the more critical (and often unquestioned) values of the "humans-as-data" worldview. For example, telling people that Facebook collects their data, listens to their conversations, tracks their movements, and the like in order to better feed and facilitate their role as Facebook-data-streams invites a certain kind of awareness. But creating an app or web-browser extension that hijacks the Facebook interface in order to capture and represent, in hypermediate fashion, the data streams themselves invites another. Think, for example, how one's experience and expectations of Facebook might change if every time a person made a post on Facebook she could see the digital residue left behind and how that residue gets taken up by the program's algorithms to make predictions, market content, or select user feeds to display. This is precisely what Data Selfie does. Created by Data X, a group co-founded by Hang Do Thi Duc and Regina Flores Mir, Data Selfie is an extension for the Google Chrome and Firefox browsers that tracks users' data traces and reveals what gets left behind and what the various learning algorithms can predict about their personalities based on the data.[7] The project was designed to help people explore their relationships to the data residue they leave as a matter of course when engaged in social networks and online media consumption. But what it does,

---

7. Data Selfie continues to operate in its data-gathering capacity, but its algorithmic prediction function was shut down on July 1, 2018.

in addition to capturing one's data stream (and highlighting humans-as-data orientations), is invite a certain kind of attentiveness to one's participation on Facebook and/or Facebook's "lurkerism" in relation to one's mediated life. Thus, Data Selfie points toward a hyperawareness (with a conditional potential for hyperrhetoricity) of the very worldview that underlines something like Facebook—which, while operating as a social media network for *people*, inherently reduces the human condition to a series of more and less valuable data streams (and thus an ethically suspect line of more and less valuable humans). But what this kind of New Aesthetic–esque browser extension also has the potential to do is to use hyperrhetorical mediations to foster an awareness of the depths to which Facebook is looking back out at its participants, listening to their lives, following along in their actions and activities, and the like—inviting the hyperawareness associated with the previous fourth-wall section.

The point, here, in all of this, but particularly in this contour, is to better understand the considerations and contributions of New Aestheticism. Collectively, then, one might see that under the auspices of the fourth contour the New Aesthetic (1) has a penchant for enactment in its own medium (e.g., an emerging aesthetic of the network taking place on/in/through the network), (2) privileges artifacts that turn to face their human viewers/participants (e.g., artifacts that call attention to their mediation and to human relationships with them, disrupting illusions of immediacy), and (3) routinely identifies with artifacts that possess a hyperrhetoricity (e.g., works that take shape in relation to their own privileged conditionalities and do so by calling attention to their own [and others'] guiding assumptions). Any one of these (or two or three together) can serve as inventive guides for making artifacts that participate in the logics and values of New Aestheticism, which means that the New Aesthetic may be, as this work has implicitly argued, far more widely at play than just in the visual/digital artifacts curated on Bridle's tumblr. For the New Aesthetic is about *awareness* (of mediation, of underlying systems that govern particular technological and/or sociocultural practices and preferences), about *relationships* (human–technology assemblages as well as technology-to-technology dynamics), and about *representational practices* (dissolving boundaries between the digital and the nondigital as well as between technological and biological materialities), calling attention to themselves as acts of mediation, and then staring back at humans as partners and co-participants in a hybrid world.

The question that emerges, of course, is how (and to what extent) does one use this kind of hyperawareness, hyperrhetoricity, and/or condition of hypermediacy in relation to the practices of rhetoric? To this end, I want to conclude this chapter (and this work) with something of a larger implication of the necessary shift that these kinds of considerations invite, which, at its core, is a reorienting of rhetorical practices away from the long-standing tradition of *ekphrasis* toward matters more intimately linked to medial experience (and *experience design*).

AUTHENTIC MEDIATED EXPERIENCES

As I introduced in chapter 1, *ekphrasis* comes out of the rhetorical tradition as part of the progymnasmata (a series of exercises designed to prepare students for the production and performance of oral declamations). In this regard, the *ekphrastic act* involved bringing (via description) something visual, material, or experiential clearly before the eyes or minds of an audience. In public declamations this was the job of the rhetor: to present, via description, the scene or image or act or object of importance/under question to audience (and to position it accordingly). And *ekphrasis* has, for the most part, remained at the heart of rhetoric over several millennia—with the very act of producing discourse involving, at a fundamental level, describing in words one's thinking, one's position, or one's preferred course of action (among other considerations). Further, as the practice of *ekphrasis* is, at its core, an act of translating something of the phenomenological world from one mediation to another, the bulk of the arts might be seen to operate in relation to the condition (and constraints) of *ekphrasis*—with artists and practitioners of all varieties employing various techné to translate (and/or transmediate) experience, imagination, feeling, and the like.

But when one shifts from *ekphrasis* to matters of *experience* (and experience design) as a point of emphasis, there is an accompanying rise in the value (and place) of pathos. And here I mean pathos not simply as it has been (mis) represented in the Aristotelian order—as a category for emotional appeals (*On Rhetoric* 1.2.2–4)[8]—but the more root meanings of the term, which are linked directly to experience, to that which one *undergoes* or that which one suffers/endures (Heidegger, *On the Way* 57; see also Handler Spitz 546–47).[9] In this sense, pathos more readily aligns with Dewey's embodied experience of

---

8. This reduction stems in part from Aristotle's treatment of specific emotions, which he construes in topoi-fashion: *Orge/Praotes, Philia/Ekhthra, Phobos/Tharsos, Aiskyne/Anaiskhyntia, Kharis/Akharistia, Eleos/Nemesan, Phthonos/Zelos* (see *On Rhetoric*, Book II).

9. Handler Spitz locates this original meaning of "experience" in works like Aeschylus's *Agamemnon* (line 177), Sophocles' *Ajax* (line 313), and Plato's *Theatetus* (193c) and *Republic* (612a) (547).

aestheticism—a recovery not of descriptions of stylistic judgments by a master class, but an undergoing of an affective experience rooted in everyday occurrences (and intrinsically linked to aesthetics).

But what drives this turn from *ekphrasis* to *experience (design)* is more than just a need to recover the aesthetic and embodied affectivities of everyday life. Rather, it is equally occasioned by the cultural shift in expectations of media suggested above—that is, that post-digital culture operates, by and large, with a hypermediate rather than immediate orientation to medial experience. Couple this overt attentiveness to mediation itself with a slew of multimedia practices that champion affect and felt sensibilities over categorical reason (see Ulmer's genres for electracy, as one set of examples), and one might start to grasp how a description of an idea, theory, or even an experience (the practice of *ekphrasis*) is increasingly insufficient for a post-digital audience. Rather, immersive mediations (from virtual reality platforms to material environments that get blanketed by layers of digital mediation) now allow (if not necessitate) working creatives to craft not just a description of X but an authentic mediated experience of X—in other words, to (re)produce an experience that, when undergone, leaves participants with an embodied sense of understanding. One example of this can be seen in rhetoric and media scholar Jason Helms's "Vorhandenheit" project, which invites participants to maneuver through an explication of philosopher Martin Heidegger's concepts of *zuhanden* (ready-at-hand) and *vorhanden* (present-at-hand), but in doing so the participants actually undergo the experience of the concepts themselves. Of course, Helms's work still includes elements of *ekphrasis* (as the shift under consideration here is by no means intended as an erasure of *ekphrasis*), but those descriptive elements are eventually subsumed by the experience itself, which offers an embodied mediated undergoing of *zuhanden* and *vorhanden*. In many ways, Helms's project is an enacting of the paradigm gestured to in the previous section, but one whose experience leads to a deeper (if not different) understanding.

But beyond individual projects like Helms's, technical communication scholar Liza Potts has gone so far as to advocate for the inclusion of a user-experience design expert on all digital humanities projects. While Potts is concerned in most cases with making sure that those projects operate with an attentiveness to the experience of the interface—as she sees this as critical to the kinds of knowledge building that digital humanities projects may accomplish—her argument is far more poignant, as computational, networked, screen-based delivery systems have necessitated a reframing and reformatting of cultural and scholarly ways of knowing and representing that knowing. For example, at this point in human history all digital-visual representations (academic and non) are, at their root, manipulated (and remediable) mediated creations. Their very coming-to-be (whether as representation, simulation, or other) is fundamentally dependent upon mediation—with each artifact subject to all sorts of influences, agendas, interpretations, and the like. What matters, then, is no longer the authenticity of a moment, which has become perpetually suspect in post-digital culture where everything is infinitely mediated and infinitely available for further mediation. Rather, what matters is the experience that an artifact offers or of which it is suggestive (again, see Helms and *Rain Room* as two such examples). Therefore, post-digital practitioners must be mindful not just of the descriptions they provide but of the experiences they produce—which include not only the authors' own sensorium that takes stock of and helps manipulate new mediating technologies toward particular ends but also that of their audiences (particularly human audiences), whose sense perception is augmented/altered by that very mediation.

In other words, every rhetorical artifact, particularly of the digitally mediated variety, offers a particular kind of mediated experience, but how one makes sense of that experience through the human sensorium is itself "enhanced" by the very medial conditions that have contributed to the creation of the artifact itself and the experience it offers. At work here, then, is a practice that produces its own conditionality. What emerges for post-digital rhetoricians as a result is a need for an orientation that includes less an attentiveness to the fidelity of representation (via the act of alphabetic and verbal description) and instead a focus on the experience that an artifact or creation can provide (and the ways in which that artifact can produce experiential homologies or invite accretions of value in relation to other rhetorical ecologies).

Further, this orientation should also include an understanding (as the New Aesthetic suggests) of the very potentialities of that experience being interdependent with the seeping of computational values and practices into the human condition, which contributes both to its production and to any attempts to make sense of the creation. Meaning, the crafting of an experience (as a rhetorical practice, homological or otherwise) must also play within the mediated expectations (and ways of experiencing that mediation) brought to the encounter by a post-digital audience.

CRAFTING EXPERIENCE

One way to help attune rhetoricians to these considerations, then, is by turning to craft—to the *crafting* of particular mediated experiences. Craft knowledge, of course, has been primarily associated with "'lower forms' of knowledge"—with having "little theoretical knowledge of its own" (Johnson 674). But as writing scholar Kristin Prins has argued, craft actually allows for an attentiveness to the relationships among human and nonhuman materialities (152) because it implies a kind of embodied creationism—it involves a human laboring act. Craft, as rhetoric and compositionist Robert Johnson has argued, is both a type of knowing and a formation of knowledge, and, just as important, is of and in the human domain (677).

When this human laboring act comes into contact with computational platforms and algorithmic procedures, what occurs, as designer Wes McGee suggests, is the opening of a "wide range of new workflows" that introduce new habits of practice (in Openshaw 272)—including new ludic habits of practice—and, as I suggested in chapter 5, a fundamental shift in labor. That is, part of what computational mediations have done is to take on some of the labor burden of making/doing. In many cases these labor shifts are subtle—from autofill to autocorrect—but in some cases they are quite extensive: for example, think about how much labor is offloaded into digital photography apps, which routinely render sepia images in the blink of an eye (an otherwise labor-intensive process). On the one hand, as suggested earlier, this shift in labor allows digital rhetors to focus their energies elsewhere: to spend more time tinkering with ideas, playing with technology, creating multiple versions, and being increasingly attentive to the crafted experience. On the other hand, the shift in labor and accompanying workflows alters the very conditions of craft knowledge itself. For if craft is understood as a capacity for action that brings together embodied habits of practice and special (if not specialized) ways of knowing—"know[ing] the materials of the trade," "understand[ing] the forms of various genres and media[tions]," and being aware of the dual orientations of (1) process and product, and (2) the making of selves (subjectivities) and the making of cultures (Johnson 685; 684)—then new computational practices that take on human labors and establish new human–technology workflows also augment the materials of the trade, the forms and experiences of mediation, and the cultures and subjectivities that might take shape. A craft orientation can help facilitate, then, the making of artifacts as offering uniquely mediated experiences because craft requires an understanding of the materialities and mediations involved, as well as how shifts in those elements introduce new craft products and new craft processes. And this (hyper)awareness of process—of altered workflows that include technological co-laborers—actually makes it easier for craftspersons to use an exposure of process for hypermediate purposes (for the making of hypermediate experiences).

Now, while craft allows for an embodied orientation to materialities and mediations, perhaps an equally valuable approach to the making of mediated experiences would be, as I suggested earlier in relation to Potts, through something like experience design, which operates more explicitly with an attentiveness to architecture and aesthetics. For example, in interaction design, usability studies, and the like, there is a highly complex, delicate, and dynamic interconnectedness that exists between the grammars, procedures, logics, frames, techniques, and so forth (architecture as structure) and matters of representation, tone, mood, visual metaphors, and so on (aesthetics as style). The default inclination, since at least Aristotle's *Metaphysics,* has been to treat these constituents separately—the lingering effect of the dominant Western form/matter model. But as media theorist Matthew Fuller has argued in *Media Ecologies: Materialist Energies in Art and Technoculture* and "Commonality, Pixel Property, Seduction: As If," the two cannot be, nor should they be, separated, particularly when trying to create meaningful representations—or, in the case of this chapter, meaningful (and rhetorical) mediated experiences. To counter this division, specifically in *Media Ecologies,* Fuller uses philosopher Gilbert Simondon's notion of individuation to suggest that the materials of any given situation—which include working creatives (humans), technologies, institutional and political contexts, cultural aesthetics, and so on—"produce their own capacities of formation," and do so "in relation to the morphogenetic affordances around them" (18). In terms of the New Aesthetic, the morphogenetic affordances include human–technology assemblages and the ways in which humans have "naturalized" computational values and practices—creating not only techno-infused epistemologies but also particular aesthetic expectations for mediated engagement. There are, of course, any number of treatises on experience design that offer basic principles or guidance, and this work is by no means discouraging readers from picking up with those considerations in more detail (particularly the works of Donald Norman and Nathan Shedroff). But this work is not about experience design itself; rather, in this context, what matters is how the phenomenon of the New Aesthetic introduces additional considerations to an experience design orientation.

For example, one key element introduced here is that post-digital rhetoricians are no longer designing artifacts for the primary experience of immediacy. Take any number of digital textbooks or accompanying "learning suites," which regularly offer "pop-up" video explanations (of the talking-head variety), interactive explanatory animations, hypertextuality as matter of user convenience, and so on. The experience of media, even relatively traditional media like textbooks that have been remediated for electronic delivery, now include a notable level of hypermediate possibilities—from additional layers of information sitting "on top" a particular content to meaning itself occurring through / in relation to the metaphors offered by visual cues and buttons. While this perpetual disruption of the *through* orientation would have been destabilizing (if not devastating) to popular culture in Richard Lanham's moment of "digital rhetoric" coinage, today's post-digital natives situate medial awareness as (increasingly) "natural" to screen-based mediations: news broadcasts include layers of related and nonrelated information situated on top of and below the main camera feed; YouTube videos are littered with onscreen and interruptive advertisements, overlays, texts, and the like; corporate websites regularly include redirects and pop-out windows that explain information, offer related services, or provide additional context; and even static print-culture media, through programs like LAYAR and Aurasma, now include the possibilities of playable media as hypermediate elements. Thus, from smartphones to computer games, television shows to digital textbooks, people are perpetually engaged in hypermediate relations with their media—through both internal (onscreen) and external (social media) mediations. What matters is no longer a mediated artifact's ties to realism, nor its ability to efface the interface— matters aligned with immediacy—but rather an attunement to how different technologies and humans are individuated in radically different ways from moment to moment, with each of those moments being increasingly mediated and yet experienced as authentic rather than artifice. Take the application Snapchat as an example; part of what makes it so engaging is not simply that it offers real-time image sharing (as one can do that in any number of other applications) but that it allows for new ways of experiencing and augmenting image/text exchanges. While the viewing time limits are unique in their own way, it is actually the quick filters (the mapping and masking dynamic) of Snapchat that make the application itself an experience. This is perhaps most evident when playing with the app in real time with a friend or family member, as the two-person augmentations (whether captured and shared via the network or not) offer an authentic mediated experience. Moreover, once one has undergone a Snapchat engagement, it becomes increasingly difficult to separate that experience from the expectations one brings to other digital-image-based mediated exchanges. This is not to say that users expect Facebook, for example, to offer the same experience as Snapchat, but that the affordances and capacities for expression (and, perhaps, for playing with the application as itself an authentic experience) seep into the milieu of image-oriented human–technology expectations.

However, while experience design has risen in prominence in the past decade for everything from the making of textiles to web design, what the

New Aesthetic provides is (1) a set of considerations that work deliberately across digital and nondigital materialities, (2) an attunement to a culture rooted in hypermediacy (not immediacy), and (3) operative contours that may help working creatives employ hypermediacy rhetorically (as part of mediated experiences). For the hyperawareness of the mediating act is not only part of the expectations that audiences bring to digital artifacts and digitally mediated engagements; it is itself a way of adding context, clarity, and condensation to the commentary or critical engagement offered by the artifact itself (i.e., part of its hyperrhetorical capacities). What all this suggests, then, is a change in how rhetors understand audiences' expectations of mediated artifacts.

To account for this shift, what the New Aesthetic contours offer is something of a post-digital remake of the clarity, brevity, and sincerity (C-B-S) system central to the *ekphrastic* practice of the last three-hundred-plus years of alphabetic literacy and print-culture rhetorics. In other words, when alphabetic writing is given primacy for rhetorical practices, the C-B-S system functions as one idealized set of operative values. Of course, as Lanham argued, these elements were never fully present/achieved in any particular production (*Analyzing Prose* 217), but they nonetheless operated in harmony and helped guide rhetors toward the production of a particular kind of text-based experience (C-B-S as a decorum for writing-as-immediacy). But post-digital rhetoricians need something grounded more fully in the human sensorium, as the experience of digital artifacts is not only different from that of text but also not beholden to the scriptures of *ekphrasis*.

Per the indications of the New Aesthetic, this "something else" includes a greater attentiveness to the embodied experiences of particular mediated artifacts and to the hyperawareness of mediation itself (manifest in relation to both material and nonmaterial conditions of production)—and here is where the New Aesthetic contours begin to take on a more systemic intent or purpose. But whereas the C-B-S elements operated in harmony—presenting product values for which to strive—the contours of the New Aesthetic orient making activities through a fluid mix of complementary connections and competing tensions, with various combinations of the contours (and even singularities) guiding post-digital rhetoricians toward making effective and affective mediated experiences in/of/for a hypermediate culture. Given this dynamic, what is perhaps most stable across the contours is the way in which each helps in the pursuit of mediated experiences that invite (if not insist on) an awareness of mediation, of materiality, of manifested implications, and the like. Which means that post-digital practitioners who allow the contours to influence their practices of making mediated (and remediable) experiences should not try to hide their rhetorical or representational maneuvers but rather should foreground the mediation itself as (critical to) the experience. To put this in McLuhan's terms: the experience of the medium is (becoming) the message. Thus, what the New Aesthetic offers is one set of operative guides for the doing of post-digital rhetoric.

WORKS CITED

Adamson, Glenn. "Craft in the Digital Age." Openshaw, pp. 286–88.

Aima, Rahel. "Breaking the Fourth Wall: Duende and the New Aesthetic." *The New Aesthetic Revisited: The Debate Continues!* The Creators Project, 4 May 2012. https://creators.vice.com/en_us/article/the-new-aesthetic-revisited-the-debate-continues. Accessed 12 June 2014.

Anderson, Daniel, and Jentery Sayers. "The Metaphor and Materiality of Layers." *Rhetoric and the Digital Humanities,* edited by Jim Ridolfo and William Hart-Davidson, U of Chicago P, 2015, pp. 80–95.

Andrews, Ian. "Post-digital Aesthetics and the Return to Modernism." *Ian Andrews,* 2000. http://www.ian-andrews.org/texts/postdig.html. Accessed June 2015.

Aristotle. *Metaphysics.* Translated by W. D. Ross, 1908. http://classics.mit.edu/Aristotle/metaphysics.html, Accessed 8 Dec. 2016.

———. *On Rhetoric: A Theory of Civic Discourse.* Translated by George Kenney, Oxford UP, 1991.

Arroyo, Sarah J. *Participatory Composition: Video Culture, Writing, and Electracy.* Southern Illinois UP, 2013.

Barnard, Malcolm. *Approaches to Understanding Visual Culture.* Palgrave Macmillan, 2001.

Bassett, Caroline. "Not Now? Feminism, Technology, Postdigital." Berry and Dieter, pp. 136–50.

Bateson, Gregory. *Steps to an Ecology of Mind.* Ballantine Books, 1972; U of Chicago P, 2000.

Baumgarten, Alexander Gottlieb. *Reflections on Poetry.* Translated by Karl Aschenbrenner and William B. Holther, U of California P, 1954.

Baxandall, Michael David Kighley. *Painting and Experience in 15th Century Italy: A Primer in the Social History of Pictorial Style.* Oxford UP, 1972.

Bay, Jenny, and Thomas Rickert. "Dwelling with New Media." *RAW: Reading and Writing New Media,* edited by Cheryl Ball and Jim Kalmbach, Hampton Press, 2010, pp. 117–40.

Benkler, Yochai. *The Wealth of Networks: How Social Production Transforms Markets and Freedom.* Yale UP, 2006.

Berry, David M. *Critical Theory and the Digital.* Bloomsbury, 2014.

———. "The Postdigital Constellation." Berry and Dieter, pp. 44–57.

Berry, David M., and Michael Dieter, editors. *Postdigital Aesthetics: Art, Computation, and Design.* Palgrave Macmillan, 2015.

Berry, David M., Michel van Dartel, Michael Dieter, Michelle Kasprzack, Nat Muller, Rachel O'Reilly, and José Luis de Vicente. *New Aesthetic, New Anxieties.* V2_ Publishers, Rotterdam, Netherlands, 2012.

Betancourt, Michael. "Automated Labor: The 'New Aesthetic' and Immaterial Physicality." *ctheory.net,* 5 Feb. 2013. http://ctheory.net/ctheory_wp/automated-labor-the-new-aesthetic-and-immaterial-physicality/. Accessed 14 Dec. 2013.

Bishop, Claire. "Digital Divide." *Artforum,* Sept. 2012, pp. 435–41.

Bitzer, Lloyd F. "The Rhetorical Situation." *Philosophy and Rhetoric,* vol. 1, no. 1, 1968, pp. 1–14.

Bogost, Ian. *Alien Phenomenology, or, What It's Like to Be a Thing.* U of Minnesota P, 2012.

———. "The New Aesthetic Needs to Get Weirder." *The Atlantic,* 13 Apr. 2012.

Bolter, Jay David, and Diane Gromala. *Windows and Mirrors: Interaction Design, Digital Art, and the Myth of Transparency.* MIT P, 2003.

Bolter, Jay David, and Richard Grusin. *Remediation: Understanding New Media.* MIT P, 1999.

Borenstein, Greg. "What It's Like to Be a 21st Century Thing." *In Response to Bruce Sterling's "Essay on the New Aesthetic."* The Creators Project, 6 Apr. 2012. https://creators.vice.com/en_us/article/in-response-to-bruce-sterlings-essay-on-the-new-aesthetic. Accessed 14 June 2014.

Bosma, Josephine. "Post-Digital Is Post-Screen—Towards a New Visual Art." *Josephine Bosma,* 29 Oct. 2013. http://www.josephinebosma.com/web/node/98. Accessed 20 Oct. 2015.

Bourdieu, Pierre. *Distinction: A Social Critique of the Judgment of Taste.* Translated by Richard Nice, Harvard UP, 1984.

Boyle, Casey. "The Rhetorical Question Concerning Glitch." *Computers and Composition,* vol. 35, 2015, pp. 12–19.

———. "Writing and Rhetoric and/as Posthuman Practice." *College English,* vol. 78, no. 6, July 2016, pp. 532–54.

Bridle, James. "#sxaesthetic." *Booktwo.org,* 15 Mar. 2012. http://booktwo.org/notebook/sxaesthetic/. Accessed 4 June 2014.

———. "The New Aesthetic." *Really Interesting Group,* 6 May 2011. http://www.riglondon.com/2011/05/06/the-new-aesthetic/. Accessed 3 June 2014.

———. "The New Aesthetic and Its Politics." *Booktwo.org,* 12 June 2013. http://booktwo.org/notebook/new-aesthetic-politics/. Accessed 4 June 2014.

———. "The Render Ghosts." *Electronic Voice Phenomena.* Mercy & Penned in the Margins Project, 14 Nov. 2013. http://www.electronicvoicephenomena.net/index.php/the-render-ghosts-james-bridle/. Accessed 3 July 2014.

———. "Waving at the Machines." *Web Directions,* 5 Dec. 2011. https://www.webdirections.org/resources/james-bridle-waving-at-the-machines/. Accessed 12 June 2014.

Brooke, Collin Gifford. *Lingua Fracta: Toward a Rhetoric of New Media.* Hampton Press, 2009.

Brouwer, Joke, Arjen Mulder, and Lars Spuybroek. *Vital Beauty: Reclaiming Aesthetics in the Tangle of Technology and Nature.* V2_ Publishers, Rotterdam, Netherlands, 2012, pp. 120–29. 2012.

Brown, James Jr. *Ethical Programs: Hospitality and the Rhetorics of Software.* U of Michigan P, 2015.

Burke, Kenneth. *Permanence and Change: An Anatomy of Purpose.* 3rd ed., U California P, 1984.

Cascone, Kim. "The Aesthetics of Failure: 'Post-Digital' Tendencies in Contemporary Computer Music." *Computer Music Journal,* vol. 24, no. 4, Winter 2000, pp. 12–18.

Ceraso, Steph. "(Re)Educating the Senses: Multimodal Listening, Bodily Learning, and the Composition of Sonic Experiences." *College English,* vol. 77, no. 2, Nov. 2014, pp. 102–23.

Chayka, Kyle. "The New Aesthetic: Going Native." *In Response to Bruce Sterling's "Essay on the New Aesthetic."* The Creators Project, 6 Apr. 2012. https://creators.vice.com/en_us/article/in-response-to-bruce-sterlings-essay-on-the-new-aesthetic#1. Accessed 14 June 2014.

Cloninger, Curt. "A Manifesto for a Theory of the 'New Aesthetic.'" *Mute,* 3 Oct. 2012. http://www.metamute.org/editorial/articles/manifesto-theory-'new-aesthetic'.

Coleman, Beth. *Hello Avatar: Rise of the Networked Generation.* MIT P, 2011.

Collamati, Anthony. *Camera Creatures: Rhetorics of Light and Emerging Media.* Dissertation, Clemson University Tigerprints, 2012.

Cox, Geoff. "Postscript on the Post-digital and the Problem of Temporality." Berry and Dieter, pp. 151–62.

Cramer, Florian. "What Is 'Post-Digital'?" Berry and Dieter, pp. 12–25.

Davies, Russell. "SXSW, the New Aesthetic and Writing." *Russell Davies.* Russell Davies, 14 Mar. 2012. http://russelldavies.typepad.com/planning/2012/03/sxsw-the-new-aesthetic-and-writing.html. Accessed 4 June 2014.

De Joode, Rachel. Interviewed by Jonathan Openshaw. Openshaw, pp. 136–39.

Demetz, Gehard. Interviewed by Jonathan Openshaw. Openshaw, pp. 74–77.

Dewey, John. *Art as Experience.* Lectures, 1934. Perigee Books, Berkley Publishing Group, 1980.

Downs, Clair. "Remember Hipstamatic? It's Still Alive." *Motherboard,* 9 Oct. 2017. http://motherboard.vice.com/en_us/article/wjx95x/hipstamatic-instagram-what-happened-to-hipstamatic. Accessed 22 Apr. 2018.

Drucker, Johanna. *Graphesis: Visual Forms of Knowledge Production.* Harvard UP, 2014.

Dunne, Anthony. *Hertzian Tales: Electronic Products, Aesthetic Experience, and Critical Design.* Royal College of Art, 1999; MIT Press, 2006.

Edbauer, Jenny. "Unframing Models of Public Distribution: From Rhetorical Situation to Rhetorical Ecologies." *Rhetoric Society Quarterly,* vol. 35, no. 4, 2005, pp. 5–24.

Edbauer Rice, Jenny. "Rhetoric's Mechanics: Retooling the Equipment of Writing Production." *College Composition and Communication,* vol. 60, no. 2, Dec. 2008, pp. 366–87.

Ehrenberg, Rachel. "Square Pixel Inventor Tries to Smooth Things Out." *Wired News,* 28 Jun. 2010. https://www.wired.com/2010/06/smoothing-square-pixels/. Accessed 18 July 2014.

Eno, Brian. "The Studio as Compositional Tool." *Audio Culture: Readings in Modern Music,* edited by Christoph Cox and Daniel Warner, Continuum, 2004, pp. 127–30.

Eyman, Doug. *Digital Rhetoric: Theory, Method, Practice.* U of Michigan P, 2015.

Farman, Jason. "When Geolocation Meets Visualization." Morey and Tinnell, pp. 176–99.

Friedberg, Anne. "On Digital Scholarship." *Cinema Journal,* vol. 48, no. 2, Winter 2009, pp. 150–54.

Fuller, Matthew. "Commonality, Pixel Property, Seduction: As If." *Pixel Plunder,* Sep. 2001. http://year01.com/archive/plunder/essay.html. Accessed 10 Nov. 2015.

———. *Media Ecologies: Materialist Energies in Art and Technoculture.* MIT P, 2005.

Gannis, Carla. "A Code for the Numbers to Come." *The New Aesthetic Revisited: The Debate Continues!* The Creators Project, 4 May 2012. https://creators.vice.com/en_us/article/the-new-aesthetic-revisited-the-debate-continues. Accessed 12 June 2014.

George, James. "The New Aesthetic Needs New Wranglers." *In Response to Bruce Sterling's "Essay on the New Aesthetic."* The Creators Project, 6 Apr. 2012. https://creators.vice.com/en_us/article/in-response-to-bruce-sterlings-essay-on-the-new-aesthetic#1. Accessed 14 June 2014.

Gibson, William. *Neuromancer.* Ace Books, 1984.

———. *Spook Country.* Putnam's, 2007.

Gitelman, Lisa. *Always Already New: Media, History, and the Data of Culture.* MIT P, 2006.

Golumbia, David. "Judging Like a Machine." Berry and Dieter, pp. 123–35.

Greenfield, Adam. *Everyware: The Dawning Age of Ubiquitous Computing.* New Riders, 2006.

Guffey, Elizabeth. *Retro: The Culture of Revival.* Reaktion Books, 2002.

Haas, Christina. *Writing Technology: Studies on the Materiality of Literacy.* Erlbaum, 1996.

Hammer, Steven. "Writing (Dirty) New Media / Glitch Composition." *Technoculture: An Online Journal of Technology and Society,* vol. 4, 2014, https://tcjournal.org/vol4/hammer-unglitched.

Handler Spitz, Ellen. "Apres-Coup: Empathy, Sympathy, Aesthetics, and Childhood: Fledgling Thoughts." *American Imago,* vol. 64, no. 4, 2008, pp. 545–59.

Hayles, N. Katherine. "Cybernetics." *Critical Terms for Media Studies,* edited by W. J. T. Mitchell and Mark B. N. Hansen, U Chicago P, 2010, pp. 144–56.

———. *Electronic Literature: New Horizons for the Literary.* U of Notre Dame P, 2008.

———. *How We Became Posthuman: Virtual Bodies in Cybernetics, Literature, and Informatics.* U of Chicago P, 1999.

———. *How We Think: Digital Media and Contemporary Technogenesis.* U of Chicago P, 2012.

———. "Hyper and Deep Attention: The Generational Divide in Cognitive Modes." *Profession,* 2007, pp. 187–99. doi:10.1632/prof.2007.2007.1.187.

———. *Writing Machines.* MIT P, 2002.

Heidegger, Martin. *On the Way to Language.* Translated by Peter D. Hertz, Harper and Row, 1971.

Helms, Jason. "Vorhandenheit." *MoMLA: From Gallery to Webtext,* edited by Virginia Kuhn and Victor Vitanza. *Kairos: A Journal of Rhetoric, Technology, and Pedagogy,* vol. 17, no. 2, Spring 2013.

Henze, Eno. Interviewed by Jonathan Openshaw. Openshaw, pp. 40–43.

Hernan, Luis. "Digital Ethereal: A Creative Exploration of Wireless Spectres." http://www.digitalethereal.com. Accessed 12 Dec. 2016.

Hodgson, Justin, Scott Nelson, Andrew Rechnitz, and Cleve Wiese. "The Importance of Undergraduate Multimedia: An Argument in Seven Acts." *Kairos: A Journal of Rhetoric, Technology, and Pedagogy,* vol. 16, no. 1, Fall 2011.

Holmevik, Jan. *Inter/vention: Free Play in the Age of Electracy.* MIT P. 2012.

Jackson, Robert. "The Banality of the New Aesthetic." *Furtherfield: For Arts, Technology, and Social Change,* 15 Apr. 2012. http://archive.furtherfield.org/features/reviews/banality-new-aesthetic. Accessed 12 June 2014.

Johnson, Robert R. "Craft Knowledge: Of Disciplinarity in Writing Studies." *College Composition and Communication,* vol. 61, no. 4, June 2010, pp. 673–90.

Jones, Steven E. *The Emergence of Digital Humanities.* Routledge, 2014.

Jurgenson, Nathan. "The IRL Fetish." *The New Inquiry,* 28 June 2012. https://thenewinquiry.com/the-irl-fetish/. Accessed 11 July 2014.

Kant, Immanuel. *Critique of Judgment.* 1790, Prussia. Translated by Werner S. Pluhar, Hacket, 1987.

Knight, Aimée. "The New Aesthetic . . . Perhaps." 10 Apr. 2012. http://aimeeknight.com/2012/04/10/the-new-aestheticperhaps. Accessed 15 Nov. 2015.

———. "Reclaiming Experience: The Aesthetic and Multimodal Composition." *Computers and Composition,* vol. 30, Issue 2, June 2013, pp. 146–55.

Kuhn, Virginia. "The Rhetoric of Remix." *Transformative Works and Cultures,* no. 9, 2012.

———. "Web Three Point Oh: The Virtual Is the Real." *Cybertext Yearbook 2013—High Wired Redux,* edited by Cynthia Haynes and Jan Holmevik, U of Jyväskylä, 2013.

Kwastek, Katja. "How to Be Theorized: A Tediously Academic Essay on the *New Aesthetic.*" Berry and Dieter, pp. 72–85.

Lanham, Richard. *Analyzing Prose.* 2nd ed., Continuum, 2003.

———. *The Economics of Attention: Style and Substance in the Age of Information.* U of Chicago P, 2006.

———. *The Electronic Word: Democracy, Technology, and the Arts.* U of Chicago P, 1993.

Losh, Elizabeth. "Nowcasting/Futurecasting: Big Data, Prognostication, and the Rhetorics of Scale." *Rhetoric and the Digital Humanities,* edited by Jim Ridolfo and William Hart-Davidson, U of Chicago P, 2015, pp. 286–95.

———. *Virtualpolitik: An Electronic History of Government Media-Making in a Time of War, Scandal, Disaster, Miscommunication, and Mistakes.* MIT P, 2009.

Lyon, Arabella. *Deliberative Acts.* Pennsylvania State UP, 2013.

Lyotard, Jean-François. *The Differend: Phrases in Dispute.* Translated by Georges Van Den Abeele, U of Minnesota P, 1988.

———. *The Postmodern Condition: A Report on Knowledge.* Translated by Geoff Bennington and Brian Massumi, U of Minnesota P, 1984.

Manovich, Lev. "The Death of Computer Art." *Rhizome,* Nov. 1996.

———. *The Language of New Media.* MIT P, 2001.

McDonald, Kyle. "Personifying Machines, Machining Persons." *In Response to Bruce Sterling's "Essay on the New Aesthetic."* The Creators Project, 6 Apr. 2012. https://creators.vice.com/en_us/article/in-response-to-bruce-sterlings-essay-on-the-new-aesthetic. Accessed 14 June 2014.

McGee, Wes. Interviewed by Jonathan Openshaw. Openshaw, pp. 270–73.

McGonigal, Jane. *Reality Is Broken: Why Games Make Us Better and How They Can Change the World.* Penguin, 2011.

McLuhan, Marshall. *Understanding Media: The Extensions of Man.* MIT P, 1964.

McLuhan, Marshall, and Quentin Fiore. *The Medium Is the Massage: An Inventory of Effects.* Bantam Books, 1967.

McNeil, Joanne. "New Aesthetic at SXSW." *Joanne McNeil.* Joanne McNeil, 14 Mar. 2012. http://www.joannemcneil.com/new-aesthetic-at-sxsw/. Accessed 4 June 2014.

Miller, Daniel. "Technology and Human Attainment." Openshaw, pp. 198–99.

Miller, Paul D. *Rhythm Science*. MIT P, 2004.

Minard, Jonathan. "Straining to Envision the New Aesthetic." *In Response to Bruce Sterling's "Essay on the New Aesthetic."* The Creators Project, 6 Apr. 2012. https://creators.vice.com/en_us/article/in-response-to-bruce-sterlings-essay-on-the-new-aesthetic. 14 June 2014.

Mirocha, Lukasz. "Communication Models, Aesthetics, and Ontology of the Computational Age Revealed." Berry and Dieter, pp. 58–71.

Morey, Sean. "Digital Ecologies." *Ecology, Writing Theory, and New Media: Writing Ecology*, edited by Sidney I. Dobrin, Routledge, 2011, pp. 105–21.

Morey, Sean, and John Tinnell. *Augmented Reality: Innovative Perspectives across Art, Industry, and Academia*. Parlor Press, 2017.

Mulliken, Jasmine. *The Mapping Dubliners Project*. 2012. http://mulliken.okstate.edu. Accessed 12 Mar. 2017.

Norman, Donald A. *The Design of Everyday Things*. Basic Books, 1988.

———. *Emotional Design: Why We Love (or Hate) Everyday Things*. Basic Books, 2004.

Ong, Walter J. *Orality and Literacy: The Technologizing of the Word*. Methuen, 1982.

Openshaw, Jonathan. *Postdigital Artisans: Craftsmanship with a New Aesthetic in Fashion, Art, Design and Architecture*. Frame Publishers, 2015.

Paul, Christiane, and Malcolm Levy. "Genealogies of the New Aesthetic." Berry and Dieter, pp. 27–43.

Pinkas, Daniel. "A Hyperbolic and Catchy New Aesthetic." Berry and Dieter, pp. 86–95.

Portanova, Stamatia. "The Genius and the Algorithm: Reflections on the New Aesthetic as a Computer's Vision." Berry and Dieter, pp. 96–108.

Potts, Liza. "Archive Experiences: A Vision for User-Centered Design in the Digital Humanities." *Rhetoric and the Digital Humanities*, edited by Jim Ridolfo and William Hart-Davidson, U of Chicago P, 2014, pp. 253–65.

Prins, Kristin. "Crafting New Approaches to Composition." *composing (media) = composing (embodiment)*, edited by Kristin Arola and Anne Francis Wysocki, Utah State UP, 2012, pp. 145–61.

Rainie, Lee, and Barry Wellman. *Networked: The New Social Operating System*. MIT P, 2012.

Rancière, Jacques. *The Politics of Aesthetics*. Translated by Gabriel Rockhill, Continuum, 2006.

Reid, Alex. "Composing Objects: Prospects for a Digital Rhetoric." *Enculturation: A Journal of Rhetoric, Writing, and Culture*, no. 14, 10 Oct. 2012. http://enculturation.net/composing-objects.

Rickert, Thomas. *Ambient Rhetoric: The Attunements of Rhetorical Being*. U of Pittsburgh P, 2013.

Rieder, David M. *Suasive Iterations: Rhetoric, Writing, and Physical Computing*. Parlor Press, 2017.

Satrom, Jon. *Creative Problem Creating: Jon Satrom at TedxDePaulU*. 13 May 2013. http://www.youtube.com/watch?v=OFwNtXpuMq4. Accessed 5 May 2015.

Selber, Stuart. *Multiliteracies for a Digital Age*. Southern Illinois UP, 2004.

Serres, Michel. *The Parasite*. Translated by Lawrence R. Schehr, Johns Hopkins UP, 1982.

Shedroff, Nathan. *Experience Design 1*. New Riders, 2001.

Shipka, Jody. *Toward a Composition Made Whole*. U of Pittsburgh P, 2011.

Sicart, Miguel. *Play Matters*. MIT P, 2014.

Stafford, Barbara. *Good Looking: Essays on the Virtues of Images.* MIT P, 1996.

Staniak, Michael. Interviewed by Jonathan Openshaw. Openshaw, pp. 132–35.

Sterling, Bruce. "An Essay on the New Aesthetic." *Wired,* 2 Apr. 2012. https://www.wired.com/2012/04/an-essay-on-the-new-aesthetic/. Accessed 3 June 2014.

Syverson, Margaret A. *The Wealth of Reality: An Ecology of Composition.* Southern Illinois UP, 1999.

Takeda, Maiko. Interviewed by Jonathan Openshaw. Openshaw, pp. 90–93.

Terrett, Ben. "SXSW, the New Aesthetic and Commercial Visual Culture." *Noisy Decent Graphics,* 15 Mar. 2012. http://noisydecentgraphics.typepad.com/design/2012/03/sxsw-the-new-aesthetic-and-commercial-visual-culture.html. Accessed 4 June 2014.

Tinnell, John. "Post-Media Occupations for Writing Theory: From Augmentation to Autopoiesis." *Ecology, Writing Theory, and New Media: Writing Ecology,* edited by Sidney I. Dobrin, Routledge, 2011, pp. 122–42.

Tufekci, Zeynep. "Why the Great Glitch of July 8th Should Scare You." *The Message,* 8 July 2015. https://medium.com/message/why-the-great-glitch-of-july-8th-should-scare-you-b791002fff03. Accessed 25 July 2015.

Turkle, Sherry. *Life on the Screen: Identity in the Age of the Internet.* Simon and Schuster, 1995.

Ulmer, Gregory L. *Heuretics: The Logic of Invention.* Johns Hopkins UP, 1994.

———. *Internet Invention: From Literacy to Electracy.* Longman, 2003.

———. *Teletheory: Grammatology in the Age of Video.* Routledge, 1989; Atropos Press, 2004.

Vartanian, Hrag. "A Not-So-New Aesthetic, or Another Attempt at Technological Triumphalism." *The New Aesthetic Revisited: The Debate Continues!* The Creators Project, 4 May 2012. https://creators.vice.com/en_us/article/the-new-aesthetic-revisited-the-debate-continues. Accessed 12 June 2014.

Verbeek, Peter-Paul. "The Limits of Humanity: On Technology, Ethics, and Human Nature." Lecture, Universiteit Twente, 15 Oct. 2009. https://www.utwente.nl/en/bms/wijsb/staff/verbeek/oratie_eng.pdf. Accessed 3 Jan. 2016.

Virilio, Paul. *Open Sky.* Translated by Julie Rose, Verso, 1997.

Vitanza, Victor J. "Three Counter-theses; Or, a Critical In(ter)vention into Composition Theories and Pedagogies." *Contending with Words,* edited by Patricia Harkin and John Schilb, MLA, 1991, pp. 139–72.

———. "Writing the Paradigm. Review of *Heuretics: The Logic of Invention,* by Gregory L. Ulmer." *Alt-X Network and the Electronic Book Review,* 1996. http://www.altx.com/ebr/ebr2/r2vitanza.htm. Accessed 10 Sept. 2014.

"We Believe." *Apple.* iPad 2 Commercial, 2011.

Weishaus, Joel. "IMAGING EmerAgency: A Conversation with Gregory Ulmer." *Postmodern Culture,* vol. 9, no. 1, Sept. 1998.

Weiss, Dennis M. "Seduced by the Machine: Human-Technology Relations and Sociable Robots." *Design, Mediation, and the Posthuman,* edited by Dennis M. Weiss, Amy D. Propen, and Colbey Emmerson Reid, Lexington Books, 2014, pp. 217–32.

Welch, Kathleen. *Electric Rhetoric: Classical Rhetoric, Oralism, and a New Literacy.* MIT P, 1999.

Wysocki, Anne Frances. "Opening New Media to Writing: Openings and Justifications." *Writing New Media: Theory and Applications for Expanding the Teaching of Composition,* edited by

Anne Frances Wysocki, Johndan Johnson-Eilola, Cynthia L. Selfe, and Geoffrey Sirc, Utah State UP, 2004.

Yancey, Kathleen Blake. "Looking for Sources of Coherence in a Fragmented World: Notes toward a New Assessment Design." *Computers and Composition,* vol. 21, no. 1, 2004, pp. 89–102.

———. "Made Not Only in Words: Composition in a New Key." 2004 CCCC Chair's Address. *College Composition and Communication,* vol. 56, no. 2, Dec. 2004, pp. 297–328.

Young, Liam. "Shadows of the Digital: An Atlas of Fiducial Architecture." Openshaw, pp. 14–16.

Zappen, James P. "Digital Rhetoric: Toward an Integrated Theory." *Technical Communication Quarterly,* vol. 14, no. 3, 2005, pp. 319–25.

Zigelbaum, Jamie, and Marcelo Coelho. "The Rasterized Snake Eats Its Analog Tail." *The New Aesthetic Revisited: The Debate Continues!* The Creators Project, 4 May 2012. https://creators. vice.com/en_us/article/the-new-aesthetic-revisited-the-debate-continues. Accessed 12 June 2014.

INDEX

1s and 0s, 24–25, 101; reductionism, 133

8-bit graphics, 11, 56, 99, 107

a priori: conditions, 28; knowledge, 29; principles, 31; disembodied value, 33

Accelerationism, 32n17

access agency, 80, 84

Achituv, Romy, and Camille Utterback, 158. See also *Text Rain*

Adamson, Glenn, 73

Adobe: Illustrator, 94; InDesign, 94, 102; Photoshop, 94, 102, 136; Premiere, 136

aesthetic: bodily augmentations, 90; choice, 99; expectations, 100, 168; human-technology-infused, 69; movement, 42, 44; pattern, 101; representation, 162; values, 100

aesthetic markers, 98, 123; of information culture, 23; borrowing of, 56

aesthetic sensibility, 69, 147; emerging, 30

aesthetics of error, 107

agency, 122, 151; agential mediatory, 122; co-agential mediating technologies, 124; degree of, 118; human, 64; technological, 64; merging of agencies, 115; of the action, 114; human and computers combining, 114; techno-human, 152; technological and human, 113; technological co-agency, 116; varying degrees of, 117

Aima, Rahel, 150; becoming the object of the gaze, 151; feminized subjectivity, 151

algorithmic: gaze, 90; media, 67; sensorium, 131

algorithmization, 9, 103, 109, 122, 140

Allen, Woody, 148, 150–51

ambient: rhetoric, 135n9; signals, 85

anamorphosis, 104–5, 107; anamorphic play, 104

Anderson, Daniel, and Jentery Sayers, 102

Anheuser Busch Superbowl commercial, 3

Apple, 49–50, 119; and App of the Year award, 119

APxD mkII, 115–16

Aristotle, 29, 164, 164n8, 168

Arnall, Timo, Jørn Knutsen, and Einar Sneve Martinussen, 130

Arroyo, Sarah, 133n8, 138 table 1

at/through, 116–17n3

audience, 38, 135, 147; aesthetic sensibilities, 21; and identity, 160; and medial experiences, 145; expectations, 155; expectations of medial experience, 33; expectations of mediated artifacts, 170; hypermediacy-oriented, 160; hypermediate-oriented, 161; rhetorical, 109; shift in medial expectations, 66; audience-based consideration, 146

Aurasma, 79, 131, 169

authentic: experience, 98; medial experience, 158; mediated experience, 88, 165, 169; authenticity of a moment, 166

autocorrect, 116–17, 167

autofill, 117, 167

autopoiesis, 114; autopoietic, 115, 126

avant-garde, 43, 75, 112; technological, 101